Ori Preuss

Bridging the Island: Brazilians' Views of Spanish America and Themselves, 1865-1912

TIEMPO EMULADO
HISTORIA DE AMÉRICA Y ESPAÑA
12

Ori Preuss

BRIDGING THE ISLAND: BRAZILIANS' VIEWS OF SPANISH AMERICA AND THEMSELVES, 1865-1912

Iberoamericana - Vervuert - 2011

The Sverdlin Institute of Latin American History and Culture
Tel Aviv University

Published in collaboration with the Sverdlin Institute
of Latin American History and Culture, Tel Aviv University

Library of Congress Cataloging-in-Publication Data
Preuss, Ori.
Bridging the island : Brazilians' views of Spanish America and themselves, 1865-1912 / Ori Preuss.
p. cm. -- (Tiempo emulado. Historia de América y España ; 12)
Includes bibliographical references and index.
ISBN 978-1-936353-02-6 (alk. paper)
1. National characteristics, Brazilian--History--19th century. 2. National characteristics, Brazilian--History--20th century. 3. National characteristics, Latin American--History--19th century. 4. National characteristics, Latin American--History--20th century. 5. Brazil--Relations--Latin America. 6. Latin America--Relations--Brazil. 7. Brazil--Civilization. 8. Brazil--History--1889-1930. 9. Latin America--Foreign public opinion, Brazilian. 10. Public opinion--Brazil--History. I. Title.
F2510.P76 2011
981--dc22
2011000873

Amor de Dios, 1 – E-28014 Madrid
Tel.: +34 91 429 35 22
Fax: +34 91 429 53 97
info@iberoamericanalibros.com
www.ibero-americana.net

9040 Bay Hill Blvd. Orlando, FL 32819
Tel. (+1) 407 217 5584
Fax. (+1) 407 217 5059
info@iberoamericanalibros.com
www.ibero-americana.net

Vervuert, 2011
Elisabethenstr. 3-9 – D-60594 Frankfurt am Main
Tel.: +49 69 597 46 17
Fax: +49 69 597 87 43
info@iberoamericanalibros.com
www.ibero-americana.net

ISBN 978-84-8489-481-0 (Iberoamericana Editorial Vervuert)
ISBN 9978-1-936353-02-6 (Iberoamericana Vervuert Publishing Corp.)

Depósito Legal: SE-3090-2011

Cover design: Carlos Zamora
Frontispiece: "Brazil and the Argentine Republic on July 9, 1888". Revista Ilustrada, July 07, 1888. Courtesy of Fundação Casa de Rui Barbosa, Archive

This book is printed on acid-free paper.

Printed by Publidisa

CONTENTS

In memory of Teddy Preuss

ILLUSTRATIONS

Acknowledgments

Many people proffered their help along the road back and forth between Tel Aviv, Miami and Rio de Janeiro leading to this book. I owe a deep debt of gratitude to my two mentors at the University of Miami, Steve Stein, and the late Robert M. Levine whose untimely death is a true loss, for their wise and caring guidance. Both left an imprint on me and on this project. Also at the University of Miami, I am thankful to professors Hugh Thomas, William C. Smith and Soledad de Mateo for their teaching; to Lenny del Granado for her precious assistance in so many ways, and to fellow students at the Department of History—Aleksi Siltala, Nikolas Kozloff, Dia Mercidi, Douglas Trefzger, John Crocitti and Mercedes Vigón—for the countless interesting conversations, heated discussions and many good laughs we shared.

Especially warm words of thanks are due to my first mentor at Tel Aviv University Tzvi Medin; to my colleagues there Rosalie Sitman, Gerardo Leibner, and Tal Goldfajn; and to my friend Hillel Eyal for their rare integrity, invaluable moral and intellectual support, and friendship throughout the years. I am thankful as well to the staff and students of The Sverdlin Institute of Latin American History and Culture, particularly Nomi Hasson, and to the Institute's former director Raanan Rein.

To the people at Xargol Books—Gaby Silon, Jonathan Nadav, and above all the late Dan Daor—I am indebted for the fortunate parallel path of literature and translation, that finally converged with the one of history. I keep going back to those enlightening, fun hours spent with Che, Gaucho Dorda, and all the rest.

I would also like to express my gratitude to Barbara Potthast for her interest and faith in this work; to Hilda Sabato for her constructive criticism; and to João Paulo Rodrigues, Thomas Whigham, Jim Green and Mauricio Tenorio for generously reading and commenting upon earlier versions of the text. While I was unable to incorporate all their suggestions, those I did surely improved the final result; to Frank McCann, Tom Cohen, Jeff Lesser, Francisco Luiz Teixeira Vinhosa, Alexandra de Mello e Silva, Lúcia Lippi Oliveira, José Murilo de Carvalho, Fábio Koifman, Nísia Trindade Lima, Marcos Chor Maio and Sérgio Murilo Zarro, for their assistance during my first ventures into the field of Brazilian history and in navigating my way in the archives and research institutions of Rio de Janeiro; to Amy Chazkel, Jerry Dávila, James Woodard, Peter Beattie, and Erica Windler, for their good company and wise advice at various junctures; and to Ingrid Fey for sharing her knowledge.

Dona Lucia Monte Alto Silva at the Arquivo Histórico do Itamaraty, Luiz Antônio Macedo Ewbank at the Museu Histórico e Diplomático do Itamaraty, Sátiro Nunes at the Arquivo Nacional, Maria Leal at the Oliveira Lima Library, the entire incredibly helpful staffs of the Fundaçao Casa de Rui Barbosa and the Ibero-Amerikanisches Institut, all deserve special thanks.

Much of the research for this book was carried out with the support of The Institute of Latin American History and Culture at Tel Aviv University; The Department of History at the University of Miami, and Yad Hanadiv Humanities Fellowship awarded me by the Rothschild Foundation in Jerusalem, for which I am deeply grateful.

Finally, I would like to acknowledge the kind and patient assistance of Kerstin Houba at Vervuert-Iberoamericana, with the publication process; Elisabeth Enenbach's careful editing of the manuscript; and Nurit Hershkovits' masterful treatment of the images.

I dedicate this book to my dearest ones, my wife Revital, my children Tair and Shahar, and my mother Adina, and to the memory of my father Teddy who opened the world for me with his stories. In my dreams I still travel with you on that unfulfilled journey of ours to the Iguaçu Falls.

A note on Portuguese spelling

As a rule, modern Brazilian Portuguese spelling is employed in the body of the text of the book, whereas original orthography of cited authors and titles is used in the captions of the figures, in the footnotes, and in the bibliography. Thus, for example, Campos Sales in the first case versus Campos Salles in the second, and *O País* versus *O Paiz.* Translations are all mine unless otherwise mentioned.

INTRODUCTION

THE ISLAND OF BRAZIL

> Looking toward the rising sun–with its population centers located much closer to Europe than to other American countries, and separated from these by differences of origin and language–neither the physical Brazil, nor the spiritual one, forms a system with these nations. Geologists say that the River Plate and the Amazon were once two long, connected seas. *Brazil, an immense island*, was then a continent in its own right [...] the Brazilian massif has profound roots and eternal foundations that are uniquely its own. This is why the volcanic eruptions of the other system do not reach the Brazilian shores.[1]

Some twenty years ago, after four months of traveling from Lima, south to Punta Arenas and north to Buenos Aires, I crossed the bridge connecting the Argentine town of Puerto Iguazú and the Brazilian town of Foz de the Iguaçu. By now, most of the details of that crossing from the most Europeanized part of Spanish America into Afro-Luso America have been forgotten. What remains in my mind is mainly a memory of the mixed sense of similarity and difference that I experienced as I stepped into Brazilian territory. That same mixed sense also marked my previous border crossings within Spanish America from Chile to Argentina in Patagonia and even

1. Eduardo Prado, *A ilusão americana* (São Paulo: Brasiliense, 1958 [1893]), p. 10; my italics.

more so the passage from the Peruvian town of Tacna to the Chilean town of Arica in the Atacama desert, a testimony to the power of state boundaries to produce cultural distinctions. Yet here, at the meeting point between Portuguese- and Spanish-speaking America, the sense of difference was far more pronounced. One crosses the river from one bank to the other and forthwith finds oneself in a different land.

Back then, I knew little about the social realities responsible for that impression of novelty, much less about their deep historical roots. Harking back in part to the colonial period, and greatly reinforced by a uniquely peaceful path to independence and an expansion of its slave plantation economy, the singularity of newly autonomous but still monarchical Brazil in relation to the newborn Spanish American republics had drawn the attention of observers right from the start. When the English traveler Maria Graham came to recount her visit to Brazil and Chile during the first days of Latin American independence, she decided to write the "narratives concerning Spanish and Portuguese America" separately under the logic of "the countries themselves being as different in climate and productions, as the inhabitants are in manners, society, institutions, and government."[2] Ensuing developments on both sides of the equation only strengthened the picture of two distinct realms. "While the Spanish American republics have been rent asunder with internal strife, and while blood, carnage, and revolution have not ceased to be the order of the day within them," wrote another foreign visitor in the 1840s, "Brazil has remained united, and, with comparatively slight exceptions, has pursued her onward course with increasing prosperity." Nevertheless, the visitor expressed doubts about the young Empire's ability to perpetuate its distinct fortune "since elements of disorder exist in Brazil, which have the terrible capacity, unless effectually restrained, of starting into action, and, by their ruinous progress, throwing her fairest prospects into gloom, if not crushing for ever the power of her now flourishing and almost idolized dynasty."[3]

2. Maria Graham, *Journal of a Voyage to Brazil, and Residence There During Part of the Years 1821, 1822, 1823* (London: Longman & C. & J. Murray, 1824), p. IV.

3. Daniel P. Kidder, *Sketches of Residence and Travels in Brazil Embracing Historical and Geographical Notices of The Empire and its Several Provinces*, 2 vols. (Philadelphia: Sorin and Ball, 1845), vol. II, p. 403.

Indeed, as we shall see, the sharp contrast between the state of things in Brazil and the state of things in the countries surrounding it would diminish dramatically toward the end of the nineteenth century, a period during which, concomitantly, the integrative idea and the name "Latin America" acquired substantial presence in Brazilian political and intellectual discourse for the first time. This notwithstanding, the notion of Brazil as an island continued to hold sway, to varying degrees, in learned circles both outside and inside the country, as is evident in the bold isolationist statement from 1893 by an influential Brazilian polemicist cited in the epigraph (after all, the subjective assertion of difference is often a case of denying objective similarities). On that basis, more diverse political, cultural, and scholarly positions with regard to Brazil's proper place within the concept and reality of Latin America have developed, ranging from outright rejection–which had been the almost completely predominant stand since independence–to serious questioning, reluctant approval, and positive endorsement.[4] But there is something that all these stands have in common and that is the mutual relationship inherent in them between interpretations of Brazil and interpretations of Spanish America. In other words, the long history of comparisons between Portuguese and Spanish America, from the early nineteenth century onward, is also the history of defining what Brazil *is* and what it *is not*, the history of the constitution of the Brazilian self. Yet it has rarely been studied as such. For modern scholarship, in the same vein as Maria Graham, has tended to set the narrative of Brazil apart from the narratives of the Spanish American countries, charting sometimes similar but ultimately separate paths of historical evolution. In particular, students of the transitional period spanning the decline of

4. Antônio Cândido's brief essay "Os brasileiros e a nossa América," *Recortes* (São Paulo: Companhia das Letras, 1993), pp. 130-139, provides an insightful introduction to the evolution of a more diverse, "systematic reflection on Latin America" in Brazil at the turn of the nineteenth century. I see now that Leslie Bethell has published "O Brasil e a ideia de 'América Latina' em perspectiva histórica," *Estudos Históricos* 22:44 (2009), pp. 289-321, a useful overview of the subject from the nineteenth century to our own time, arguing categorically (p. 321) "that neither Spanish American nor Brazilian intellectuals, and neither Spanish American nor Brazilian governments considered Brazil part of 'América Latina' at least until the second half of the twentieth century." As will be seen, my reading of some of the same texts and other sources as well has led me to a different emphasis.

slavery and monarchy and the consolidation of the first republic (roughly 1870-1914) have drawn many parallels and distinctions between the two blocks, but have paid little attention to how Brazilians perceived and interpreted those similarities/differences at the time as part of their self-identification.[5]

The Close Otherness of Nineteenth-Century Latin Americans

While rooted in Brazil's idiosyncrasies the scholarly neglect of cultural circulation between Portuguese- and Spanish-speaking America, and of causal links between their histories, is also symptomatic of wider trends in the study of national and supranational identities in nineteenth-century Latin America as a whole. Strongly informed by dependency or postcolonial theory, this scholarship has generally revolved around highly asymmetrical relations of power–be those relations of domination, confrontation, or negotiation–both between center and periphery and within each country of the periphery. Whether writing with a top-down or a bottom-up approach, implicitly or explicitly, historians and literary critics have directed their attention to two main axes of interaction, the first connecting Latin America's upper classes with Europe and the United States, and the second connecting these upper classes with their respective "peoples." Mary Louise Pratt's assertion that "the newly independent elites of Spanish America" –and for that matter of Portuguese America as well–"faced the necessity for self-invention in

5. An interesting case in point is José Murilo de Carvalho's seminal work about imperial Brazil *A construção da ordem: A elite política imperial/Teatro de sombras: A política imperial*, 2nd revised ed. (Rio de Janeiro: Editora UFRJ, Relume-Dumará, 1996). "When studying nineteenth-century Brazil," it is stated in the beginning of the book (p. 11), "we come across something that contemporary Brazilians were more aware of than subsequent researchers. That is, the remarkably distinct evolution of the Spanish and Portuguese colonies in America, which would have such profound influence on the future of the countries of this region." Carvalho perceptively identifies the lacuna but does not fill the gap. In what follows his statement, the reader finds many comparisons between the Brazilian Empire and the Spanish-speaking republics but almost no reference to Brazilian attitudes toward their neighbors during that period.

relation both to Europe and the non-European masses they sought to govern," exemplifies this basic double-axis scheme.[6]

The point is that the nearly obsessive interest in vertical relations between peripheral elites and the center, or between peripheral elites and the lower classes of their individual countries, as justified as it may be, obscures the significance of a third axis of interaction, more horizontal in terms of power, across state borders among those elites themselves. This largely ignored axis is of special importance due to the region's postcolonial reality of sharp cultural and ethnic cleavages *within* "national" boundaries, and a high degree of cultural and ethnic closeness from *without*, throughout the nineteenth century and well into the twentieth. Not only did the Latin American state precede the nation, as most historians now agree, but it was born in what Anthony Smith has designated a "culture area,"[7] the product of more than three hundred years of colonial rule. Independence in the region took place against a background of shared historical experience and a high level of cultural, linguistic, and religious uniformity, which proved to be propitious ground for collective identifications beyond

6. Mary Louise Pratt, *Imperial Eyes: Travel Writing and Transculturation*, 2nd ed. (London: Routledge, 2008), p. 110. Rigorous critical studies about Latin American nationalisms and national identities were rare until the 1990s, but have proliferated since then. A notable and highly influential example of the bottom-up approach that concentrates on popular nationalism is Florencia E. Mallon, *Peasant and Nation: The Making of Postcolonial Mexico and Peru* (Berkeley: University of California Press, 1995). A paradigmatic elite-centered study is E. Bradford Burns, *The Poverty of Progress: Latin America in the Nineteenth Century* (Berkeley: University of California Press, 1980). Recent important contributions with a self-declared focus on the elites include Rebecca Earle, *The Return of the Native: Indians and Myth-Making in Spanish America, 1810-1930* (Durham: Duke University Press, 2007); and Juan Pablo Dabove, *Nightmares of the Lettered City: Banditry and Literature in Latin America, 1816-1929* (Pittsburgh: University of Pittsburgh Press, 2007). This is to name but a few works that concentrate on the nineteenth century and cover more than one country. For an insightful historiographical overview, see Nicola Miller, "The Historiography of Nationalism and National Identity in Latin America," *Nations and Nationalism*, 12:2 (2006), pp. 201-221.

7. Anthony D. Smith, *National Identity* (Reno: University of Nevada Press, 1991), pp. 171-173. Smith stresses the importance of this phenomenon, noting that (p. 172) "whereas political and economic unities are planned and organized, families of cultures and culture areas appear inchoate and uninstitutionalized but are no less real and potent for those in their orbit." Yet it is a minor theme in his book.

the level of the state straight from the beginning.[8] Put differently, nineteenth-century Latin America constituted a case of close Otherness (both objective and subjective) between groups and individuals of diverse nationalities.

This was especially true with regard to the Europeanized, predominantly white sectors of the elite, who were so strongly attached to French or English culture and profoundly alienated from the "colored" masses, a point recently emphasized by Miguel Angel Centeno. "If we think of Latin America, as having four 'nations' at the time of independence–Spanish, Creole, Indian and African–," he notes, "the first two were often united in their opposition to the last two."[9] And it was still true, perhaps even more so, toward the end of the nineteenth century, when the accelerated pace of ideational and economic internationalization; improvements in transportation and communication; and increasing menace of Western imperialism all brought Latin American statesmen and intellectuals closer together, both physically and mentally. Their common outward-looking fantasies of civilization mixed with fears of its might, and inward-looking nightmares of barbarism are familiar to us. Yet we still know relatively little about the way in which they viewed each other's efforts

8. On supranational identities in the region during the independence period, see Simon Collier, "Nationality, Nationalism, and Supranationalism in the Writings of Simón Bolívar," *Hispanic American Historical Review*, 63:1 (1983), pp. 37-64, and José Carlos Chiaramonte, "Formas de identidad en el Río de la Plata luego de 1810," *Boletín del Instituto de Historia Argentina y Americana Dr. Emilio Ravignani*, 3:1 (1989), pp. 71-92. For the second half of the nineteenth century and the early twentieth, see Arturo Ardao, *Génesis de la idea y el nombre de América Latina* (Caracas: Centro de Estudios Latinoamericanos Rómulo Gallegos, 1980); Walter Mignolo, *The Idea of Latin America* (Malden, MA: Blackwell, 2005), chap. 2; Nicola Miller, *In the Shadow of the State: Intellectuals and the Quest for National Identity in Twentieth-Century Spanish America* (London: Verso, 1999), chap. 5; and Miller, "The Historiography of Nationalism," p. 216. Again, what is notable about the latter works and others on the topic is their emphasis on elite reactions to external or internal threats, the much lesser amount of attention paid to transnational exchanges among the elites themselves, and a strong focus on Spanish America, to the exclusion of Brazil.

9. Miguel Angel Centeno, *Blood and Debt: War and the Nation-State in Latin America* (University Park: Pennsylvania State University Press, 2002), pp. 90-91, 175, passim. A similar point is made by Francisco-Xavier Guerra, "The Implosion of the Spanish Empire: Emerging Statehood and Collective Identities," in Luis Roniger and Tamar Herzog, eds., *The Collective and the Public in Latin America* (Brighton: Sussex Academic Press, 2000), pp. 71-94.

to get over the latter and realize the first, what was said between them, and how, in turn, these transnational gazes and dialogues within the periphery fashioned individual state identities as well as regional solidarities. In what follows, I attempt to shed some light on these questions from the supposedly extraneous and therefore least relevant standpoint: the "island" of Brazil.

* * *

The present study does not attempt to (un)cover the entire range of Brazilian elite references to Spanish America from the late 1880s to the early 1910s,[10] nor does it purport to probe deeply into the inner lives or ideas of certain individuals. Its aim is more modest: to trace some major shifts and continuities in outlooks through several figures who played key roles in this regard, interweaving their reflections on Brazil's neighbors with other forms of Luso–Hispano-American interaction in the realms of culture and foreign affairs. The focus is on men who combined national thought and political action in the nineteenth-century Latin American tradition of the "writer-statesman."[11] Quintino Bocaiuva (1836-1912), Eduardo Prado (1860-1901), Joaquim Nabuco (1849-1910), Rui Barbosa (1849-1923), José Maria da Silva Paranhos Jr., the Baron of Rio Branco (1845-1912),

10. I leave out, for example, *A America latina: Males de origem* (1905), by Manoel Bomfim, a dissident anti-racist and anti-oligarchic voice in Brazilian social thought during the early republic who differed on certain fundamental points from the dominant intellectual currents that I focus on here. His book is the one text concerning Latin America from the period that has received considerable scholarly attention as such. See, for instance, Cândido, "Os brasileiros e a nossa América," pp. 137-139; Flora Süssekind, "Shifting Frontiers–Manuel Bonfim [sic] and *A América Latina*: An Introduction," *Journal of Latin American Cultural Studies*, 11:1 (2002), pp. 65-76.

11. Doris Sommer, *Foundational Fictions: The National Romances of Latin America* (Berkeley: University of California Press, 1991), pp. 4-7; Angel Rama, *The Lettered City*, ed. and trans. by John Charles Chasteen (Durham: Duke University Press, 1996), p. 77. Both scholars stress the close relationship between writing and governing in nineteenth-century Latin America as a whole–a tradition that extended, as Rama shows, into the period under study here. For the Brazilian case, see Angela Alonso, *Idéias em movimento: A geração 1870 na crise do Brasil-Império* (São Paulo: Paz e Terra, 2002), pp. 29-30; and João Paulo Coelho de Souza Rodrigues, *A dança das cadeiras: Literatura e política na Academia Brasileira de Letras* (Campinas: Editora da Unicamp, 2001), pp. 15-30.

and Oliveira Lima (1867-1928) were all instrumental in the evolution of Brazil's self-understanding, either as central leaders of the republican and monarchist camps during the conflictual years surrounding the fall of the monarchy in 1889, and/or as high-profile diplomats during the 1900s, after an oligarchic consensus blurred distinctions between the two parties and their respective visions.[12] However, their role in the construction of Brazil's national identity should not be reduced to that of "architects," along the lines of rational constructivist approaches which stress the elements of "artifact, invention and social engineering" in the making of nations.[13] For, if expressions of ethnic and national identities are often symbolic tools in political struggles, they may also be, at the same time, psychological responses to situational triggers and attempts to create order in the social universe.[14] This point, informed by anthropological and socio-psychological research, is no less relevant to national identity formation among political and intellectual leaders, exclusivist in their imaginings of the nation as they may be, than to other social sectors. The white elite males mentioned above strongly identified themselves with a certain Brazil, even if not with many aspects of Brazilian life. Making sense of the changing national reality and speculating about its historical causes and future outcomes were, therefore, conscious as well as unselfconscious acts of both collective and individual self-definition. Like their Spanish-speaking counterparts in other countries of the continent, grappling with questions of racial inferiority,

12. On the centrality of these figures see Nicolau Sevcenko, *Literatura como missão: Tensões sociais e criação cultural na Primeira República* (São Paulo: Brasiliense, 1983), pp. 46-47.

13. The quote is from a central exposition of these approaches: E. J. Hobsbawm, *Nations and Nationalism since 1780*, 2nd ed. (Cambridge: Cambridge University Press, 1992), p. 10.

14. Thomas Hylland Eriksen, *Ethnicity and Nationalism: Anthropological Perspectives* (Chicago: Pluto Press, 1993), p. 76. Other works that stress the emotional and psychological dimensions of collective identity formation, which I have used throughout this book, include Thomas J. Scheff, "Emotions and Identity: A Theory of Ethnic Nationalism," in Craig Calhoun, ed., *Social Theory and the Politics of Identity* (Oxford: Blackwell, 1994), pp. 277-303; Rogers Brubaker, Mara Loveman and Peter Stamatov, "Ethnicity as Cognition," *Theory and Society* 33:1 (2004), pp. 31-46; William Bloom, *Personal Identity, National Identity and International Relations* (Cambridge: Cambridge University Press, 1990).

material backwardness, and political misrule, these Brazilians wrote not only for others but also for themselves.[15]

Structured chronologically around international and transnational events, this book analyzes discussions–both public and behind the scenes, official and non-official–that accompanied each of these occurrences in the form of diplomatic documents, private correspondence, lengthy essays and newspaper articles, carefully choreographed ceremonies and more spontaneous street demonstrations, state iconography, and illustrated magazines. Intimately tied to partisan struggles and international relations, these documents, which have been left on the margins of scholarship, can enrich our understanding of Brazilian self-perceptions at the turn of the nineteenth century. Not only were they exceptionally sensitive to short-term historical settings and less prone–although by no means immune–to the predominant racial and environmental determinisms of the period, but they were also designed to mobilize people and could reach a larger audience than other, more purely intellectual "foundational" texts of Brazilian national thought. Thus, although this is a study of the uppermost echelons of Brazil's political-intellectual elite, it does attempt to address, to a certain extent, the difficult issue of a broader reception. As the last chapter will show, the foreign policy discourse of those years functioned as a reproduction site of national myths that continue to live on in the Brazilian popular imagination today.

But first things first: chapter 1 provides the historical background that is necessary for understanding the impact of future events. The starting point is the Paraguayan War (1864-70), also known as the War of the Triple Alliance, in which Brazil fought alongside Argentina and Uruguay against Paraguay. While the influence of this major conflict on Brazilian attitudes toward Spanish America still awaits detailed study, a perusal of key published documents from the period and of recent academic research shows that it constituted a critical moment in the history of Luso-Hispano-American relations. Joining forces with two Spanish American nations against "barbarism," as the allies' propaganda proclaimed, ran against Brazil's self-perception

15. A point made even more radically by Aline Helg, "Race in Argentina and Cuba, 1880-1930: Theory, Policies, and Popular Reaction," in Richard Graham, ed., *The Idea of Race in Latin America* (Austin: University of Texas Press, 1990), p. 61.

as an island of civilization in Latin America. At the same time, the protracted military campaign exposed the structural and ideological weaknesses of the slaveholding Empire.

The chapter further traces the intensification of these tendencies in the following two decades. With the rise of scientific liberal reformism in Brazil, monarchy and slavery, the two central institutions that set the country apart from Spanish America and loomed large in the country's self-image, came to represent impediments to progress and suffered increasing attacks. At the same time, the Spanish American "age of caudillos" was coming to an end. The integration of Latin America into the world economy led to growing levels of political stability and material progress in many parts of the region, seriously undermining its negative image and even turning it on its head. In Brazil there was a widening sense that the neighboring republics were progressing while the Empire stood still. As a result of these interrelated processes, from inside as well as outside the country's borders, Brazilian leaders sought to reverse its political and cultural isolationism.

These developments serve to explain the optimistic discourse of South American solidarity and progress that appeared in Brazil in the aftermath of the abolition of slavery on May 13, 1888, which constitutes the focus of interest of chapter 2. The chapter opens with a detailed description of important, yet largely forgotten occurrences, namely, the celebrations of the end of Brazilian slavery in several Spanish American capitals (which reached the most dramatic proportions in Buenos Aires) and Brazilian retribution for this show of support. In Rio de Janeiro there was an outburst of passionate rhetoric of Brazilian-Argentine friendship that expressed a strong sense of relief and renewal. In Brazilian eyes, this chapter shows, late-nineteenth-century Argentina came to represent an emerging Latin America that aroused interest, elicited positive judgments, and encouraged transnational identification; three interrelated trends which continued, as is further shown through a review of discussions in the press, in Congress, and in public rallies, beyond the euphoric climate of May-July 1888.

If the abolition of slavery opened an optimistic, positive avenue of identification with Spanish America, the coming of the republic a year and a half later through a military coup inaugurated a pessimistic, negative avenue of identification, a theme that I discuss in chapter 3. In the aftermath of November 15, 1889, Brazilians were thrown into an unfamiliar reality of political and economic turmoil that shattered some vital components of their country's self-image. Facing a sudden break from the old order, an abrupt eruption of what for them had been unknown or repressed qualities of the nation, intellectual leaders of all political stripes were forced to make sense of a radically different sociopolitical context, give it meaning, and redefine their own national identity. In so doing, they turned their eyes toward their neighbors, concentrating mainly on the less promising aspects of Spanish America's past and present.

The focus is on leading figures of the monarchist camp. A close reading of their private papers and journalistic writing–largely overlooked in treatments of Brazil's national identity–reveals how the history of Spanish America served them both psychologically, as a conceptual framework, and instrumentally, as propaganda material–that is, for both cognitive and ideological purposes. While republicans stressed once and again the non-violent character of the revolution, adhered to American[16] values of peace and liberty, and promoted rapprochement with prosperous Argentina, which everybody envied, events on the ground were more reminiscent of Spanish America's "age of caudillos." At least this is what the opposing camp felt, thought, and proclaimed. Monarchist leaders responded to the turmoil of the early 1890s by discovering the relevance of the Spanish American experience to Brazil as a negative reference point. Underlying this awakening about the anarchic and authoritarian nature of their neighbors' life was an assumption of common essence, which the emotionally and ideologically charged debate between monarchists and republicans over Brazil's national identity further reworked and reinforced. The military presence in the government, political instability, violence, repression, and financial collapse were all seen and described as signs of Hispano-Americanization, of becoming like *them* and therefore a part of Latin America in a very negative and unwanted way.

16. The terms "America," "American(s)," and "Americanism" are used throughout this book in a hemispheric sense.

In the early 1890s, the old imaginary line separating civilization from barbarism no longer lay along the Brazilian national border. It did not fade but moved, as Brazilian elite members started to develop a common vision of two different Latin Americas. This vision would become well established during the next decade, a theme that I explore in chapter 4 through the study of what I call "close encounters of the peripheral kind": encounters across state borders between Portuguese- and Spanish-speaking Americans, encounters that grew in number and visibility during the 1900s. First, I provide a discussion of Brazilian and Spanish-American reactions to the rise of U.S. expansionism, which is essential for understanding the intra-Latin American interaction of the period. Then I proceed to focus on two particular events–the exchange of presidential visits between Brazil and Argentina in 1899/1900 and the Third Pan-American Conference in Rio de Janeiro in 1906–closely examining visual works and literary texts that were produced on and for these occasions as a window onto Self-Other perceptions.

Such a textual analysis shows that Brazilian views of Spanish America and of Brazil itself within the Latin American context had grown more complex. If the abolition of slavery marked the inauguration of what I have called a positive pattern of identification with Spanish America, and if the initially caudillistic nature of the republic inaugurated a negative pattern of identification, a much more stable and confident Brazil in the early 1900s witnessed the emergence of more synthetic perceptions. By then, members of the Brazilian elite had come to perceive themselves, and their nation, as a part of a Latin America that was neither entirely anarchical, weak, and backward, nor fully ordered, vigorous, and advanced. This shared consciousness, infused with varying degrees of pessimism and optimism, was translated by leading men-of-state-and-letters into different ideological formulas: Americanism, Latin Americanism, and Luso-Americanism, represented by Joaquim Nabuco, Oliveira Lima, and Rio Branco, respectively.

The closing chapter of the book, which explores the final stage in the evolution of Brazilian elite perceptions of Spanish America and of their own reality between 1888 and 1912, argues in favor of the eventual dominance of Luso-Americanism. Consequently, the focus is on the diplomatic undertakings and public image of the Baron of

Rio Branco, Brazil's dominant foreign minister from 1902 to 1912. Whereas Oliveira Lima and Joaquim Nabuco clearly identified themselves and their country with Latin America or America as a hemisphere, Rio Branco promoted and symbolized Brazil's singularity in the continent. If Lima and Nabuco's contrasting Pan-Americanisms represented a high point in the opening-up of Brazil's national identity following the collapse of the country's double slaveholding-imperial wall, Rio Branco's foreign policy and the discourse surrounding it signified the reconstitution of the country's distinctiveness. This chapter is a critical survey of the Baron's spoken, written, and illustrated road to becoming a national symbol of a new-old insular Brazil, powerful but peaceful. The winning Luso-American formula he embodied expressed the regained and secure national identity of an island, but an island with bridges connecting it to Spanish America.

Chapter 1
The Island of Brazil and Spanish America: First Bridges, 1865-1888

A Proud Monarchy, a Shameful Slavocracy

In 1824, once the tumult of battle between Simón Bolívar's forces and the Spanish army at Ayacucho had subsided, Brazil remained the single monarchic relic in a republican continent. Since these early days of Latin American independence–as is often argued in the historiography–the institution of the monarchy loomed large in the self-image of the Brazilian elite. The stability and unity achieved by the regime created a feeling of superiority vis-à-vis the Spanish American world, which had disintegrated into numerous turbulent republics. The imperial elite saw and represented Brazil as a monarchical island of civilization surrounded by a Spanish-speaking republican domain, which it equated with anarchy, political divisiveness, lack of civil rights, caudillism, and–in sum–barbarism.[1]

1. This argument is presented succinctly and in an almost identical form by numerous scholars. Exceptionally elaborate is Ron Seckinger's discussion of the Brazilian elite's view of Spanish America during the immediate aftermath of independence, in *The Brazilian Monarchy and the South American Republics, 1822-1831: Diplomacy and State Building* (Baton Rouge: Louisiana State University Press, 1984), pp. 26-39. Making a general statement about the nineteenth century, Emília Viotti da Costa mentions that "the example of other South American states [...] served to buttress the argument of Brazilians who considered a centralized state the best form of government," in her *The Brazilian Empire: Myths and Histories* (Chicago: Chicago University Press, 1985), p. 220; and so does José Ribeiro Júnior, who claims that "The Latin American experiences intimidated the Brazilian elites," in his "O Brasil

Domingo Faustino Sarmiento, Argentina's future president (1868-74), founding intellectual father, and leading opponent of caudillo Juan Manuel de Rosas's dictatorial rule (1829-32, 1835-52), captured something of this haughty mentality–partly a façade in his interpretation–when he passed through Rio de Janeiro in 1846. "Rosas is called here an intruder, a barbarian, and a poor devil, as the Brazilians pretend to ignore the existence over there of something called the Argentine Republic," noted the South American passenger in his travel accounts. The Empire had pretensions to dominate America with its navies, diplomacy and trade, seeing "the *casteçao*s as a degeneration of the Portuguese race and Spanish as a dialect of the language of Camões." But Sarmiento did not only document Brazilian ambitions and condescending views toward their neighbors; he also identified what were, in his view, serious points of weakness as well–principle among them the corrupting influences of slavery. "Slaves are to be found where there are no dynamic forces," he asserted, and their white owners "pay dearly for this injustice," thus putting his finger on an often-silenced source of unease for Brazilians themselves.[2]

If the monarchy was a source of pride and self-confidence, slavery, the second central institution of the country, was destined to produce mainly opposite sentiments. Slavery was the one face of Brazil that the elites preferred to hide, as were the hundreds of thousands of black slaves who sustained the Brazilian economy, their numerous mulatto descendants, and their rich African traditions. Rather, it was the Indian, few in number and geographically removed that became the Monarchy's national symbol. Yet suppressing the essential qualities of the nation ran into difficulties. As the nineteenth century pro-

monárquico em face das repúblicas americanas," in Carlos Guilherme Mota, ed., *Brasil em perspectiva*, 2nd ed. (São Paulo: Difusão Européia do Livro, 1969), p. 154. On the manipulation of Spanish America's negative image by regime-affiliated historians during the Second Empire (1840-1889), see Stanley Stein, "The Historiography of Brazil 1808-1889," *Hispanic American Historical Review* 40:2 (1960), p. 245. An intriguing treatment of the issue from a regional perspective and at the grassroots level is provided in John Charles Chasteen, *Heroes on Horseback: A Life and Times of the Last Gaucho Caudillos* (Albuquerque: University of New Mexico Press, 1995), pp. 48-52.

2. Domingo Faustino Sarmiento, *Viajes por Europa, África y América, 1845-1847* (Madrid: ALLCA XX, 1996[1849]), pp. 58, 67.

gressed, slavery became increasingly identified with cultural barbarism and material backwardness and gradually disappeared from the Americas. At the same time, scientific racist theories emanating from Europe and the United States, which asserted white supremacy, gained ground among the Latin American elites. Upper-class Brazilians, always sensitive to foreign opinion, were becoming more aware of the contradictions between the racial, social, and political reality of their country and what they wanted it to be. By 1870, members of a new generation of political and intellectual leaders started calling for reform.[3]

The aforementioned contradictions of the Brazilian Empire were fully exposed during the War of the Triple Alliance, which was yet another episode in a long history of Portuguese, and later Brazilian, armed conflicts with Spanish Americans over control of the River Plate system. Brazil's fears of Argentine intentions to revive the Viceroyalty of the River Plate–a colonial administrative unit which had also included Paraguay and Uruguay–accompanied and fueled these clashes. Yet during this war, the Empire fought alongside its traditional rival and Uruguay against Paraguay, which was eventually defeated. The terrible nature of the struggle, which lasted from 1864-1870 and decimated 60 to 69 percent of Paraguay's population,[4]

3. On attitudes toward slavery, see Robert Conrad, *The Destruction of Brazilian Slavery, 1850-1888* (Berkeley: University of California Press, 1972); Barbara Weinstein, "The Decline of the Progressive Planter and the Rise of Subaltern Agency: Shifting Narratives of Slave Emancipation in Brazil," in Gilbert Joseph, ed., *Reclaiming the Political in Latin American History* (Durham: Duke University Press, 2001), esp. pp. 92-95; Andrew Kirkendall, *Class Mates: Male Student Culture and the Making of a Political Class in Nineteenth-Century Brazil* (Lincoln: University of Nebraska Press, 2002), pp. 139-145. On structural and ideational developments, see Viotti da Costa, *The Brazilian Empire*; Richard Graham, *Britain and the Onset of Modernization in Brazil, 1850-1914* (Cambridge: Cambridge University Press, 1972); José Murilo de Carvalho, "Brazil 1870-1914: The Force of Tradition" *Journal of Latin American Studies* 24, Quincentenary Supplement (1992), pp. 145-162; On racial thinking and national identity, see Sommer, *Foundational Fictions*, chap. 5; Lilia Moritz Schwarcz, "A Mestizo and Tropical Country: The Creation of the Official Image of Independent Brazil," *European Review of Latin American and Caribbean Studies*, 80 (2006), esp. pp. 35, 39; Thomas E. Skidmore, *Black into White: Race and Nationality in Brazilian Thought* (New York: Oxford University Press, 1974).

4. Thomas Whigham and Barbara Potthast, "The Paraguayan Rosetta Stone: New Insights into the Demographics of the Paraguayan War, 1864-1870," *Latin American Research Review* 34:1 (1999), pp. 174-186.

did not prevent the allies from presenting it as a clash between civilization and barbarism. Speakers for these governments claimed that they were fighting to liberate the Paraguayan people from the tyrannical rule of their dictator, Francisco Solano López. However, this message could not be easily promoted by the only independent American country where legal slavery was still widely practiced, and whose army relied partially on liberated slaves who had been granted freedom to fight and die in the battlefield instead of on the plantation.[5]

Paraguayan agents in Europe turned the Brazilian justification for the war on its head, claiming that their country fought for the sake of freedom against slavery, and the same argument was made on the battlefield itself. When the allied heads of state called on a Paraguayan commander of a besieged town to surrender in the name of the aforementioned emancipatory cause, he threw it back at them. "If your excellencies are so anxious to grant freedom to the Paraguayan people, as you claim," said the reply, "why don't you start by liberating the unhappy negroes of Brazil, who comprise the majority of its population and who sigh under the hardest and most dreadful slavery in order to enrich several hundred grandees of the Empire and allow them to idle away their time."[6] Tacitly or not so tacitly, race was

5. Francisco Alambert, "Civilização e barbárie, história e cultura: Representações literárias e projeções da guerra do Paraguay nas crises do segundo reinado e da primeira república," and Léon Pomer, "A guerra do Paraguay e a formação do estado na Argentina," both in Maria Eduarda Castro Maglhães Marques, org., *A guerra do Paraguay: 130 anos depois* (Rio de Janeiro: Relume-Dumará, 1995), pp. 83-96, 118; Thomas Whigham and Hendrik Kraay, "Introduction: War, Politics, and Society in South America, 1820s-60s," in Whigham and Kraay, eds., *I Die with My Country: Perspectives on the Paraguayan War, 1864-1870* (Lincoln: University of Nebraska Press, 2004), p. 16. The contradiction between the Empire's liberalist pretensions abroad and the continuation of slavery at home became especially pronounced after the Count d'Eu, commander of Brazilian forces in Paraguay and the emperor's son-in-law, asked the provisional government which replaced Solano López to abolish slavery in Paraguay. See Lidia Besouchet, *José Maria de Silva Paranhos: Visconde do Rio Branco* (Rio de Janeiro/Brasília: Nova Fronteira/INL, 1985), pp. 106-107, 162-163.

6. Antonio Estigarribia, "Resposta dos sitiados," reproduced in José Maria da Silva Paranhos, (Visconde do Rio Branco), *A convenção de 20 de fevereiro demonstrada à luz dos debates do Senado e dos successos da Uruguayana* (Rio de Janeiro: B.L. Garnier, 1865), pp. 244-245.

another issue in the context of the War. Paraguayan propaganda depicted the Brazilian soldiers and officers, as well as the emperor himself, as monkeys.[7]

Such attacks on Brazil as a "slavocratic empire," an isolated relic of the past in the New World, including racial insults, did not come only from the Paraguayan enemy but also from the allies. "Federation or Death! Long Live General Urquiza! Down with the [Brazilian] Slavers who Oppose Him! Long Live the Union of the Americas!" said a slogan of federalist rebels who rose up against the Argentine government in 1866.[8] This was in the same spirit as *The Dissentions of the River Plate Republics and the Machinations of Brazil*, a pamphlet published the year before in Paris by Argentina's leading jurist, Juan Bautista Alberdi. The ongoing conflict endangered "American interests," he warned. Slavery in particular, consecrated by Brazilian legislation, threatened the social principle of civil liberty, which by then–according to Alberdi–had become an American one. But the liberal thinker had other concerns as well. Spanish Americans should join forces against Brazil, he proclaimed, in order to avoid a humiliating defeat at the hands of an empire of the Portuguese race, strongly altered by the mixture with peoples of color. After all, they "do not want to be transformed into Luso-Americans of dark skin and thick lips."[9]

7. On Paraguayan propaganda, see Paulo de Carvalho Neto, "Folclore da guerra do Paraguai," *Journal of Inter-American Studies* 3:2 (April 1961), p. 274. Note that, according to the war memories of the Brazilian officer Dionísio Cerqueira, Paraguayan propaganda actually reached the hands of Brazilian troops. See *Reminiscências da campanha do Paraguay, 1865-1879* (Rio de Janeiro: Biblioteca do Exército Editora, 1980 [1910]), p. 122.

8. Cited in David Rock, "The Collapse of the Federalists: Rural Revolt in Argentina 1863-1876," *Estudios Interdisciplinarios de América Latina y el Caribe* 9:2 (July-Dec., 1998), p. 11. According to Ricardo Salles, European authors who documented the war associated the cowardly behavior of the Brazilian forces with their racial composition and so did Argentines, Uruguayans, and Paraguayans. See *Guerra do Paraguay: Escravidão e cidadania na fomação do exército* (Rio de Janeiro: Paz e Terra, 1990), p. 136.

9. "Las disensiones de las repúblicas del Plata y las maquinaciones del Brasil," in Juan Bautista Alberdi, *Historia de la guerra del Paraguay* (Buenos Aires: Ediciones de la Patria Grande, 1962), pp. 84, 115-116. For similar attacks on Brazil as a slave-owning society in a free America by other Argentine intellectuals, see Nicolas Shumway, *The Invention of Argentina* (Berkeley: University of California Press, 1991), p. 236.

While the reception of such ideological criticism and racial mockery among Brazilians still awaits detailed study, some modern scholarship and key primary sources indicate that they did not remain indifferent.[10] About a year after the Paraguayan War had ended, Brazil passed the Law of the Free Womb, a crucial legislative step toward the total abolition of slavery. The main figure behind the law, Prime Minister the Viscount of Rio Branco (the father of the Baron of Rio Branco), had recently returned from his fourth diplomatic mission to the Plata region. Defending the law before Parliament, he said that once the fighting ended, he found himself "amid no less than fifty thousand Brazilians who had been in contact with the neighboring peoples, and I know"–added Rio Branco–"for myself and from the confessions of the most enlightened of them, how often the permanence of this odious institution [i.e., slavery] in Brazil vexed and humiliated us before foreigners."[11]

Brazilian sensitivity to Spanish American judgments–and not only to European or North American judgments–also surfaced in Joaquim Nabuco's *O Abolicionismo*, the most important text of the abolition-

10. On Brazilian sensitivity to Spanish American racial insults in the specific context of the war, see Peter Beattie, *The Tribute of Blood: Army, Honor, Race, and Nation in Brazil, 1864-1945* (Durham: Duke University Press, 2001), pp. 61-63; and Lilia Moritz Schwarcz, *As Barbas do imperador: D. Pedro II, um monarca nos trópicos* (São Paulo: Companhia das Letras, 1998), pp. 313-314. Also relevant is the public exchange of insults by two future foreign ministers, Estanislao Zeballos of Argentina and the Baron of Rio Branco of Brazil in 1875, as described by Alvaro Lins, *Rio Branco*, 2nd revised ed. (São Paulo: Companhia Editora Nacional, 1965), p. 68. Leading literary critic José Veríssimo wrote some years later about the "nickname 'monkeys' by which several friendly or brother nations adorn us," *A educação nacional*, 3rd ed. (Porto Alegre: Mercado Aberto, 1985 [1890]), p. 131. Helio Lobo mentions slavery as one of the main reasons for Brazil's isolation in America and adds that "a slavocratic empire" was a common epithet in both formal and informal Spanish American usage. *O Pan-americanismo e o Brasil* (São Paulo: Companhia Editora Nacional, 1939), p. 44.

11. A speech in the Chamber of Deputies, June 14, 1871, cited in Joaquim Nabuco, *Um estadista do Império*, 2 vols., 5th ed. (Rio de Janeiro: Topbooks, 1998 [1898-1900]), vol. 1, p. 658. Nabuco brings this quote to support his argument that the first legislative initiatives toward the abolition of slavery, taken from 1865 to 1866, were strongly linked to condemnations of slavery by other American countries that had offended the Brazilian national honor. For the same argument, see also Raimundo Teixeira Mendes, *Benjamin Constant: Esboço de uma apreciação sintética da vida e da obra do fundador da República brazileira*, 2nd ed. (Rio de Janeiro : Séde central da Igreja pozitivista do Brazil, 1913 [1892]), p. 165.

ist movement in Brazil, in which the author singled out the harm of "the reputation we have throughout South America as a country of slaves." From this reputation, broadcast to the entire world, added Nabuco, "arose the cynicism with which the myth was generally received that we had gone to Paraguay to establish freedom; from this results the channeling of immigration toward the Plata." A lengthy footnote, occupying half the page, in which he counterposed a description of the visit of former Argentine president Nicolás Avellaneda to a Brazilian slave plantation in 1882 with data concerning European immigration to Argentina, further revealed that it was not only slavery itself that preoccupied Nabuco. In his mind, as in the mind of other opponents of slavery, abolition was a precondition for white immigration and white immigration, in turn, a precondition for South American progress. Hence his warning that if the current state of things was to persist, "within twenty years Argentina will be a stronger, more advanced and more prosperous nation than Brazil."[12]

Advancing Spanish American Republics, Stagnant Luso-American Empire

The Paraguayan War not only heightened sensitivities about slavery and race, but also had other, more visible effects on Brazilians' perceptions of their neighbors and themselves. To begin with, the protracted armed struggle exposed the inefficiency and backwardness of Emperor Dom Pedro II's Empire, thus undermining the status of the monarchy as a source of pride. Second, joining forces with the recently established Eurocentric liberal government of Argentina, with its ideological justification of fighting to bring freedom to

12. Joaquim Nabuco, *Abolitionism: The Brazilian Antislavery Struggle*, trans. by Robert Conrad (Urbana: University of Illinois Press, 1977 [1883]), p. 163. On abolition and the ideal of whitening through immigration, see Giralda Seyferth, "Construindo a nação: Hierarquias raciais e o papel do racismo na política de imigração e colonização," in Marcos Chor Maio and Ricardo Ventura Santos, eds., *Raça, ciência e sociedade* (Rio de Janeiro: Editora FIOCRUZ, 1996), pp. 41-58; and Skidmore, *Black into White*, pp. 21-27, 124-144.

Paraguay, produced cracks in the alleged Brazilian monopoly on civilization in Latin America.[13]

These cracks had already appeared in the very first moments of the war, as is evident in the case of Francisco Otaviano de Almeida Rosa, the Brazilian minister plenipotentiary for Triple Alliance matters in Argentina and Uruguay, the man who negotiated and signed the treaty with the two countries at Buenos Aires in May 1865. Soon after he arrived there, Otaviano's original apprehensions about Argentine expansionism gave way to a positive assessment of Argentina, and a resolute defense of the alliance against criticism at home. As revealed in his correspondence, by February 1866 he was convinced that joining forces would help "the two races," the Argentine and the Brazilian, to overcome their mutual hatred and would constitute a basis for reconciliation and friendship. Significantly, this aspiration for a new kind of relationship with the Argentines emerged alongside a fresh perception of their character. In Otaviano's description, they were the "Yankees of the South," a dynamic and enterprising people with a great future ahead under its new liberal leadership. As both a statesman and a poet, he articulated his vision of regional unity and grandeur also in verse:[14]

O majestoso Prata bem claro nos ensina,
Nesta junção feliz de rios tão distantes,
Que os sul-americanos, por uma lei divina,
Devem viver unidos, se querem ser gigantes.

The majestic River Plate clearly reveals to us,
In this happy juncture of rivers so distant,

13. Fernando A. Novais, "O significado da 'guerra do Paraguay' na história do Brasil," in *A guerra do Paraguay: 130 anos depois*, p. 81. To be sure, Brazilians had already fought alongside Spanish Americans in the campaign against Rosas's government in Argentina in 1852. Still, this military episode, probably because of its much more limited scope and successful conclusion, as well as the fact that Brazil's ally was a caudillistic government–and not a "civilized" Unitarian government such as Mitre's–did not have an effect of the sort that the Paraguayan War had on Brazilian public opinion.

14. This account of Otaviano's change of heart is based on Francisco Doratioto, *Maldita guerra: Nova história da guerra do Paraguai* (São Paulo: Companhia das Letras, 2002), pp. 165-167.

That South Americans, by divine law,
Ought to live united, if they aspire to be giants.[15]

At about the same time that Otaviano was dispatching his first letters from the Plata to Rio de Janeiro, Emperor Dom Pedro II and his entourage were traveling in the opposite direction to meet with Presidents Bartolomé Mitre of Argentina and Venancio Flores of Uruguay near the Brazilian town of Uruguaiana, where the allied forces were besieging an invading Paraguayan division. The three parties met on September 11, 1865. The emperor's French son-in-law, the Count d'Eu, who was present at the site, documented the encounter in his diary. He was not sure what the two heads of states and their general command would think of the Brazilian side. However, "the impression *they* made on *us*,"–of this he was certain–was "decidedly favorable." Although fashioned in the midst of a military campaign, his account of the meeting focused on cultural rather than strategic matters. The face-to-face encounter aroused in him a sense of revelation and an ethnographic impulse: "We are so accustomed to hearing criticism about the lack of civilization of these Spanish Americans in Rio de Janeiro and in Europe," he wrote, "that it is a nice surprise to find courteous and elegantly dressed people among them." The Count was especially fascinated by Mitre, whose gentlemen-like, tidy attire he described in detail. Everything about this Argentine, who could speak with ease about natural history, the fine arts, and literature, radiated elegance and thoughtfulness. This was in stark contrast, the prince noted, to Flores, whose physical appearance and culture suggested indigenous blood, scantily developed intelligence and poor education. The Uruguayan leader reinforced the old stereotype of Spanish American primitivity; the Argentine leader destroyed it.[16]

It is of symbolic significance that the Emperor and his son-in-law approached the international border but did not cross it. Apparently, there were limits to how far the imperial leadership could go, not

15. Cited in Ibid., p. 166.

16. Conde D'Eu (Prince Gastão de Orléans), *Viagem militar ao Rio Grande do Sul* (Belo Horizonte: Editora Itatiaia; São Paulo: Editora da Universidade de São Paulo, 1981), pp. 80-82, 87. The two Spanish American leaders left quite similar impressions on the Emperor himself. See Roderick J. Barman, *Citizen Emperor: Pedro II and the Making of Brazil, 1825-1891* (Stanford: Stanford University Press, 1999), p. 205.

only physically but also conceptually. The Count d'Eu's discovery of sameness with the Spanish-American Other did not involve a corresponding radical problematization of the Brazilian self. This was true even of Otaviano, who went further south. Yet by the end of the war, there were voices that openly called into question not only the identity of the neighbors but of Brazil as well.

The year 1870 saw the publication of the Republican Manifesto which challenged the isolationism pursued by the monarchy. "We are from America and we want to be Americans," wrote the authors of the document that marked the resurgence of American-spirited republicanism in Brazil. Echoing similar voices heard in other parts of Latin America at the time, they emphasized the total contradiction, in theory and practice, between the monarchical form of government and the laws and interests of the New World's countries. The permanence of this regime, it was stated, would continue to cause domestic oppression as well as hostility and wars with the peoples surrounding us. "We strive to establish amicable relationships with all peoples and to live in democratic solidarity with the continent to which we belong."[17]

Historians have often quoted these closing statements from the Republican Manifesto and rightly noted that its drafters associated the republican form of government, peace, freedom, and material progress with America. Yet most students of Brazil have failed to follow in the footsteps of Joaquim Nabuco (the retired politician and nostalgic monarchist historian of the late 1890s), who had indicated that republican propaganda had some origins in the Plata region, a product of the "influence that the institutions and peoples of the *Prata* had exerted on Quintino Bocaiuva and others [...]."[18] Bocaiuva,

17. "Manifesto," *A República*, Dec. 3, 1870, in Quintino Bocaiúva, *Idéias políticas de Quintino Bocaiúva*, ed. by Eduardo Silva (Brasilia/Rio de Janeiro: Senado Federal/Casa Rui Barbosa, 1986), vol. 1, p. 330. On Americanism during this time, see Leopoldo Zea, *The Latin American Mind* (Norman: University of Oklahoma Press, 1963), pp. 77-106; Allen L. Woll, *A Functional Past : The Uses of History in Nineteenth-Century Chile* (Baton Rouge: Louisiana State University Press, 1982), pp. 104-126; Charles Hale, "Political and Social Ideas in Latin America, 1870-1930," in Leslie Bethell, ed., The *Cambridge History of Latin America*, vol. 4 (Cambridge: Cambridge University Press, 1984), p. 372.

18. Nabuco, *Um estadista do imperio,* vol. 1, p. 511. A similar observation can be found in Sílvio Romero's *Novos estudos de litteratura contemporanea* (Rio de Janeiro: H. Garnier, 1899), p. 24, and among modern scholars in Raimundo Faoro's *Os donos*

one of the authors of the Manifesto, future leader of the Republican National Party and another main character in our story, was already a well-known journalist when he set off to Buenos Aires and Montevideo in 1868, where he and another notable republican propagandist of the early 1870s, Francisco Xavier da Cunha, came into contact with some of the most prominent Argentine intellectuals of the period. Upon their return, both men attacked the Empire's foreign policy toward its southern neighbors, and more significantly–from our point of view–the perceptions underlying it as well.

Soon after he arrived in Rio, Bocaiuva delivered a public lecture about "The Institutions and the Peoples of the River Plate," which he opened by noting that the common negative image of Argentina and Uruguay was superficial and therefore unjustified. The period when these countries' politics were dominated by the sword–he informed his audience–was coming to a close, clearing the way for civilization and progress. In some respects, such as guaranteeing civil liberties, attracting and receiving immigrants, or compiling national statistics –Bocaiuva warned–Brazil was already lagging behind the two republics, and even behind "miserable" Paraguay: "In this way, gentlemen, we are at risk of remaining the ultimate sentinel of the past in this continent, guarding the grave of a great nation!"[19]

do poder: Formação do patronato político brasileiro, 13th ed. (São Paulo: Globo, 1998), p. 451. But most often than not the revival of American-spirited republicanism in Brazil is associated with growing admiration for the United States. See, for example, Francisco José de Oliveira Vianna, *O ocaso do império* (São Paulo: Melhoramentos, 1925), pp. 94-97; Moniz Bandeira, *Presença dos Estados Unidos no Brasil*, 2nd ed. (Rio de Janeiro: Civilização Brasileira, 1978), pp. 116-120; and Thomas Skidmore, "Brazil's American Illusion: From Dom Pedro II to the Coup of 1964," *Luso-Brazilian Review* 13:2 (1986), pp. 71-74. Exceptional in this regard is Hale's "Political and Social Ideas," in which he rightly places the publication of the Republican Manifesto within a general Latin American trend of the period, pointing at mutual influences among Brazil and its neighbors.

19. The lecture was published as a pamphlet titled *As instituições e os povos do Rio da Prata* (Rio de Janeiro: Typ. do Imperial Instituto Artistico, 1870), in Bocaiúva, *Idéias políticas*, vol. 1, pp. 292-297, quote, p. 297. Many years later, Bocaiúva would refer to this public assembly as the launch pad of the republican campaign. See "Como se fez a república, Um 'interview' com o general Quintino Bocaiúva," *A Ilustração Brasileira*, Nov. 15, 1909, in *Idéias políticas*, vol. 1, p. 641. For Francisco Xavier da Cunha's views, and for information regarding his, and Bocaiúva's, stay in the River Plate, see his *Propaganda contra o imperio; Reminiscencias na imprensa e na diplomacia, 1870 a 1910* (Rio de Janeiro: Imprensa Nacional, 1914), which contains many arti-

The point here is not so much to reinforce Nabuco's suggestion of a cause-and-effect relationship between the close encounter with Argentines and Uruguayans and the rise of republicanism, as it is to stress the new role assigned to Spanish America in Brazil's ongoing discussion about its desired regime and its insertion in the New World. If, until the Paraguayan War, political and economic conditions across the borders had served mainly as a warning against the replacement of the monarchy–and thus had also encouraged isolationism–they were now seen and presented by some as proof that such a change was essential.

Objective processes taking place across the border nurtured these varying perceptions and ideological tendencies. Bocaiuva's earlier observations turned out to be almost prophetic, as they came to reflect the reality of several Spanish American countries in the 1880s much more accurately than the established imperial image of them as anarchical, caudillistic, and barbarian *republiquetas*. The levels of political stability and modernization achieved by Argentina, Chile, and Mexico suggested that Spanish American republicanism did not necessarily equal anarchy, while Luso-American monarchism did equal backwardness. Thus Brazil's singularity within Latin America, which had bolstered the self-confidence of its elites, could be interpreted by the monarchy's opponents as a burden.

The republicans were not the only ones to notice and point out the changing circumstances of Spanish America. The renowned modernizer Tavares Bastos, for example, warned in the early 1860s that in the event a republic were to be established in Brazil, "*caudilhos* will inherit *caudilhos*, like in Mexico [...] and in the *Rio da Prata*."[20] Yet in his *A Província: Estudo sobre a decentralização do Brasil* (1870), he expressed a completely different view and usage of Argentina's recent history. His loyalty to the monarchy did not prevent the ardent reformer from making several references to what he perceived as the

cles he published in republican newspapers during the early 1870s (see pp. 71-94, 135-145). For a succinct description of the republican-monarchist debate regarding Spanish America by another important republican, see José Affonso Mendonça de Azevedo, *Vida e obra de Salvador de Mendonça* (Brasília: Divisão de Documentação, Seção de Publicações, 1971), p. 178.

20. Aureliano Cândido de Tavares Bastos, *Os males do presente e as esperanças do futuro*, 2nd ed. (São Paulo: Companhia Editora Nacional, 1939[1862]), p. 46.

better position of the neighboring republic concerning legislative and educational systems, material infrastructure, and attractiveness to immigration –"white," he stressed, in the same vein as Nabuco– thanks to its federal political structure.[21]

In this way, the Argentine experience was transformed from a warning signal against barbarism into a road map for progress. Again, bringing up information concerning Brazil's traditional rival reflected an approach that was not merely instrumental. Much as in Bocaiuva's case, Tavares Bastos's growing appreciation of this country went hand in hand with a call for a reversal of Brazil's policy toward the Plata, urging rapprochement with the entire continent, as well as with an outright expression of American consciousness. And although the interest and admiration for the United States by this writer-statesman far exceeded those he felt for any other American country, it should be noted that his frame of reference was explicitly hemispheric, and included Spanish America as well. To what extent this had to do with his visit to the Plata on a diplomatic mission in 1864 remains an open question.[22]

Some years later, another articulate Brazilian made a different kind of journey south. In 1882, Rio de Janeiro's *Gazeta de Notícias* published a series of travel notes by a young law graduate, the son of one of São Paulo's wealthiest and most influential families, who had already established for himself a reputation as a conservative political writer. Eduardo Prado set out on a grand tour, which first stopped in Montevideo, Buenos Aires, Valparaíso, and Santiago. About ten years later, the same Eduardo Prado would publish his famous treatise, *A ilusão americana* (*The American Illusion*), in which he inscribed the previously quoted description of Brazil as an island within Latin America. Although traces of this arrogant isolationist attitude are strongly pres-

21. Aureliano Cândido de Tavares Bastos, *A província: Estudo sobre a decenralização do Brasil*, facsimile ed. (Brasília: Senado Federal, 1996[1870]), pp. 187, 195, 219, 245, 251, 258, 264, 278, 297, 318, 321, 328. A pertinent analysis of Tavares Bastos's Americanism–although it compares, rather than relates, his thinking to Spanish American trends–can be found in Luiz Verneck Vianna, "Americanistas e iberistas: A polêmica de Oliveira Vianna com Tavares Bastos," *A revolução passiva: Iberismo e americanismo no Brasil* (Rio de Janeiro: Revan, 1997), pp. 125-172.

22. Carlos Pontes, *Tavares Bastos*, 2nd ed. (São Paulo/Brasília: Ed. Nacional/INL, 1975), pp. 98-100, 106, 141-142; Tavares Bastos, *A província*, pp. 12-15, 21.

ent throughout Prado's travel accounts, replete with condescending references to Spanish American social and political practices, his observations were not entirely negative, and betrayed a degree of identification with some sectors of these other nations' societies.

The Brazilian visitor was impressed, for example, by the dedication and intelligence of the faculty of the University of Montevideo, whom he sympathetically described as "a weak and small center of resistance against the militarism" that dominated Uruguay. During his stay in Chile, whose material achievements and political culture he praised, Prado witnessed the solemn opening session of the National Congress and noticed that the president held up the same traditional eyeglass that the Brazilian emperor used to wear on such occasions. For Prado, this ceremonial detail demonstrated "how republican the Brazilian Monarchy [was]."[23] Here was another case in which a Spanish American country elicited a positive judgment, yet not because it was different from Brazil, but rather the opposite–it was very Brazilian.

Obviously, unlike Tavares Bastos and Bocaiuva, Prado's visit to the neighboring countries was not accompanied by any call for American solidarity, let alone for replacing the already "republican" Empire with a republic. Nevertheless, his 1882 articles heralded a period of increasing contact with the reality of Spanish American countries, and a growing awareness of their achievements, both among supporters and opponents of the monarchy in Brazil. It was more than just a coincidence that in the same year, the director of the Empire's National Museum, Ladislau Netto, left for Buenos Aires in order to explore this city's anthropological museums, and that on board the boat which carried the distinguished servant of the Crown was also Argentina's former President, Nicolás Avellaneda, returning home after a visit to Brazil.[24]

In the late nineteenth century, information about the latest developments on the other side of the border reached the Brazilian elites

23. On Prado, see Darrel Levi, *The Prados of São Paulo, Brazil: An Elite Family and Social Change, 1840-1930* (Athens: University of Georgia Press, 1987), p. 125. For his own words, see Eduardo Prado, *Viagens: América, Oceania e Asia* (São Paulo: Salesiana, 1902), pp. 31, 94, respectively.

24. *Correio do Brasil* (Lisbon), Nov. 20, 1882, p. 6.

in various ways. New publications arrived at the Brazilian Historical and Geographical Institute and the National Library, as well as falling into the hands of individuals by way of private and institutional donations or exchanges. Direct encounters took place aboard the growing number of ships connecting Valparaíso, Buenos Aires, and Montevideo with Europe and the United States, which passed through Brazilian ports. These boats also carried the latest editions of Chilean, Argentine, and Uruguayan newspapers that were reproduced occasionally by Rio de Janeiro's pro-regime and most respected daily, the *Jornal do Comércio*. Likewise, telegraph lines enabled this newspaper to report on the previous day's events in the capitals of the above-mentioned countries on a daily basis.[25] In this sense, Rio was closer to Buenos Aires than to most other towns in Brazil.

* * *

During the first days of 1888, the *Jornal do Comércio* published on its front page special summaries of the previous year's occurrences in South America. Focusing on major political developments, economic performance, and modernization, the authors of these accounts observed new degrees of stability in Argentina and Uruguay, continuous order in Chile and Venezuela, and a general

25. On Spanish American titles entering Brazilian public and private collections, see the "Bibilioteca Nacional" section of the *Relatorio do Ministerio do Imperio* (Rio de Janeiro: Imprensa Nacional), for the years 1885, 1886, 1888; José Alexandre Teixeira de Mello, "Relatorio dos trabalhos annuaes de 1889 e 1890," *Revista do Instituto Historico e Geographico Brasileiro*, vol. LIII, part II (1891), pp. 576-579; Q. Bocayuva, "in the name of the editors of *O Paiz*," to Vicente G. Quesada, Rio de Janeiro, May 28, 1885, Vicente G. Quesada papers, Ibero-Amerikanisches Institut, Berlin [Hereafter cited as VQP], box 2. On shipping, see James R. Scobie, *Argentina: A City and a Nation*, 2nd ed. (New York: Oxford University Press, 1971), p. 108; and Graham, *Britain*, pp. 88-89. For personal accounts of Spanish American–Brazilian encounters aboard ships, see Alberto Blancas, *Anécdotas y recuerdos* (Buenos Aires: Editorial Tor, 1936) p. 131; and Vicente G. Quesada, *Mis memorias diplomáticas, misión ante el gobierno del Brasil*, 2 vols. (Buenos Aires: Imprensa de Coni hermanos, 1907-1908), vol. 1, p. 98-100. In 1883, the Brazilian telegraph system was connected with those of Argentina and Uruguay; see A. Tavares de Lyra, "Correios, telegraphos e telephonos," in Instituto Historico e Geographico Brasileiro, *Diccionario historico, geographico e ethnographico do Brasil* (Rio de Janeiro: Imprensa Nacional, 1922), pp. 760-761.

"reproductive" trend in all these countries as well as in Paraguay.[26] It was in this climate that the Brazilian Empire would eliminate slavery and win Spanish American applause.

26. "Retrospecto político de 1887," *Jornal do Commercio*, Jan. 7, p. 1, and Jan. 13, 1888, p. 1.

Chapter 2
The End of Slavery and the Hopeful Beginnings of a Latin American Consciousness in Brazil

La fiesta de la libertad

The sense that their neighbors were marching forward while Brazil stood still, and the resulting discontent with rejection by them, is essential for understanding the burst of American–and more specifically South American–solidarity that followed the abolition of slavery in Brazil on May 13, 1888. Most Brazilians rejoiced in the abolition. For the next couple of days, streets and plazas throughout the land filled with celebrating crowds, while erudite editorials and public speeches interpreted the event as a national triumph marking the integration of the country into the civilized world.[1]

So far this is a familiar story. What has been left untold is that Brazilians, as they were very soon to discover, did not celebrate alone and that this supposedly national occasion was, in fact, transnational. Newspapers in several South American capitals reported the event in highly favorable terms, dubbing it as a victory not only for Brazil but for the principle of freedom in America. In Asunción, and still more so in Santiago de Chile, there were public acts of tribute.[2] Yet noth-

1. For example, various articles in "Ave libertas!: Homenagem da Escola Normal de São Paulo," a special supplement to *A Provincia de São Paulo*, May 15, 1888; as well as Eduardo Silva, *Prince of the People* (London: Verso, 1993), pp. 158-159; and Conrad, *The Destruction of Brazilian Slavery*, pp. 270-274.

2. "Honor al Brasil," *La Nación* (Asunción), May 19, 1888; "La manifestación al Brasil del 21 de Mayo," *La Nación* (Asunción), May 23, 1888; "La abolición de la

ing equaled the swiftness and the magnitude of the Argentine reaction. On May 17, which the Argentine government declared a national holiday, at about the same time that 20,000 people convened for an open-air mass in Rio de Janeiro, a crowd estimated at 20,000 to–40,000 marched through the decorated streets of Buenos Aires to the Brazilian legation to show their support. Leading the parade was former president Bartolomé Mitre, who, upon arrival at the legation, gave a public address in which he praised the long and ceaseless efforts of the liberal Brazilian Empire to abolish slavery. Mitre also stressed the great contribution of the Paraguayan War, in which he had served as commander of the allied forces, "to wipe away this hereditary stain [i.e., slavery] from [Brazil's] forehead." To support this argument, the Argentine leader quoted from the Viscount of Rio Branco's defense of the Law of the Free Womb before the Brazilian Parliament in 1871. Mitre repeated verbatim Rio Branco's words about how the Brazilian forces felt humiliated before their Spanish-speaking allies during the 1865-1870 campaign because of slavery.[3]

Translated into Spanish, words formerly in Portuguese now rang out in the Argentine capital with the new purpose of improving relations with Brazil, and soon afterward made their way back to Rio de Janeiro. Mitre's speech, together with other congratulatory notes from all over Argentina, were collected and published in Buenos Aires as a booklet entitled *La fiesta de la libertad*. The Brazilian plenipotentiary, the Baron of Alencar, sent 500 copies of this volume to his minister in Rio de Janeiro, followed by a dispatch saying that Mitre's speech merited attention both for its spirit and its content and warranted a formal expression of gratitude. Two weeks had passed

esclavitud en el Brasil," "Teatros-Función de Gala en honor del Brazil," *Ferro Carril* (Santiago de Chile), May 18, 1888; "La manifestación al ministro del Brasil," *Ferro Carril* (Santiago de Chile), June 30, 1888; "No más esclavos," *Libertad Electoral* (Santiago de Chile), 17 May, 1888; "No más esclavos," *El Siglo* (Caracas), May 21, 1888; "La América está de plácemes," *La Opinión Nacional* (Caracas), May 21, 1888. These articles were enclosed in dispatches sent by Brazilian ministers in the respective capitals to the minister of foreign relations in Rio de Janeiro.

3. "Discursos en la legación. Discurso del General Mitre," transcript enclosed in Brazilian Minister Barão de Alencar, Buenos Aires, to Minister of Foreign Relations Rodrigo Augusto da Silva, Rio de Janeiro, May 31, 1888, Arquivo Histórico do Itamaraty [Hereafter cited as AHI].

since the mass celebration in the streets of the Argentine capital, and Alencar was still strongly impressed by the events. "Even today," he wrote to his superior, "I still cannot manage to give your Excellency an at least partial idea of this ovation."[4]

The Brazilian government, although satisfied with the public celebrations and the compliments it received, reacted with caution. The Empire responded positively, for instance, to an Argentine proposal that both countries confer medals commemorating the Paraguayan War on the participating soldiers of the other, and on May 17, a protocol was signed. Yet, when the Argentines pressed the issue further and requested that the agreement bear the date of the abolition of slavery in Brazil in order to reinforce the impression of spontaneity, the Brazilians initially refused. In July, the matter was still under discussion. In a conversation he held with the Baron of Alencar that month, the Argentine foreign minister expressed his resentment at the Brazilian insistence that the exchange of medals convey a more restrained message than the neighboring republic had hoped to convey through the change of dates.[5]

In contrast to the lukewarm official response, many reform-minded political groups and individuals in Rio de Janeiro responded enthusiastically to the news from Buenos Aires. Especially responsive were abolitionist leaders loyal to the monarchy, as well as republicans and military men who, in less than two years, would bring down the regime. A few army officers, for example, planned an extraordinary parade to be held on May 25, Argentina's national holiday. News of a severe deterioration in the health of the emperor, who was then in Europe, led to the cancellation of this specific march but did not prevent dozens of notable politicians, state offi-

4. Barão de Alencar to Rodrigo Augusto da Silva, May 23 and 31, 1888, AHI. A detailed description of the various events in Buenos Aires can be found in *Jornal do Commercio*'s "Telegrammas" section, May 18, 1889, p. 1.

5. Barão de Alencar, Buenos Aires, to Minister of Foreign Relations Rodrigo Augusto da Silva, Rio de Janeiro, June 14 and July 21, 1888, AHI; Da Silva, Rio de Janeiro, to Alencar, Buenos Aires, June 30, 1888, AHI; For more evidence on Brazil's restraint in responding, see the letter from Estanislao Zeballos to Enrique Moreno, dated July 12, 1888, in Fermín Vicente Arenas Luque, *Enrique B. Moreno, un gran diplomático argentino*, 2 vols. (Buenos Aires: Editorial "La Facultad," 1945-1946), vol. 1, pp. 324-335.

cials, high- and low-ranking officers, and journalists from arriving at the residence of the Argentine minister, Enrique B. Moreno, on that day in order to pay their respects.[6] Among the participants in this "pilgrimage," as they themselves referred to it, were the editors of the popular *Revista Ilustrada*, which celebrated the occasion with a full-page drawing of Moreno rising above the national flags and emblems of the Platine republic and the Luso-American Empire. The latter were tied together with a ribbon bearing the dates May 25 and May 13. Below, an inscription read, "two glorious dates that establish a fraternal bond between the Argentine and Brazilian nations [Figure 2.1]."[7]

Representatives of the Abolitionist Confederation also came to the Argentine diplomat's house. One of them, Rui Barbosa, a law graduate who had already made a name for himself as a liberal deputy and journalist and whose criticism of the regime verged on the republican, gave a short speech which appeared the next day in the abolitionist and increasingly anti-monarchist daily *O País.* The main issues that Rui Barbosa raised in this speech, and in another text he published on July 9, recurred in numerous articles and public statements released by the Rio de Janeiro press on, and between, the two commemorative days of Argentina's struggle for independence. Like other political figures of all political colors, Rui highlighted the extraordinary, authentic, and popular nature of the celebrations in Buenos Aires, and expressed deep gratitude for this act in the name of Brazil. He also praised the neighboring republic's high level of civilization in almost mystical terms, stated that the end of slavery signaled the end of hostile relations between the two countries, and

6. "Manifestação solemne em homenagem à República Argentina," *O Paiz*, May 19, 1888; "Homenagem à República Argentina," *O Paiz*, May 26, 1888; "Homenagem à República Argentina," *Jornal do Commercio*, May 23, 1888. The Argentine envoy to Brazil, *Enrique B. Moreno*, was very active in promoting the amicable dialogue between the two countries, as well as his own prestige. He was prompt in compiling the many relevant news articles that appeared in the Rio de Janeiro press between May 13 and early June, and republishing them in book form: Legación de la República Argentina, *La fiesta de la libertad en el imperio do Brazil; Testimonios de amistad fraternal á la República Argentina. Colección hecha por Enrique B. Moreno* (Rio de Janeiro: Imprensa Nacional, 1888).

7. *Revista Illustrada*, June 2, 1888, pp. 2, 8.

FIGURE 2.1.
"Two glorious dates": May 25 and May 13.
Revista Illustrada, June 2, 1888.
Courtesy of Arquivo da Casa de Rui Barbosa.

branded the ensuing manifestations of friendship on both sides of the River Plate a great contribution to "American solidarity."[8]

Not so unanimously expressed, though, were Rui's association of Argentina's progress with its republican form of government and his subtle suggestion that Brazil should make one more decisive step, beyond abolition, in order to fully integrate itself into the continent of freedom. These propositions he shared only with ardent opponents of the monarchy like Silva Jardim, Lauro Sodré,[9] and the chief editor of *O País*, Quintino Bocaiuva. The latter's newspaper led the Argentinophile-Americanist campaign, bringing it to a climax on the ninth of July with a special honorific issue, allegedly printed in 100,000 copies, of which many were to be sent for distribution in Buenos Aires.[10] The opening article was titled "Historical Sketch of the Argentine Republic–The Ascending March of Its Progress and Greatness," and its author–Bocaiuva himself–expressed hopes that it would inform the Brazilian reader not only about the advancement of Argentina but also about the social efficacy of its institutions.[11]

Republicans were obviously exploiting the moment in order to promote their political cause, making use of Argentina's new image to identify the republican form of government with "democracy," social order, and material progress. Sympathizers with the monarchy, for their part, emphasized the liberal character of the Brazilian

8. Rui Barbosa, "Saudação a Henrique B. Moreno, Ministro da República Argentina no Império do Brasil," in *Obras completas de Rui Barbosa* (Rio de Janeiro: Ministério da Educação e Cultura, 1942–), vol. XV, t. I (1888), pp. 155-156; and "Carta ao presidente da Confederção Abolicionista," *Cidade do Rio*, July 10, 1888, in ibid., pp. 157-159. For similar views, see *La fiesta de la libertad*, passim; various original articles, as well as republished ones from other newspapers, in *Revista Illustrada*, July 14, 1888.

9. Antônio da Silva Jardim, *Propaganda republicana (1888-1889): Discursos, opúsculos, manifestos, e artigos coligidos, anotados e prefaciados por Barbosa Lima Sobrinho* (Rio de Janeiro: Ministério da Educação e Cultura/Fundação Casa de Rui Barbosa, 1978), pp. 265-268; Lauro Sodré, *Crenças e opiniões*, facsimile ed. (Brasília: Senado Federal, 1997 [1896]), p. 64.

10. Reported in the news section of the *Gazeta da Comarca* (São Fídelis, Rio de Janeiro), July 7, 1888, newspaper clipping found in Arquivo Quintino Bocaiúva, Centro de Pesquisa e Documentação de História Contemporânea do Brasil, Fundação Getúlio Vargas, Rio de Janeiro, Serie Imprensa QB 874.06.25. I was unable to verify whether any copies were actually sent to Buenos Aires.

11. Quintino Bocayuva, "A República Argentina–Esboço histórico–Marcha ascencional do seu progresso e da sua história," *O Paiz*, July 9, 1888, p. 1.

FIGURE 2.2.
"Brazil and the Argentine Republic on July 9, 1888." This image formed part of the unprecedented discourse of Brazilian-Argentine rapprochement that developed in Rio de Janeiro in the immediate aftermath of the abolition of slavery. The juxtaposition of the native Indian, personifying the Brazilian Empire, and the French "Marianne," personifying the Argentine Republic, insinuates a radical alterity between the two entities that appears to contradict the message of solidarity embodied in their reciprocal gaze and handshake. But this might have been precisely the cartoonist's intention: to suggest that in order for Brazil to fully integrate itself within South America, not only slavery but also the monarchy should be eliminated. *Revista Illustrada*, July 14, 1888. Courtesy of Arquivo da Casa de Rui Barbosa.

Empire, thus countering republican accusations. Outstanding among them was Joaquim Nabuco, whom we have already mentioned as a great champion of abolitionism and who, in spite of political differences, wrote regularly to Bocaiuva's *O País*. In an article published on May 30, 1888, he cited Mitre's reference to the Brazilian Empire–two weeks earlier at the Brazilian legation in Buenos Aires–as a "democracy with a king's crown." The discussion of this "great Latin American figure," wrote Nabuco, along with other favorable statements coming from the United States, demonstrate that "the republicans of America do not see the Brazilian monarchy as a hated exception, but rather as a school of liberalism and political tolerance, necessary for the progress of the neighboring Republics."[12] Significantly, Mitre's very same words were also cited in a laudatory semi-official biography of Emperor Dom Pedro II, published under a pseudonym by the son of the Viscount of Rio Branco, the Baron of Rio Branco–at that time still a minor diplomat and historian–one year later in Paris.[13]

That the monarchy's advocates summoned Mitre as a character witness indicated a new line of defense against republicanism that would not have been possible earlier. As already mentioned, the neighboring countries' advancements had been acknowledged by republicans and monarchists alike. This common change in what can be defined on the basis of Tzvetan Todorov's typology of relations to the Other as the dimension of knowledge ("the epistemic level"), allowed another transformation in the dimension of value judgment ("the axiological level"): segments of Spanish America came to be considered at least as equal, if not superior, to Brazil. Bocaiuva's, and now also Nabuco's, usage of Argentina as a source of political legitimation at home was conditioned by this shared transition from a negative to a positive value judgment. Yet, the similarities between republicans and monarchists, in terms of their attitude toward Spanish America, did not remain limited to the two mentioned dimensions. Common patterns extended also to the dimension of action

12. Joaquim Nabuco "A magnanimidade argentina," *O Paiz*, May 30, 1888.

13. B. Mossé, *Dom Pedro II, imperador do Brasil*, trans. by Herminia Lessa (São Paulo: Edições Cultura Brasileira, n.d.[1889]), p. 192.

("the praxeological level"). In this area, a transition from distancing to rapprochement was clearly taking place.[14]

As for the republicans, a simultaneous change in all three dimensions was already evident in their 1870 Manifesto, yet back then the context was different. Now, 18 years later, in the climate produced by abolition, Quintino Bocaiuva could proudly remind *O País*'s readers how he had used to be mocked as "*archi-philo-platino*," contrasting this past reaction with the honor he received at present as a champion of Brazilian-Argentine rapprochement.[15] Almost simultaneously, in the Chamber of Deputies, another republican, Afonso Celso, declared himself to be "the Argentines' greatest friend in Brazil" and an "enthusiast of their wonderful progress." Celso, son of the man who would soon become the Empire's last prime minister, made this statement during an interpellation he made to the foreign minister on July 6. In his interrogation he pressed the minister to accept an invitation to the South American Congress of International Private Law, to be held in Montevideo the next month, and to take advantage of the warming regional atmosphere in order to finally resolve the old dispute with Argentina over the territory of Missões.[16]

This border question had been a major source of the "spirit of jealousy and ill-feeling" that existed between the two sides, as the United States envoy in Rio de Janeiro observed in late 1887. Although at this point tensions had started to subside, some months later negotiations over the issue were still dragging on.[17] It was against this background that, in the immediate aftermath of abolition, Nabuco and another devotee of the Empire, André Rebouças, decided to take action on the matter. Much of the energy that these

14. Tzvetan Todorov, *The Conquest of America: The Question of the Other*, trans. by Richard Howard (New York: Harper Perennial, 1992), pp. 185-186.

15. Bocayuva, "A República Argentina."

16. Brazil, *Annaes do Parlamento Brazileiro, Camara dos Srs. Deputados–Terceira sessão da vigesima legislatura de 4 de julho a 2 de agosto de 1888*, vol. 3 (Rio de Janeiro: Imprensa Nacional, 1888), session of July 6, pp. 47-50.

17. Mr. Jarvis, Rio de Janeiro, to Mr. Bayard, Washington, Nov. 10, 1887, No. 55, in U.S., Department of State, *Papers Relating to the Foreign Relations of the United States Transmitted to Congress with the Annual Message of the President, Dec. 3, 1888* (Washington, 1889), pp. 55-56; Amado Luiz Cervo, *O parlamento brasileiro e as relações exteriores: 1826-1889* (Brasília: Editora Universidade de Brasília, 1981), pp. 122-132.

two had dedicated to ending slavery they now channeled toward the termination of the Missões controversy.

Rebouças, a mulatto engineering professor at the Polytechnic School, entrepreneur, longtime companion of Nabuco in the leadership of the abolitionist movement, and intimate of Emperor Dom Pedro II, started to draft a unique plan for the final settlement of the question. His obsession with modern technology, his interest in promoting European immigration, as well as the principle of rural democracy on which he hoped to reshape Brazil all received their due expression in this project. It included the construction of a new railway to mark the border, while territory on both sides of it would be "neutralized" and divided into modest agricultural lots to be inhabited by immigrants from "Europe's most advanced countries."[18] It is hard to miss the symbolism embedded in this picture of a train, perhaps the sublime expression of modernity at the time, running parallel to the border–clearly separating the two nations, while at the same time bringing them together on a ride up the track of civilization. Once again, this time among monarchists, we witness the linkage between projects of national renewal and hopes of regional peace, hopes which Rebouças had already written in his diary while in Uruguay during the Paraguayan War.[19]

Nowhere was this amalgam of national, regional, and continental aspirations more evident than in the thinking of Joaquim Nabuco, although in his case there was less emphasis on concrete material enterprises. In 1882, he had already expressed to one of his acquaintances the wish to establish a non-partisan, truly "liberal" journal that would serve to remove the misconceptions of the past, and instead teach "sound economic principles" and proven "social laws."

18. André Rebouças, *Diário e notas autobiográficas*, eds. Ana Flora and Ignacio José Verissimo (Rio de Janeiro: José Olympio, 1938), pp. 313-316, 332-340, 373-374. On the imagery aspects of modernity, especially trains, see Francisco Foot Hardman's *Trem Fantasma: A modernidade na selva* (São Paulo: Companhia das Letras, 1982), where there is also a treatment of Rebouças, pp. 79-84. On Rebouça's concept of rural democracy, see Maria Alice Rezende de Carvalho, "André Rebouças: Un americanista del imperio," in Víctor A. Arriaga Weiss and Ana Rosa Suárez Argüello, eds., *Estados Unidos desde América Latina: Sociedad, política y cultura* (Mexico City: Colegio de Mexico, 1995), pp. 197-216.

19. Rebouças, *Diário*, pp. 91, 101.

This "American and South American" newspaper, which was never actually launched, might have also assumed the task of improving relations with "countries like Argentina and Chile" in the context of its overall mission to propel Brazil along the way of progress.[20]

Three years later, Nabuco presented in the Brazilian congress a triple plan of "Abolition, Federation, and Peace," designed to save the monarchy by reforming its social, economic, and political structure, as well as its traditional interventionist foreign policy in the Plata region.[21] At the time, he hardly developed the third article of the plan, but once the grand task of abolition had been accomplished, he made "American peace" a new mission. He promoted this cause in Congress, through *O País*, and, after leaving the newspaper that became too republican for him in January 1889, also during his honeymoon in Uruguay, Argentina, and Paraguay.[22] His public speeches and articles from that period offer the most elaborate version of a voluminous, quite uniform, but still inchoate and superficial Americanist discussion that developed in Rio de Janeiro immediately after May 13, 1888, and continued to flow in different directions over the next several years.[23]

20. Joaquim Nabuco to Barão Homem de Melo, London, Nov. 28, 1882, in Joaquim Nabuco, *Cartas a amigos*, ed. and annotated by Carolina Nabuco, 2 vols. (São Paulo: Instituto Progresso Editorial, 1949), vol. 1. p. 95.

21. Joaquim Nabuco, "Projeto da monarquia federativa," Sep. 14, 1885, in *Discursos parlamentares* (Rio de Janeiro: Imprensa Nacional, 1949), pp. 429-430. Nabuco was working in coordination with Rebouças, who, in a letter written on Jan. 1, 1885, even before Nabuco was elected to Parliament, had pointed out that the promotion of "peace through arbitration" would be the most important task on his friend's future agenda, together with the abolition of slavery. In the same letter, Rebouças also mentioned that they might have to create a "Society of Peace Advocates" to make propaganda and "prevent a devastating war with Argentina." Arquivo de Joaquim Nabuco, Arquivo Nacional, Rio de Janeiro [Hereafter cited as AJN] 001-74/259.

22. A letter sent to Nabuco by Rebouças on July 6, 1889 suggests that the honeymoon was indeed not very intimate: "The telegrams arriving from Montevideo," wrote the latter from Rio, "say that you are propagating the confraternity of the peoples of South America." As is evident, the cooperation between the two friends toward peace in the region continued. Rebouças encouraged Nabuco in his mission, and, in order to help him, enclosed a copy of the plan he [Rebouças] had prepared for the solution of the Missões controversy. AJN 001-74/598.

23. My discussion of Nabuco's ideas is based on "A magnanimidade argentina," *O Paiz*, May 31, 1888; "A organização da paz," *O Paiz*, June 3, 1888; "A nação Argentina," *O Paiz*, July 9, 1888; "A república em Pernambuco," *O Paiz*, Dec. 16,

Nabuco drew a moral-historical trajectory, expanding in time and space, which led from the glorious days of Latin American independence, through the joint struggle against Solano López's tyranny, to the abolition of slavery in the present, and further on toward an American future of peace, freedom, and progress. According to Nabuco, on the day of abolition, Brazil was reborn as a civilized nation, leaving behind not only its barbarous past as a slave-owning society, but also its traditional rivalries with Spanish America.

Here was an exemplary case of "creating national genealogies" by reminding the community of what it has to forget, a phenomenon that Benedict Anderson finds typical of nineteenth-century nationalisms. Like Ernest Renan's French audience, Nabuco's Brazilian readers "were told to have already forgotten" what Nabuco "assumed that they naturally remembered."[24] The interesting difference is that Nabuco was producing a genealogy for two communities, one national (Brazilian), and another transnational (South American and American). While mentioning the battle of Ituzaingó, where forces of the United Provinces of the River Plate clashed with the Brazilian army in 1827, Nabuco declared that the Empire's "traditional policy" of interventions in its neighbors' affairs was like indecipherable "hieroglyphs" to his contemporary countrymen: "We, peoples of South America, tend to forget fast." He then likened the relationship between pre- and post-abolitionist Brazil to the one between a cocoon and a butterfly, and added, "The sun of America that had the power to suddenly break the three-centuries-long night of slavery, rose on us only on May 13, 1888."[25]

The repeated use of the metaphors of night and day, darkness and light, black and white to describe the transformation that Brazil had

1888, transcribed in Fernando da Cruz Gouvêa, *Joaquim Nabuco entre a Monarquia e a República* (Recife: Fundação Joaquim Nabuco, Editora Massangana, 1989), pp. 384-388; "Argumentos republicanos – I – A única exceção na América," *O Paiz*, Dec. 20, 1888, in ibid., pp. 388-392; and on the following documents found at AJN: "Discurso proferido no Paraguay," 001.13-74/14; "Discurso no Instituto Geográfico Argentino," 001.13-74/17; "Impressões do Prata," 001.13-74/18; "Discurso em Buenos Aires," 001.13-74/19.

24. Benedict Anderson, *Imagined Communities: Reflections on the Origin and Spread of Nationalism*, 2nd rev. and extended ed. (London: Verso, 1991), p. 200.

25. Joaquim Nabuco, "A nação argentina." N.B. that this article appeared in the aforementioned special edition of *O Paiz* that was to be distributed also in Argentina.

just gone through was not unique to Nabuco. Their recurrence may well have bespoken another source of relief. In the previous chapter, we saw some clues suggesting that it was not only slavery itself, but also the ensuing racial miscegenation that caused concern in Brazil about being left behind its Southern neighbors. One of the solutions was to increase the white element in the population through European immigration. Whitening was another ideal, besides "liberal" order and material progress, that united Brazilian statesmen and intellectuals with their Spanish American counterparts. Black and mixed populations were perceived as a serious obstacle to national development by elites throughout the continent.[26] From this perspective, Brazil, with its large share of blacks and mulattos, seemed much worse-off than some other countries in the region, according to the predominant thought of the day.

And yet, as Thomas Skidmore and other students of racial thought in Brazil have shown, there had been very little direct and open discussion of "the Negro question" and whitening before the abolition of slavery.[27] It is only after May 13, 1888 that a "scientific" racial discourse on national identity became predominant. This fact may partially answer why one hardly encounters any explicit expressions of racial inferiority vis-à-vis Argentina or Chile during these early days of the transition to free labor. Social groups, like individuals, are often silent about their most troubling questions, or express them only indirectly. This would appear to have been the case with the numerous black and white metaphors. Slavery was repeatedly referred to as *a mancha negra*, not simply "the stain" but "the *black* stain," that had been finally removed. Besides joy and relief about the elimination of a backward and barbaric institution that set them apart from a free America, Brazilians seem to have been expressing some more silent expectations. The destruction of slavery, they thought, could facilitate the assimilation of dark-skinned Brazilians with a

26. See, for example, George Reid Andrews, *Afro-Latin America, 1800-2000* (New York: Oxford University Press, 2004), chap. 4.

27. Thomas Skidmore, "Racial Ideas and Social Policy in Brazil, 1870-1940," in Richard Graham, ed., *The Idea of Race in Latin America* (Austin: University of Texas Press, 1990), pp. 8-9; Dain Borges, "Intellectuals and the Forgetting of Slavery in Brazil," *Annals of Scholarship* 11 (1996), pp. 44-46; Seyferth, "Construindo a nação," p. 48.

growing stream of European immigrants, who until then had emigrated in much bigger numbers to Argentina.[28]

Such was the rhetoric that abolition itself and the Argentine reaction to it had aroused. This national, international, as well as transnational event released some genuine feelings and gave strong impetus to ideas that had been in the making for some time. Slavery was perceived by many, even if they did not actively support abolition, as a wall separating Brazil from the civilized world in general, and from the Americas and South America in particular. Its destruction, it was hoped, would elevate the traditional outcast of the region to an equal status with its neighbors, in terms of both socioeconomic structure and racial composition, and thus open the way for its recognition and integration in the region.

Experienced and interpreted on that basis, the friendly celebrations in Buenos Aires brought a great sense of relief and renewal, especially in view of their extraordinary magnitude and the fact that they came from Brazil's traditional rival and most powerful neighbor. The moment was propitious for the instant formulation of an integrative liberal discourse, imbued with a strong positivistic spirit, *bilaterally* centered but *continental* in scope, whose basic elements could be drawn from their shared pasts. The proximity of Argentine commemorative dates to the moment of abolition contributed to a discussion about liberty that lumped national independence (May 25, July 9) with individual freedom (May 13). In addition, Mitre's central role in the celebrations called for the evocation of the 1865-1870 campaign for the "liberation" of Paraguay as a unifying experience between the two former allied nations. These historical events came to resemble milestones in a unilinear process, inevitably leading toward a higher stage of civilization seen as both conditioned by and conducive to peace.

28. Skidmore, *Black into White*, pp. 21-27, 124-44. From 1871 to 1888, Argentina received 451,000 immigrants, while Brazil accepted 193,000. In the next decade, about one million immigrants entered Argentina, almost double the figure for Brazil. These figures must have seemed even less favorable to Brazilians who wanted to whiten their people, if we remember that in 1890 Brazil had a total population of 14.3 million, while Argentines numbered about 4 million (ibid., pp. 140-142). See also the proceedings of a meeting of the Central Society of Immigration at the time, reported in *Jornal do Commercio*, April 7, 1889.

Men like Rui Barbosa and Bocaiuva, on one side, and Rebouças and Nabuco, on the other, could not agree about what type of regime would be ideal for such a future to be achieved. Yet this controversy did not prevent reform-minded republicans and monarchists from sharing the vision of integrating their country with the environment of its close neighbors. Recognition of South American advancements, as already stressed above, lay at the basis of this vision. But the single most important factor in igniting the Brazilian imagination was Argentina's transition from anarchic caudillism to remarkable political stability and glowing prosperity. This, in particular, served as an assurance that the southern countries of America with their composite populations and Iberian traditions, were no less capable of marching forward than their Anglo-Saxon sister to the north.

"A miraculous people who, in fifteen years, had achieved the most astonishing national transformation remembered in the history of civilization." This is how *A Cidade do Rio*, just one of many similar voices, described the Argentines in an article it published on May 25, 1888. According to the popular abolitionist newspaper, Brazilians were at first so unfamiliar with Argentine history that the news concerning this instantaneous progress had seemed to them "mythological." But no more. The neighbor's passage from "revolutionary and dictatorial militarism to a civilian regime that closely follows the laws of sociology," is now fully recognized. And this new Argentina "offered herself as a witness to our investiture as a civilized nation [...] making our rehabilitation hers. This is why we celebrate today, with heart and spirit, Argentina's anniversary."[29]

Underlying the rapid and dramatic sequence of events were, then, long-term trends. The Argentina of the late 1880s came to represent an emerging Latin America that aroused more interest, extracted more positive judgments, and better encouraged identification with it than in the past. And thus, even though the outpour of overblown rhetoric that followed abolition finally subsided after several weeks, these three interrelated trends continued.

29. "O paiz do bom senso," in *La fiesta de la libertad*, pp. 225-229.

"A Cheap Rio-Paris or even a Poor Man's Buenos Aires"

In July 1888, the Empire finally accepted Argentina's and Uruguay's invitation, sent in March, to participate in the aforementioned South American Congress of International Private Law in Montevideo. The foreign minister significantly referred to this fact in the Brazilian parliament, in reply to Afonso Celso's interpellation, as *a rupture* from Brazil's traditional approach to exclusively American congresses.[30] In the Montevideo congress (January 1889), Brazil joined Argentina, Bolivia, Chile, Paraguay, Peru, and Uruguay in signing agreements destined to regulate practices concerning patents, literary and artistic property rights, trademarks and the judicial process for individual crimes. The convention itself and the issues on the agenda may attest to the increasing interaction among and mutual interests of South American oligarchies.

A short time afterward, in February, an Exposition of South American Geography was inaugurated at the Polytechnic School in Rio de Janeiro in the presence of Emperor Dom Pedro II–who closely examined the material presented, including dozens of books from Argentina, Bolivia, Chile, Paraguay, and Venezuela. Under the section of Political and Commercial Geography, one could find historical works such as Barros Arana's multi-volume *Historia General de Chile* (1884-87) and a new edition of Bartolomé Mitre's *Historia de Belgrano* (1887) alongside more practical works like the *Primer Censo General de la Provincia de Santa Fé* (1888).[31] A month later, this census was submitted for discussion at a session of the Sociedade Central de Imigração by André Rebouças, who expressed his desire to show "this admirable work to each of our deputies and each of our senators, and ask them, 'Isn't it possible to implement in the

30. Brazil, *Annaes do Parlamento,* 1888, vol. 3, session of July 6, p. 52.

31. Sociedade Brasileira de Geografia, *Catalogo da exposição de geographia sul-americana realizada pela Sociedade de geographia do Rio de Janeiro e inaugurada em 23 de fevereiro de 1889* (Rio de Janeiro: Imprensa Nacional, 1891), pp. XVII-XIX, 173, 181, 351. See also, for example, the large segments from the Argentine president's then-recent message to his congress that were reproduced by the *Jornal do Commercio,* July 10 and 16, 1889, accompanied by detailed data tables.

provinces of São Paulo, Bahia, and Minas Gerais that which has been done with such perfection in the Argentine province of Santa Fé[?]'"[32]

Indeed, Spanish American texts of a more practical nature, replete with statistics and surrounded by a scientific aura, seem to have held the biggest sway over educated Brazilians. In July 1889, Rio de Janeiro's *Jornal do Comércio*, dedicated its "Folhetim" section to the recently published *Censo general de la población, edificación, comercio e industrias de la ciudad de Buenos Aires*. This work is "a real patriotic monument," wrote the reviewer, who went on to quote and discuss data concerning the population, schooling, sewage systems, water supply, hygiene, street lighting, and especially European immigration. He also added a citation from Mitre's *Historia de Belgrano*, in which the latter described Argentine society as a product of the mixture between whites, Indians, and Africans. Of these three agents, though, according to Mitre, only the whites played an active role in Argentine history and had prevailed in the process of miscegenation thanks to their inherent racial superiority and the continued flow of new arrivals from Europe. Then the Brazilian reviewer came up with his own conclusion: "The same causes produce the same effects no matter where. When reading the history of Buenos Aires's advancements, we therefore get the sense that we are watching, in many respects, the future trajectory of civilization in our own city, *mutatis mutandis*." More than a useful guide, the Argentine census seems to have been a source of envy as much as a boost to Brazilians' self-confidence: if the Argentines could do it, then so could they.[33]

Some other indications that Spanish American works reaching Brazil were not mere diplomatic ornaments, and that leading Brazil-

32. Proceedings of a meeting of the Sociedade Central de Immigração, reported in *Jornal do Commercio*, April 7, 1889. Similar opinion was sounded in the Senate in June by Rebouça's colleague in the society, Alfredo d'Escragnolle Taunay, who raised claims about immigrants leaving Brazil for Argentina and presented Argentina as a model to be followed–alongside the United States–with respect to immigration policy. Reported in *Jornal do Commercio*, June 1, 1889, p. 1.

33. "Folhetim do *Jornal do Commercio*–Bibiliographia," *Jornal do Commercio*, July 10, 1889, p. 1. About the prestige of statistics as a sign of the times, see Mauricio Tenorio-Trillo, *Mexico at the World's Fairs: Crafting a Modern Nation* (Berkeley: University of California Press, 1996), pp. 127-130.

ians were coming to treat certain neighboring countries as role models, can be found in three series of articles that Rui Barbosa published in his *Diário de Notícias* between April and October of 1889. One was dedicated to Chile's financial conditions and policy, and the other two to the history of relations between the Church and state in Argentina and to that country's handling of immigration. Significantly, each of his series, although subtitled "*estudo*," was based almost solely on a single recently published work by Argentine and Chilean authors, which may attest to Rui's scant familiarity with the subject matter. Yet, it was exactly this kind of ignorance that Rui set out to correct through his essays, in which he presented the courses of action taken by Chile and Argentina as examples to be followed.[34]

In the same vein, when Joaquim Nabuco came back from his mid-1889 journey to Argentina, Paraguay, and Uruguay, he confessed to his limited knowledge of the Plata region, but referred to his visit there as "preparatory."[35] Indeed, he would return to Argentina within two years. In the meantime, he would have the opportunity to become better acquainted with the country and its educational system through the more than 60 books he had received from the Argentine Consejo Nacional de Educación.[36]

Circumstantial evidence suggests that Nabuco's first journey signaled an intensification of a trend the beginnings of which were

34. Rui Barbosa, "O Casamento civil na República Argentina," *Diário de Notícias*, April 14 ,16, 18, 1889, in *Obras completas*, vol. XVI, t. II, pp. 1-12, 27-56; "A imigração na República Argentina," *Diário de Notícias*, July 1-4, 7, 1889, in ibid., vol. XVI, t. IV, pp. 1-38, 61-9; "Estudos Chilenos," *Diário de Notícias*, Oct. 16, 17, 19, 21, 23, 1889, in ibid., vol. XVI, t. VII, pp. 165-172, 181-186, 201-206, 219-223. Barbosa's active intellectual interest in Spanish American affairs can be traced at least as far back as 1883, when he asked a Brazilian colleague with ties to Vicente Quesada and Ernesto Quesada, editors of the *Nueva Revista de Buenos Aires*, for information about subscribing to this journal devoted to Latin American literature, history and international law. Ruy Barbosa to Franklin Tavora, July 10, 1883, VQP box 2.

35. Joaquim Nabuco, "Impressões do Prata." This handwritten document is, in all probability, a draft for a newspaper article which starts, "My friends kindly ask me to disseminate my impressions of the River Plate region [...]"

36. "Lista de livros remetidos a Joaquim Nabuco pelo Consejo Nacional de Educación [de Argentina]," AJN, 001.14-74/10; Consejo Nacional de Educación to Joaquim Nabuco, Aug. 16, 1889, AJN 001-74/612. According to this letter, the books were sent upon request by an Argentine acquaintance of Nabuco, which makes it plausible that the request had originated from Nabuco.

already discussed in chapter 1. He arrived at Buenos Aires about a year after a group of Brazilian journalists who had gone there during the jubilant days of abolition, and who had caused their hosts some frustrations. Among the latter was Estanislao Zeballos, one of Argentina's leading men-of-state-and-letters, soon to be nominated for the post of foreign minister. In a letter to his friend Moreno, in Rio de Janeiro, he complained that the Brazilian guests were spending their time mainly moving from one *fiesta* to another. Zeballos was especially anxious to get rid of one of them whom he wished would at last terminate his "official tasks" of eating and mingling with high society, so that the guest could go back to Brazil "to give his wife a party at home." "They are all very nice people," he suddenly changed the tone, "but we were expecting people of the rank of Nabuco and Bocaiuva."[37]

The Argentine expectations were eventually fulfilled. Although Nabuco's visit to the Argentine capital resembled in many ways that of his predecessors, his journey appears to have marked a new stage in the transnational movement within South America, at least in the eyes of his contemporaries. For example, when the abolitionist leader arrived in Montevideo, one of the city's newspapers placed the event within a wider context of a departure from the past custom of having scant, mainly political, contacts between the countries of America. "The growing civilization of these societies," said the article, "along the mutual sympathy that it produces, and the greater facility of travel, are beginning to change this state of things and provide us frequent opportunities to welcome many distinguished representatives of the Empire [...]"[38]

A few weeks later, back in Rio de Janeiro, Rui Barbosa's *Diário de Notícias* observed that the warm welcome Nabuco had received in the Plata and the sight of the region's advancements seem to have destroyed his monarchist convictions. In reality, this alleged ideological metamorphosis to republicanism did not happen. Still, we should not dismiss the following sentences, which the *Diário de Notícias*'s correspondent claimed to have heard from the returning traveler:

37. Zeballos to Moreno, in Luque, *Enrique B. Moreno*, p. 234 .
38. *El Siglo*, July 2, 1889.

"there is no need to go to Paris anymore, since everything that exists there can also be found [in Buenos Aires]. Exactly the same thing!"[39]

Of course Brazilians did not think it was "exactly the same thing." The recourse to the comparison, and its contents, indicate that in terms of external manifestations of culture, Argentina was admired not for its originality but as a successful imitation of France; this "great nation of whose glory we were always a distant satellite," as Nabuco defined the nature of the relationship in a 1886 article celebrating Sarah Bernhardt's Latin American tour.[40] Indeed, the dependent character of the Brazilian upper class's ties with Europe, and particularly with France, meant that very little attention was generally paid to Spanish American *belles lettres*.[41] However, this did not mean, as scholars were misled to infer, a general lack of interest in Brazil's neighbors. For if the Eurocentrism that Rio de Janeiro's urban elite shared with the upper classes of other Latin American capitals hindered certain types of mutual knowledge, it encouraged others. Dissident writer Lima Barreto captured the essence of that dynamic some years later in his criticism of the remodeling project executed in Rio de Janeiro in the 1900s, which was aimed at creating "a cheap Rio-Paris or even a poor man's Buenos Aires,"[42] as he cynically put it. Paris first, Buenos Aires second. The Frenchified Argentine capital

39. "Uma palestra," a clipping from *Diário de Notícias*, marked Sep. 10, 1889, AJN 001.16-74/160. Rui Barbosa himself published a month later an article titled "Irmãos de além Prata," in which he generalized about Brazil's relations with the River Plate region, saying that "each man of ours who returns from the great meridional confederation" becomes a messenger of peace. This kind of visits, according to him, contributed to the victory of friendly public opinion over political rivalries. See *Obras completas*, vol. XVI, t. VII, pp. 81-83. In 1893, Eduardo Prado would write that many Brazilians who had gone to Argentina during the last years of the monarchy were misled by a façade of progress, and thus became republicans. See *A ilusão americana*, pp. 52-53.

40. Joaquim Nabuco, "Sarah Bernhardt," in *Escritos e discursos literários. L'option* (São Paulo: Instituto Progresso Editorial, 1949), p. 40.

41. Daniel S. Wogan, *A literatura hispano-americana no Brasil: 1877-1944* (Baton Rouge: Louisiana State University Press, 1948), pp. 1-7; José Honorio Rodrigues, *Conhecimento dos países hispano-americanos no Brasil* (Washington, DC: Unión Panamericana, 1956), p. 14.

42. "Um Rio-Paris barato ou mesmo Buenos Aires de tostão." Lima Barreto, "O convento," *Gazeta da Tarde*, Sep. 21, 1911, in Beatriz Resende and Rachel Valença, eds., *Toda crônica: Lima Barreto*, 2 vols. (Rio de Janeiro: Agir, 2004), vol. 1, p. 100.

constituted, in other words, a subsidiary point of reference, a subordinate model, relevant for its greater similarity to the elites' shared ideal of civilization. Similar, but not identical.

"We may well suspect," as Angel Rama has noticed, "that Latin American understandings of the ideal city could not but differ substantially from European models, both actual and imaginary. Rather then reproducing precise copies of European models, as has so often been said, the renovated cities on the western shore of the Atlantic resulted in something partly original, offspring of a desire not strictly tied to the sources of its inspiration, a desire that, in striving to realize itself, must necessarily produce a muddy amalgam compounded of dreams and stubborn material realities."[43] True, everybody wanted their capital city to be Paris, but Paris *in America*, in South America, conscious of the particular circumstances of the region that the positivist mindset of the day deemed important.[44] Some of the most practical means for achieving the common European ideal were therefore not to be found beyond the Atlantic but across the River Plate or the Andes. This is how Chile, and more so Argentina, acquired the perceived *status* of a model-within-a-model (irrespective of actual imitation, which is beyond the scope of this work); perhaps not as central or visible as the European model, but a model all the same. And around this hybrid model, born out of marriage between Old World fantasies and New World realities, a wider identity, stretching beyond the limits of the Southern Cone, started to evolve.

43. Rama, *The Lettered City*, p. 83. The argument regarding copies differing from their originals has been made for the colonial period as well. See Mignolo, *The Idea of Latin America*, p. 63.

44. According to Angel Rama, the enormous popularity of positivist sociology in Latin America should be credited not only to its explanatory force but also to its easy compatibility with the region's mentality and to the fact that "it permitted a continued focus on *a closed regional context*." Rama farther argues, with regard to the period under discussion, that internationalization had its limits and that "(in part because of the positivist inflexions of the late nineteenth century) unalloyed ideological imitation, irrespective of local traditions and historical experience, would not now be repeated." See *The Lettered City*, pp. 56, 81. This argument is in accordance with Leopoldo Zea's thesis that Latin American intellectuals chose positivism as a practical philosophy that could provide answers to the specific problems of their time and space. In other words, historical relativism led to the acceptance of positivism. See *The Latin American Mind*, esp. chap. 7.

Not Just One America: North and South, Anglo-Saxons and Latins

Neither Brazil, nor any other "*Latin* nation," Joaquim Nabuco said to the members of the Brazilian Parliament in August 1888, would have come out with its unity intact had it gone through the terrible internal crisis that the United States experienced at the beginning of the 1860s, nor the lesser presidential-election controversy it faced in 1876. Only there, in the United States, thanks to "the Anglo-Saxon spirit," could a federal republican regime be viable. The other countries of the continent, said Nabuco, could not have overcome such crises since "the *Latin* race is incapable of restraining its passions, which, when reaching the high point, lead to the eruption of civil wars."[45]

At the same time, other reformist leaders were also making allusions to the notion of Latinity, albeit with an exactly opposite tone. According to Rui Barbosa, for example, Chile and Argentina constituted "a double argument that clears the *Latin* race from the unfounded stigma of political disability."[46] Similarly, Bocaiuva's *O País* crowned Brazil's Southern neighbor as "pride of the *Latin* race *in America*," and Afonso Celso grounded his call to improve relations between the peoples of South America in their "common origin."[47] In the aftermath of abolition, reformist leaders in Brazil reiterated their–and by extension also their country's–sense of belonging to America, but rarely doubted the *essential* differences that set Portuguese and Spanish Americans apart from their Anglo-Saxon brothers to the north. This was the case regardless of whether they admired the United States or described it with contempt.[48]

"While many Latin Americans may have admired British, German, and U.S. efficiency and technology," as Ingrid Fey explains in

45. Joaquim Nabuco, "Um projeto de federação," Aug. 8, 1888, in *Discursos parlamentares,* p. 497.

46. Rui Barbosa, "República Argentina," Diário de Notícias, May 25, 1889, in *Obras completas,* vol. XVI (1889), t. I, p. 489.

47. Visconde de S. Salvador de Mattosinhos, "Homenagem à República Argentina, oblação," *O Paiz*, special issue, July 9, 1888; my italics. Brazil, *Annaes do Parlamento,* 1888, vol. 3, session of July 6, p. 48. My italics throughout.

48. Brazilian approaches to the United States and their relationship to the formation of a Latin American identity are discussed in chapter 4.

her study of the Latin American community in turn-of-the-century Paris, "few would exclaim that although their home was in Latin America, their souls were English, German, or Yankee. By contrast many Latin American elites acknowledged their soulful connections to France, and particularly to Paris. For example, Buenos Aires did not want to be known as the New York or London of Latin America, but as the *Paris* of South America. It sought the distinction of being the first 'Latin' city of the Americas, a sister of the first 'Latin' city of Europe, which was, of course Paris."[49] What Buenos Aires had been looking for, it received from distinguished visitors from Rio de Janeiro. Joaquim Nabuco was not the only one to identify the Argentine capital with the French one (or at least to provoke others to do so). Ladislau Netto, the director of the National Museum–who, as the reader might recall, went south to Buenos Aires back in 1882 to explore the city's anthropological museums, also joined the post-abolitionist euphoria of May 1888 and sang its praises: "[...] There is, in the heart of this Istanbul of the River Plate"–*porteños* might not have been so pleased with this compliment, but they surely enjoyed what followed–"something of Athens, the old Paris of that Attica [...] Something of Paris, the modern Athens of that France [...]"[50]

Obviously, and this has already been suggested, the Brazilians' relatively novel fascination with Buenos Aires had to do with their older and much greater fascination with France. In turn, France's spell, it is important to note, did not only derive from what it *was* but also from what it *was not*: "France was Latin, but not Spanish or Portuguese; and it was modern, but not Anglo-Saxon."[51] But let us now leave this discussion of relationships along the axis connecting the

49. Ingrid E. Fey, "First Tango in Paris: Latin Americans in Turn-of-the-Century France, 1880-1920," (PhD diss., University of California Los Angeles, 1996), p. 7. For the Chilean case see, Manuel Vicuña Urrutia, *El París americano: La oligarquía chilena como actor urbano en el siglo XIX* (Santiago, Chile: Universidad Finis Terrae/Museo Histórico Nacional, 1996), pp. 87, 105, 118; and for the Argentine and the Brazilian cases, Jeffrey D. Needell, "Rio de Janeiro and Buenos Aires: Public Space and Public Consciousness in *Fin-de-Siècle* Latin America," *Comparative Studies in Society and History* 37:3 (July 1995), pp. 519-540.

50. "Aos argentinos," *O Paiz*, May 25, 1888, in *La fiesta de la libertad*, p. 212.

51. Gerald Martin, "Literature, Music and the Visual Arts," in Leslie Bethell, ed., *A Cultural History of Latin America: Literature, Music, and the Visual Arts in the 19th and 20th Centuries* (New York: Cambridge University Press, 1998), p. 65.

Latin American elites to the Old World, which has drawn so much scholarly attention, and turn to the often-ignored axis that interests us here–the intra-Latin-American one–in order to try to understand how Latinity evolved from interaction across state borders *within* the periphery.

Placed within a wider context of contemporary Western thought and international politics, Brazilians' *active* recognition of two different Americas, Anglo-Saxon and Latin, at that particular moment, may be seen as a peripheral manifestation of the dominant contemporary tendency to view the world as divided into large unequal supranational communities of race and culture that were in competition with each other.[52] Nonetheless, this alone may not account for the assertiveness of statements such as Rui Barbosa's, cited above. What is needed is an explanation more specific to Brazil and to that particular moment in time. The existing secondary literature offers here only a few observations, which focus on a somewhat later period, but they are nonetheless significant. Brito Broca pointed out, for example, that many Brazilian literati of the *belle époque* envisioned themselves and their nation as white, and more specifically Latin, as a "defense mechanism" against the threat of a racially mixed society.[53] Latinity, according to this argument, was formed along the axis connecting the elite with the masses. Thomas Skidmore's study *Black into White* highlighted a seemingly contradictory propensity among intellectuals of the period to accept the notion of "Latin degeneracy" as a corollary to the widely accepted theory of Aryan superiority,[54] thus linking the preoccupation with Latinity in Brazil to the previously mentioned axis running between educated Latin Americans, Brazilians included, and the North Atlantic centers.

52. Alan Cassels, *Ideology and International Relations in the Modern World* (London: Routledge, 1996), pp. 101-107.

53. Brito Broca, *A vida literária no Brasil –1900*, 2nd ed. (Rio de Janeiro: José Olympio, 1960), pp. 102-108. Broca's argument is repeated with some nuances by David Brookshaw, *Race and Color in Brazilian Literature* (Metuchen: Scarecrow Press, 1986), pp. 57-59; and in Needell, *A Tropical Belle Époque* (Cambridge: Cambridge University Press, 1987), p. 201. For a similar argument regarding Latin American elites in general, see Mignolo, *The Idea of Latin America*, chap. 2; Mauricio Tenorio-Trillo, *Argucias de la historia: Siglo XIX, cultura y 'América Latina'* (Mexico City: Paidós, 1999), p. 166.

54. Skidmore, *Black into White*, pp. 52-53, 62-63, 71-72.

In reality, Rui Barbosa's vindication of Latinity can be interpreted both as an outright expression of the first trend (Brazilians, like Argentines and Chileans, are Latin), as well as a contradictory expression of the second (Latins are not inferior to Aryans). But missing here is the Brazilian–Spanish American dimension, the intra-Latin American axis, which, if introduced, allows us to come up with a richer explanation, comprised of three mutually reinforcing elements. Trapped between a degrading European and North American discourse from above, and a feared or despised *povo* from below, upper-class Brazilians had good reason to embrace the friendly and reassuring messages of their Spanish American peers, who were in a similar predicament.[55] The notion of Latinity was a means to this end. It provided Brazilians with a common denominator through which they could identify with those whom they perceived to be *essentially* similar and, at least for the moment, more successful. Buttressed by rising levels of order and progress, Latinity became an inviting psychological shelter where predominantly white Luso- and Spanish American elite members could find common refuge.[56]

In fact, the self-confident members of the Generation of 1880 now ruling Argentina were already transforming the concept of two different Americas, which on their side of the River Plate had more meaning-

55. On Brazilian elite attitudes toward "the people," see, for example, Robert M. Levine, "Elite Perceptions of the Povo," in Michael L. Conniff and Frank D. McCann, eds., *Modern Brazil: Elites and Masses in Historical Perspective* (Lincoln: University of Nebraska Press, 1989), pp. 209-224, esp. p. 217; Carvalho, "The Force of Tradition," pp. 156-162; Gerald Michael Greenfield, "The Great Drought and Elite Discourse in Imperial Brazil," *Hispanic American Historical Review* 72:3 (1992), pp. 375-400; According to Jeffrey Needell, elite men had a "'middling' role of domination, between [...] Europeanized, or Europeanizing whites and the Afro-Brazilians masses. The elite men were, in this respect, rather like colonialists within their own country." See *A Tropical Belle Époque*, p. 63.

56. On identity as a defense mechanism, see Eriksen, *Ethnicity and Nationalism*, p. 76; Bloom, *Personal Identity, National Identity and International Relations*, pp. 113-114. Jorge Larraín's discussion of Axel Honneth's theory, according to which the experience of disrespect at the individual level and the resulting struggle for recognition "has the potential to become collective," in a way that "personal and collective identities meet," is also relevant here. See Jorge Larraín, *Identity and Modernity in Latin America* (Malden: Polity Press, 2000), p. 28. In "First Tango in Paris," p. 20, Fey has put forward a very similar explanation to mine–albeit with no reference to the elite-*povo* axis–for the formation of a pan-Latin American identity among Latin Americans in the French capital.

ful roots than in Brazil, into a political tool in international relations. At the same time that the United States was launching a new Pan-American movement, the Argentine delegates to the 1888-1889 South American Congress of International Private Law in Montevideo "were sketching the first lines of quite a different picture of international harmony, one which foreshadowed a strong Latin America, independent of foreign domination, solving its own problems in its own way."[57]

Imperial Brazil, as already noted, decided to participate in the Montevideo congress somewhat hesitantly, amid calls from both loyalist and republican reformers like Nabuco and Afonso Celso to reverse its traditional isolationist foreign policy. But even they were mainly responding to recent developments at home and next door. For the time being, Brazilian intellectuals hardly used the name "Latin America," the two components of which, Latinity and Americanism–themselves poorly articulated–had not been merged into a unified whole. In theoretical terms, Brazilians' perception of themselves and their neighbors was based on a negative Us and Them, rather than on a positive We and You principle: they were *not* quite European, and *not* simply American.[58] However, the dynamic just described was only in its nascent stages. Soon, this latent, embryonic Latin American consciousness would come to life and become explicitly expressed.

* * *

The main points of this chapter can be summarized through the *Jornal do Comércio*'s analyses of South America in 1888, which were much more extensive than the ones of 1887, and even more optimistic in tone. The prediction was that soon enough "[South America], like

57. Thomas F. McGann, *Argentina, the United States, and the Inter-American System 1880-1914* (Cambridge: Harvard University Press, 1957), pp. 74-77. For earlier manifestations of this thinking in Argentina, see Norberto Galasso, "Prólogo," in Manuel Ugarte, *La nación latinoamericana* (Caracas: Biblioteca Ayacucho, 1978), p. XII; Shumway, *The Invention of Argentina*, pp. 244-248.

58. According to Eriksen, "we can distinguish between two modalities of group solidarity, which we may, following Sartre (1943), call *we-hood* and *us-hood*, respectively. Being us, people are loyal and socially integrated chiefly in relation to *the other* [...] Being *we*, on the other hand, entails being integrated because of shared activities within the collectivity." *Ethnicity and Nationalism*, p. 67.

the North American countries [*sic*] of the Saxon race, will constitute one entity–intimately connected and scientifically articulated." With regard to the place of Brazil within this evolving union, the authors wrote the following: "The law of May 13 that had put us, at least in terms of social conditions, on an equal level with the most free and advanced peoples of South America, broke the ice barriers that had separated us from that community. Consequently, today it is only natural that we enter this fellowship."[59]

Slavery had no doubt posed serious limits to Brazil's ability to narrow its distance from Spanish America, at least psychologically, but improved relationships with its neighbors were not as inevitable as this article suggests. Although this rapprochement is presented as seemingly "natural," in accordance with the evolutionist mindset and language of the day, it should not make us deaf to the ideological overtones. Brazilian leaders of different leanings had many motivations, psychological, ideational, and political, to promote South American solidarity. This project could bring them various benefits, hence their need to legitimize it and couch it as being preordained.

The above prophecy is emblematic. In the guise of a scientific forecast, it includes more than a dose of wishful thinking, and a good measure of elite interests. But whatever doubts might persist with regard to its true nature, one thing is certain: as a forecast, it was far from complete. For before long, the dissolution of the "ice barriers" of slavery would be followed by the shattering of the walls of the Empire. In November 1889, within a warming climate of South American fraternity, Rio de Janeiro received the Chilean battleship *Admiral Cochrane* for an official visit. The festivities were extraordinary, reaching their climax with a magnificent ball attended by the imperial couple. Without knowing it, the monarchy was celebrating its impending death. A few days earlier, when the Chilean officers visited the Military School, the cadets shouted "viva a república... do Chile," stretching the pause between the two parts of the statement.[60]

59. "Retrospecto político do ano de 1888–América do Sul," *Jornal do Commercio*, Jan. 10, 1889.

60. Sérgio Buarque de Holanda, *Do Império a República*, tomo 2, vol. 5, of Buarque de Holanda, ed., *História geral da civilização brasileira* (São Paulo: Difusão Europeia do Livro, 1972), p. 359.

Nevertheless, the first years of the soon-to-be-born Brazilian republic would not exactly resemble the salient traits of Chilean history. Republicans and monarchists would be adapting to a new reality that would remind them more of caudillistic and anarchic *republiquetas*. Many certainties were about to disappear, and Brazilian intellectual leaders would have to redefine their nation in relation to the Spanish American experience in all aspects, both those that were promising and those that were menacing.

Chapter 3
The End of the Monarchy and the Unwelcome Hispano-Americanization of Brazil

"Hatreds of an Almost Spanish American Crudity"

On November 15, 1889, following secret negotiations with republican leaders, the Brazilian army brought down the monarchy after encountering only minimal resistance. Brazil was proclaimed a republic, and, thus, 67 years of institutional exoticism in America had come to an end. From the historian's vantage point, the republic's first years are normally seen as a disordered interim of ideological confusion, military rule, and political violence between the remarkably stable Second Empire (1840-89) and the oligarchic phase of the republic (1898-1930)–an outburst of forces that appeared prematurely, and for just a few moments, on the political stage, and then withdrew or were forced to withdraw back to base. "It is true that during the time of Floriano [Peixoto], with the so-called 'consolidation' of the Republic, there was some intransigence, with *political hatreds of an almost Spanish American crudity*," writes Gilberto Freyre, as if forced to confess to a breakdown of the national character. "But," he is quick to correct, "the tension lasted only for a short time, too short to constitute an era. Hatreds were soon dissipated in the amiable Brazilian tradition of overlooking the occasional pecadillo [...] in the spirit of easygoing international cordiality."[1]

1. Gilberto Freyre, *Order and Progress: Brazil from Monarchy to Republic*, ed. and trans. by Rod W. Horton (Berkeley: University of California Press, 1986), p. 339.

As a matter of fact, Brazilians acted with " Spanish American crudity"–to use again this most interesting wording, from our perspective–for longer than Freyre would want to admit. It took the country's oligarchies roughly a decade to create a well-functioning governing mechanism, and to consolidate their rule. Eventually, political power shifted southward, principally to the civilian elites of the states of São Paulo and Minas Gerais, while monarchist and Jacobin opposition withered almost completely away.[2] In March 1899, Joaquim Nabuco would accept his government's invitation to represent Brazil in the arbitration case concerning the disputed borderline with British Guiana. Ten years of "mourning for the Empire"–as he confessed to a friend–which had taken the form of "meditative refuge of religion and letters," would thus come to an end.[3] Nabuco's reconciliation with the republican regime, which he had for a long time feared and done much to discredit, would be sealed a year afterward when he assumed the leadership of the Brazilian legation in London. This individual move was entwined with the

Horton's translation captures the essence of the original, but since it is quite liberal, it is worth quoting the key passage in Portuguese: "[...] houvera ódio político entre os brasileiros sob formas terrívelmente cruas que, por algum tempo, acentuaram as semelhanças dos brasileiros com os sul-americanos equatoriais de língua espanhola." *Ordem e progresso*, 2 vols. (Rio de Janeiro: J. Olympio, 1959), vol. 2, p. 613; my italics. It is interesting to note that scholars continue to employ the comparison to Spanish America in order to characterize the early years of the republic, albeit with a different tone: "During the century's last decade it seemed that time in Brazil had sped up; in just a few years the same conflicts that had emerged in Spanish America over the span of the nineteenth century [...]" Robert M. Levine and Steven C. Topik, "Introduction," *The Americas* 48:2 (1991), p. 131.

2. This is the standard periodization of the First Republic. See, for example, Boris Fausto, "Brazil: the Social and Political Structure of the First Republic (1889-1930)," in Leslie Bethell, ed., *Cambridge History of Latin America* (Cambridge: Cambridge University Press, 1986), vol. 5, pp. 812-814.

3. The first quote is taken from a letter to Barão Homem de Melo, cited in Carolina Nabuco, *The Life of Joaquim Nabuco*, ed. and trans. by Ronald Hilton (Stanford: Stanford University Press, 1968), p. 239, date unmentioned. The second is from Rui Barbosa's newspaper article "A missão Nabuco," *A Imprensa*, March 13, 1899, in *Obras completas*, vol. XXVI (1899), t. IV, p. 76, which celebrated Nabuco's decision to serve the republic. Nabuco thanked Barbosa in a private letter (March 14, 1899, *Cartas a amigos*, vol. II, p. 10) that was published two days afterward, also in *A Imprensa*, adopting the latter's depiction of the last ten years of his life as a "meditative refuge of religion and letters."

republic's consolidation process, and represented the synthetic nature that the regime had started to acquire.

There was nothing new, of course, about a monarchist joining the rival camp. It is a well-known fact that many planters converted to republicanism in the immediate aftermath of abolition, and that a great number of imperial statesmen were quick to adhere to the new political order that had been established on November 15. Traffic, although meager, also went in the opposite direction. Unambiguous vehement renunciations of republicanism, such as that of Afonso Celso, which occurred shortly after his father had been forced out of office by the military, were rare.[4] Nevertheless, it was not uncommon for longtime republicans to attack the regime that they had long desired in terms that brought them very close to the monarchist opposition, and indeed the 1890s saw some collaboration between old political adversaries.[5]

Put against this background of loose boundaries between monarchists and republicans, Joaquim Nabuco's transformation from the great mourner of one regime into a dedicated servant of another should not be given much importance. Yet, to judge by Nabuco's personal correspondence from that time and by the raging reactions, both in private and public, of his contemporaries, his move *did* have significance–emotional and symbolic, first and foremost.[6] That partisan border-crossing was widely practiced does not mean that there was no meaningful border to cross. Imaginary fences separating, first, the existing monarchy from an ideal republic, and later on, the existing republic from an idealized monarchy, were built and maintained by well-spoken and vociferous minorities found within both camps. As long as the Empire was in place, republicans had dominated this

4. A detailed account of Celso's political transformation is found in his *Guerrilhas* (Rio de Janeiro: Typ. Moraes, 1895), pp. 293-337.

5. Joseph Love, *São Paulo in the Brazilian Federation, 1889-1937* (Stanford: Stanford University Press, 1980), pp. 110-112; and June Edith Hahner, *Civilian-Military Relations in Brazil, 1889-1898* (Columbia, SC: University of South Carolina Press, 1969), chap. 6, esp. pp. 118-122.

6. Luis Viana Filho, *A vida de Joaquim Nabuco* (São Paulo/Brasília: Martins/INL, 1973), pp. 241-247; According to Carolina Nabuco, "the violence of the Monarchist reaction against Nabuco exceeded all expectations." It is also important to note that Nabuco himself was not at ease with his move and felt "deeply hurt" by the criticism. "[T]he wound never healed." *The Life of Joaquim Nabuco*, pp. 242-243.

practice, but after November 15, 1889, they were joined by a well-spoken and strongly motivated monarchist opposition. The 1890s thus witnessed an intensified production and reproduction of an imaginary border that separated the imperial past from the republican present, a border that helped the people who created it to define and understand who they themselves, and their country, really were. In other words, here was a moment in which identities–individual and collective–were reshaped and even born anew.

Yet, students of national identity during the early republic have largely overlooked the highly dynamic and emotionally charged debated between political intellectuals of republican and monarchist persuasions. The focus has usually been on a fairly limited number of intellectuals who did not play an *active* role in politics, and their "scientific" discourse–which evolved within the framework of positivist and evolutionist doctrines (mainly those of Comte and Spencer) and tended to subordinate the cultural-historical dimension of the nation's character to environmental factors and, most of all, racial parameters.[7] The scholarly interest in the latter and in racial thinking has been coupled with an emphasis on long-term ideational developments and on intellectual borrowings from Europe and the United States. Consequently, the impact of the immediate local context on how these and other intellectuals of the period perceived themselves and their nation remains little attended. When it comes to the study of national identity, those dramatic years when Brazilians passionately struggled over their self-image, behaving for a while with " Span-

7. One of the most notable examples is Skidmore, *Black into White*. In this book, which rightly remains an authoritative work on the subject, Skidmore symptomatically distinguishes between "the politically oriented," who struggled for changes in the political structure and whom he discusses only briefly, and "the intellectuals" on whom he focuses (p. 98). See also Renato Ortiz, *Cultura brasileira e identidade nacional* (São Paulo: Brasiliense, 1985); Roberto Ventura, *Estilo tropical* (São Paulo: Companhia das Letras, 1991); and Roberto Schwarz, "Brazilian Culture: Nationalism by Elimination," *New Left Review,* 167 (Jan-Feb 1988), especially the discussion of Sílvio Romero on pp. 77-90. Jeffrey Lesser, *Negotiating National Identity: Immigrants, Minorities, and the Struggle for Ethnicity in Brazil* (Durham: Duke University Press, 1999), chap. 2, is exceptional in this regard in that it seeks to shift attention from race to ethnicity. A definition of the "scientific" mentality is provided in Roque Spencer Maciel de Barros, *A ilustração brasileira e a idéia de universidade* (São Paulo: Universidade de São Paulo, 1959), chap. 4.

ish American crudity," dissolve in a broad picture of intercontinental currents of thought.

The major exceptions to the described historiographical tendency are several works by José Murilo de Carvalho–especially his *A formação das almas*–and Lúcia Lippi Oliveira's *A questão nacional na Primeira República*. To these should be added a small number of much more succinct or in-passing treatments of the issue. To summarize briefly and in very general terms, historians in this group describe a dual battle, strongly tied to politics, between two opposing interpretations of Brazil. The first one, promoted by the new regime, was based on universal ideas and values, and tended to overlook the uniqueness of Brazil. The general tendency of the republicans was to eradicate signs of the Lusitanian tradition in the present, and thereby any connection with that particular past. The Brazilian identity was to be forged as part of a broader American identity based on common values and political forms that unified the New World and distinguished it from the Old. This emphasis on American identity generated a renewed appreciation of the colonial past and of the Brazilian character of the Empire in the rival camp. Monarchist intellectuals upheld the important and positive influence of the Luso-Catholic culture in America. They claimed that the separation from Portugal, together with the continuation of the monarchy, facilitated both the maintenance of European cultural and racial components as well as the development of authentic Brazilian cultural characteristics.[8]

This synthesis provides the launching pad for this chapter, but before we move on, it should be noted that the works on which it is based take an instrumentalist approach to republican and monarchist

8. My summary is based on José Murilo de Carvalho, "Brasil naciones marginadas," in Antonio Anino, Luis Castro Leiva, and François-Xavier Guerra, eds., *De los imperios a las naciones* (Saragosa: Ibercaja, 1994), and idem, *A formação das almas* (São Paulo: Companhia das Letras, 1993); Lúcia Lippi Oliveira, *A questão nacional na Primeira República* (São Paulo: Brasiliense, 1990); Freyre, *Order and Progress*; Hahner, *Civilian-Military Relations in Brazil*; Maria de Lourdes Monaco Janotti, *Os subversivos da República* (São Paulo: Brasiliense, 1986); Thomas Skidmore, "Eduardo Prado: A Conservative Nationalist Critic of the Early Republic, 1889-1901," *Luso-Brazilian Review* 12:2 (1975), pp. 149-161; Steven C. Topik, *Trade and Gunboats: The United States and Brazil in the Age of Empire* (Stanford: Stanford University Press, 1996), pp. 102-103.

discourses, treating them as competing projects of identity formation, and products of rational calculations. The leaders of both camps are seen as self-conscious producers of national imaginaries designed for consumption by others. Hence the title of José Murilo de Carvalho's book: *The Formation of the Souls*. In other words, here again, as in the formerly mentioned studies focusing on the less-politicized scientific-naturalist discourse of *brasilidade*, ideas and ideologies have been given precedence over their "emotional and cognitive motors."[9]

Building on rather than discarding previous contributions, I seek to approach intellectuals of the periods as simultaneously conscious and unconscious manufacturers of meaning geared toward both themselves and others, stressing the largely overlooked role of Spanish America in that dynamic. In the aftermath of November 15, 1889, both republican and monarchist leaders were thrown into an unfamiliar reality that shattered some vital components of the Brazilian self-image. It is not without reason that, writing some 70 years later, Gilberto Freyre still needed to turn to the notion of Hispano-Americanization in order to characterize the period. Facing a sudden break of the old order, an abrupt eruption of what for them had been unknown or repressed qualities of the nation, members of the Brazilian elite had to give meaning to a radically different sociopolitical context and redefine who they were. In doing so, they turned their eyes to their neighbors, focusing mainly on the negative traits of the ex-Spanish colonies. A close reading of their private papers, journalistic writing, and essayistic works reveals how the violent aspects of Spanish American politics served Brazilian literati both instrumentally, as propaganda material, and psychologically, as a conceptual framework–that is, both ideologically and cognitively. Out of this highly dynamic and simultaneous process of self-interpretation and interpretation of the Other, this chapter argues, a Latin American consciousness would be forged.

9. This quote is from Scheff, "Emotions and Identity," pp. 279-281. For a theoretical criticism of "narrowly instrumentalist" approaches to identity formation, see Brubaker, et al., "Ethnicity as Cognition," esp. p. 51. Interestingly, José Murilo de Carvalho himself notes in another work that the impact of the change of regime at the "mental level," including not only ideas but also feelings and attitudes, remains to be studied. See *Os bestializados* (São Paulo: Companhia das Letras, 1987), p. 26.

Diagnosing Early Spanish American Symptoms: Joaquim Nabuco

For some Brazilian men-of-state-and-letters, such as Joaquim Nabuco and his close friend André Rebouças, the republic represented a very palpable and challenging menace even before it came into being. "According to the telegrams arriving from Montevideo," wrote the latter to the first in July 1889, "you are promoting the fraternization of the peoples of South America." "Here," in Rio de Janeiro, he added, "all efforts are concentrated in allocating money to the landowners [*fazendeiros*], in preparation of an oligarchic republic."[10] As mentioned in the previous chapter, Nabuco's journey to the Plata and the optimistic message of peace, regional cooperation, and American solidarity he carried with him, had some relationship to the momentum that republicanism gathered after abolition.

It was only at this time that monarchism began to take shape, when supporters of the crown were hard pressed to formulate a justification of the existing system of government in order to confront the ever-more-threatening propaganda of their opponents.[11] A major republican argument was that the monarchy had to be eliminated because it was out of step with the institutional and moral traditions of the continent, and because it poisoned Brazil's relations with its neighbors. One way to deal with this claim was to portray the Empire as a true republic, more liberal than many of the neighboring regimes. A complementary defense line was to try to prove that the Empire could live in peace and harmony with the nearby countries and be–as it had always been–a respected member of the American and South American community. This kind of strategy went hand in hand, as we have already seen, with a change of attitude toward Spanish America that was not merely instrumental.

At the beginning of July 1888, Nabuco told his Brazilian readers that present-day Argentina was not the Argentina of the times of

10. André Rebouças to Joaquim Nabuco, July 06, 1889, AJN 001-7/598. In a letter to Barão de Penedo, written as early as May 25, 1888, Nabuco wrote to his close friend that the monarchy seemed to be in "serious danger, almost doomed." In *Cartas a amigos*, vol. 1, p. 171.

11. Maria de Lourdes Monaco Janotti, "The Monarchist Response to the Beginnings of the Brazilian Republic, *The Americas* 48:2 (Oct. 1991), pp. 225-226.

Rosas; that its history had started from scratch with the relatively recent acceleration of progress, "a wonderful phenomenon" that turned the Platine republic into "the United States of South America."[12] Similarly, a few days earlier in Congress, he had risen against the idea that Brazil should participate in the 1889 international exposition in Paris, claiming that the Empire should not preoccupy itself with the Old World, but better invest its efforts in achieving legitimacy amidst "the democratic [spirit] of the continent."[13] Yet, only one month later, again in front of the Chamber, Nabuco portrayed an image of Latin America that contrasted sharply with these highly favorable statements.

In the August speech he presented a program of constitutional reform designed to turn Brazil into a federation that would revive the monarchy, instead of destroying the monarchy in order to create a federation. The monarchy did not stand in the way of decentralization, argued Nabuco. On the contrary, it was a precondition for it, if one wished to preserve the country's unity and to continue to enjoy liberty. The speaker asked his audience to recall the history of the republics of America, a history that had been dominated by a constant struggle between federalist and unitarian principles. In all of these countries, he said, excluding the United States, presidents had to destroy provincial autonomy in order to establish their continued power. A similar destiny awaited Brazil if it were to become a republic. Every time a presidential mandate would come close to its end, the country would become submerged in the same large-scale and grave disturbances so typical of the republics of South and Central America. These internal struggles could only usher in either a dictatorship–military or oligarchical–that would guarantee unity by means of violent repression, or else, dismemberment.[14]

One wonders what happened to "the democratic spirit of the Continent" in such a short lapse of time. Judging by Nabuco's words, Spanish America had for him a split personality. The contrast becomes even more pronounced if we move again back in time to 1885. In that year, Nabuco presented his program of federalization

12. Nabuco, "A nação Argentina," *O Paiz*, July 9, 1888.

13. Brazil, *Annaes do Parlamento,* 1888, vol. 2, session of June 28, p. 438.

14. Nabuco, "Um projeto de federação," p. 497.

for the first time. One of his arguments, back then, was that the federal form of government was fundamentally American. To support this argument, he mentioned the cases not only of Canada, the United Sates, Mexico, and Argentina, but even of Central America, usually a synonym of political violence and chaos at that time.[15]

Nabuco's shift from a highly positive to an outright negative portrayal of Spanish America was evidently abrupt, but apparently not accidental. His somber warnings that a change of regime would necessarily lead the country to Spanish American–style chaos and authoritarianism repeated themselves in December 1888, this time in a series of newspaper articles that were titled "Republican Arguments" and explicitly designed to counter the rising wave of republican propaganda. Although he stated some significant reservations, to which we will refer later, Nabuco categorically ruled that, "notwithstanding, there still remains the incontestable fact: that in all these countries dictatorship had become the essential principle of political life."[16]

It seems as if the Brazilian elite's deep-rooted and monolithic view of Spanish America as anarchic and tyrannical by nature, which had been losing ground since circa 1870 and eventually broke down, had come back to life. Or maybe it had never died? The question must be asked not only with regard to Nabuco, but also to his audience, since in both cases he was making a public political appeal that needed to be effective. So how may we account for the sudden and vigorous reappearance of the old stereotype? Part of the answer is that, although less so than before, it still had a certain basis in reality. True, parts of Spanish America had achieved by then high levels of political stability and economic growth, but this was not the rule everywhere. Second, "when national stereotypes are found inadequate," as Joep Leerssen has argued, "they are not so much canceled and forgotten as giving rise to their very opposite."[17] This meant that both rival camps

15. Nabuco, "Projeto da monarquia federativa," p. 425.

16. "Argumentos republicanos – I – A única exceção na América," *O Paiz*, Dec. 20, 1888, in Gouvêa, *Joaquim Nabuco*, p. 390. Negative references to Spanish America are also found in "A república em Pernambuco," *O Paiz*, Dec. 16, 1888, and "Argumentos republicanos – II – O privilégio de família," *O Paiz*, Dec. 28, 1888, both in ibid., pp. 384-388, 392-395.

17. Joep Leerssen, "The Rhetoric of National Character: A Programmatic Survey," *Poetics Today* 21:2 (2000), pp. 278-279. On the longevity of national images, see

in the Brazilian political arena, republicans and monarchists, could evoke contrasting images of Spanish America in accordance with their respective interests.

The neighbors' portrait was not fixed. It was being contested as part of the ongoing struggle between political and ideological factions. Contrasting images could be found even within the same camp. An amalgamation of conscious manipulation and psychological needs gave rise to varying representations of Spanish America, optimistic and pessimistic, rooted in race and history. These representations were produced as much in connection with long-term processes as with very immediate circumstances. In the euphoric climate of mid-1888, supporters of the crown chose to join the celebrations and ride the wave of solidarity with their neighbors. In those circumstances, it was more tempting to highlight positive common denominators. Yet, by August, the euphoria had subsided as the republic loomed more and more menacingly. It was at this point that Nabuco, like the founders of the Empire back in the 1820s, chose to ring the alarm bell of the Spanish American experience.

Yet he did so in a different more cautious and nuanced manner that did not fully contradict his previously favorable declarations, and which reflected the very different status of Spanish America in the public discussion. In both his congressional speech in August and his *O País* articles in December, Nabuco highlighted one aspect of Spanish American history at the expense of others. The focus was less on political turmoil and much more on the authoritarian regimes that, according to Nabuco, it inevitably produced. Brazil, he explained, was, despite everything, different from the Central American republics "that one day band together to form a federation and on another day break apart into independent states"; therefore Brazil would inevitably prefer a "unionist [Francisco Solano] López" rather than "five, even ten, separationist Washingtons." Faced with the danger of dismemberment, the natural choice would be a "blood-thirsty tyrant" such as the Paraguayan.[18] For Nabuco, the

also K. E. Boulding, "National Images and International Systems," *Journal of Conflict and Resolution* 3 (1959), pp. 130-131; Bloom, *Personal Identity, National Identity and International Relations*, pp. 113-114.

18. "A república em Pernambuco," pp. 387-388.

establishment of independent republics in America, excluding the case of the United States, had led to fierce and continuous internal struggles between federalists and unitarians, the results being either political dissolution or destruction of local autonomies by a repressive central government. Although a generalization, this was not an essentializing monolithic view insensitive to changes over time and space. Nabuco's emphasis on authoritarianism fit the emergence of Spanish America from the age of caudillos into the era of authoritarian developmentalism. And even in this regard, he distinguished between different types of dictatorships: military, oligarchical, and mercantile.[19]

To add to the composite nature of the picture, Nabuco was "ready to admit, truly proud of being American, that most of these countries have developed, through their violent struggles, a virile and practical, determined and liberal character, and learned how to rule themselves."[20] Here was an original interpretation of the Spanish American civil wars as an edifying experience that could correct the inherent vices of the "Latin race." Finally, to complete the duality of the message, Nabuco summoned once again, as he did in the immediate aftermath of abolition, Argentina's former president Mitre, and this time also "a famous Chilean, Mr. Montt," as character witnesses in order to prove that Emperor Dom Pedro II enjoyed a good standing among Brazil's neighbors.[21] Authoritarian as they may have been, the more orderly and (although this was not said openly) white neighbors could apparently still serve as a source of legitimation.

What we see here is neither the inflated tribute to Argentina and American solidarity that had followed the abolition of slavery, nor the traditional stereotyping and rejection of any link with Spanish America, but rather a new synthesis of both. In late 1888, Nabuco tried to offer his audience a realistic and complex view of the surrounding Spanish-speaking sphere–not exactly an obvious choice when practicing propaganda. The words he picked might have therefore reflected not only his evolving individual perception, but possi-

19. "A única exceção na América," pp. 389-390;"Um projeto de federação," p. 497; "O privilégio de família," p. 394.

20. "A única exceção na América," p. 389.

21. Ibid., p. 391.

bly also the diminishing acceptability of crude essentialist notions about neighboring countries. These notions had to be brought up to date in order to serve as defensive weapons in the fight against the prospective Brazilian republic. The discourse about Spanish America was constructed with both old and new materials, while burning political needs at home fueled and shaped the process.

There were other driving and shaping forces, as well. Nabuco's ultimately pessimistic appraisal of Spanish America in late 1888 can be partially explained psychologically, in the same way as the positive evaluation and optimistic identification with other parts of Spanish America that had been so emphatically expressed immediately after abolition. The change in tone and approach was not simply a deliberate and well-calculated manipulation designed to influence public opinion, but also the expression of an emotional predicament at a personal level.

As the title of his series of articles clearly indicates, Nabuco was now on the defensive, reacting to the other side's attacks. This was a dramatic change for someone who had been leading the offensive against the major social institution of the country up until a few months earlier. Indeed, within a short time after the high point of May 13, Nabuco's spirit started to fall, and his energies dwindled. The movement of many planters to republicanism in reaction to abolition and his inability to convince the Liberal Party to advance further reforms filled him with a sense of futility and alienation with regard to the political system. His private letters from that time reveal these sentiments. He expresses his will to withdraw from politics, and informs Quintino Bocaiuva that he feels obliged to retire from *O País* due to the newspaper's republican stand.[22] The crisis was temporarily solved by the creation of a column entitled "Campo Neutro" (No-Man's Land), in which Nabuco published the articles under discussion. José de Patrocínio, a fellow abolitionist leader and journalist, significantly referred to the column as "Campo Santo" ("The Graveyard") and maintained that its contents resembled "the mourn-

22. Jeffrey Needell, "A Liberal Embraces Monarchy: Joaquim Nabuco and Conservative Historiography," *The Americas* 48:2 (1991), p. 168. Aurélio Nogueira, *As desventuras do liberalismo: Joaquim Nabuco, a monarquia e a república* (Rio de Janeiro: Paz e Terra, 1984), p. 130.

ful solemnity of the colonnades in a temple of monumental nostalgia to a dead faith."[23]

Put against this personal background, Nabuco's somber references to Spanish America seem quite natural–just another manifestation of an emotional state. At a certain moment, he could see the bright sky of Argentina; in another, the dark clouds of Central American chaos and repressiveness. After all, Brazil's neighbors embodied both promises and threats. Yet, to view the matter just in terms of emotional ups and downs would be too simplistic. More profound psychological developments were involved. After the abolition of slavery, the monarchy's value soared, as far as Nabuco was concerned. The more he felt alienated from the political scene, the more he identified with the Empire that had managed to get rid of its former great mark of disgrace. Abolition meant "the conquest of a new world." Like Cortés, the Empire burnt its ships, the ships that had brought Dom João VI to Brazil, and from now on she would never turn back. Like other supporters of the crown, Nabuco no longer associated slavery with the monarchy, but rather with its newly acquired opponents, the "pseudo-republican" planters.[24] Gone was the shame that the barbaric institution had inflicted. Instead, there was pride in the noble act of liberating the slaves, as well as in what now came to be perceived and presented as the Empire's admirable characteristics and valuable achievements–namely, territorial unity, political stability, and liberal rights. There was also great anxiety that all these enviable assets might be lost.

This combination of regained pride and fear for the fate of the monarchy both allowed and encouraged, as we saw in the previous chapter, rapprochement with Brazil's more successful neighbors. Yet, at the same time, it also directed attention to the less fortunate coun-

23. Cited in Carolina Nabuco, *The Life of Joaquim Nabuco*, p. 181, who finds Patrocínio's diagnosis "not inappropriate."

24. Joaquim Nabuco, "A monarquia federativa," *O Paiz*, Dec. 3, 1888, in Gouvêa, *Joaquim Nabuco*, p. 383. Nabuco would later refer to the day of the abolition of slavery as the beginning of the fourth stage in the evolution of his monarchical faith: "What the Monarchy did on that date created a bond of solidarity between her and the faction of the abolition movement to which I belonged." See *Resposta às mensagens do Recife e Nazareth*, 2nd. ed. (Rio de Janeiro: Leuzinger, 1890), p. 6. For other monarchists' views of this issue, see Viotti da Costa, *The Brazilian Empire*, pp. 203, 208.

tries of the continent, and permitted Nabuco to see and expose their defects. In the aftermath of abolition, republican propaganda–with its emphasis on the negative implications of Brazil's singularity in the continent–had grown ever more menacing, and drove Nabuco to discover the dark side of Spanish America. Faced with the call to eliminate the hereditary system and adopt instead the continent's unified form of government, it was necessary to demonstrate the failure of the republican principle in most of the hemisphere's countries–necessary, and now, for the first time after a long period in which every Spanish American vice had paled before the great Brazilian sin of slavery, also possible.

Nabuco did not awaken to the negative aspects of the continent's past and present happily, so it seems. It should be remembered that, like so many other Brazilian and Latin American intellectuals, Nabuco held on to what Antônio Cândido calls "the idea of the new country, [which] accentuated potential strength and, therefore, a still unrealized greatness." This idea was joined after independence by the complementary notion that "America had been predestined to be the country of liberty, and thus to consummate the destiny of Western man."[25] Despite all his admiration for Europe, Nabuco, just like Quintino Bocaiuva and other republican leaders, believed that he was from America and wanted to be American, with the single difference that he did not see the monarchy as a contradiction to that belief.[26] It is the very American ideal he held that made his exposure to the chronic problems of Spanish America especially tormenting and painful.

This is evidenced by a few handwritten pages found in his private archive, entitled "Mexico. United States of Mexico (1825-1861),"

25. Cândido's assertion that "this state of [post-independence] euphoria was inherited by Latin American intellectuals, who transformed it into both instruments of national affirmation and an ideological justification," is also valid for Nabuco. Antônio Cândido, "Literature and Underdevelopment," in *On Literature and Society*, ed., trans., and introduced by Howard S. Becker (Princeton: Princeton University Press, 1995), p. 119.

26. For early expressions of Americanism, see Joaquim Nabuco, "O povo e o trono: Profissão de fé política de Juvenal, romano da decadência" (1869), in idem, *Nabuco e a república*, ed. by Leonardo Dantas Silva (Recife: Fundação Joaquim Nabuco, Editora Massangana, 1990), pp. 20, 22, 32, passim. This text exhibits republican principles that had been abandoned by the 1880s.

"Republics of Central America, 1824-1860," and "Republics of South America." Albeit undated, the content of these notes strongly suggests that they belong to the same period as the congressional speech and the newspaper articles under discussion.[27] They are informative in nature, comprising mainly information drawn from Mitre's *Historia de San Martín* (1887-88) and some other unidentified sources concerning the history of these Spanish–speaking countries from the early- to the mid-nineteenth century. In view of the fact that most of the space is filled with names and dates associated with the political upheaval of the post–independence period in Spanish America, it would appear at first that Nabuco was simply gathering evidence in support of some preestablished notions. But if we read these ostensibly dry, objective chronicles more closely, we find that they are intertwined with a few isolated comments that are highly subjective. The most significant one appears in the middle of an inventory of border and regime changes in Central America, immediately after a reference to General Francisco Morazán's execution: "Why such widespread crime? What can explain this great amount of horrors in America?"[28] asks Nabuco, seemingly shocked in the face of these dreadful occurrences.

Full of sentiment, this interjection suggests that whatever the initial motivation for taking these notes, Nabuco did not remain indifferent to the facts he was copying, but began to ask questions about them. His questions about Spanish America's past appear to be, in fact, questions about Brazil's future. Evidently, the growing threat to the monarchy's existence did not entail only public action to save it, but also an individual effort to assess what might be lying ahead.

Obviously, underlying both Nabuco's public addresses and personal ruminations from late 1888 was apparently the notion that Brazil had something fundamental in common with the Spanish-speaking countries surrounding it, namely, the encounter between the "violent" Latin character and American circumstances. Other-

27. From the AJN: "Mexico. Estados Unidos Mejicanos (1825-1861)," 001.12-74/51; "Republicas da America Central, 1824-1860," 001.12-74/52; "Republicas Sul-Americanas," 001.12-74/53. So far, I have not found any mention of these documents in studies about Nabuco.

28. "Republicas da America Central," AJN 001.12-74/52,1.

wise, what could account for his assumption that the former Portuguese colony was destined to reproduce the torturous experience of the other Iberian parts of the continent, were it to become a republic? This Spanish American–derived interpretation of Brazil was seemingly in contradiction with Nabuco's usual insistence on his country's singularity in Latin America due to its distinct historical experience; a contradiction that reflected, in turn, a deeper conflation of historical and ahistorical principles of thought. Whatever the complexities and ambiguities of Nabuco's view, the main significance of his newspaper articles and the personal notes under discussion is the opening of a new course of identification with Spanish America, different from the one we have previously encountered. This was not the optimistic identification that relied on recent Argentine achievements and highlighted common American values, but rather, one that reflected a pessimistic sense of sameness rooted in shared historical experience and common racial origins.

Most interestingly, Nabuco's growing awareness of Spanish America's chronic illnesses did not go hand in hand with condescension toward these countries. He denounced, or more accurately, lamented some of their acquired attributes–mainly their political culture–and not Spanish Americans themselves, or their more innate qualities. This distinction is made by Nabuco himself only in other terms, when he says that what he knows about certain American republics inspires in him "profound pain about the barbarization of these proud and noble nations."[29]

The usage of the noun *barbarization*, rather than the adjective *barbarian* is significant. For Nabuco, Spanish America had deteriorated to barbarism; it was not born in such a state. Something had gone wrong on the way, and therefore could also be fixed. While Nabuco's comparative historical analysis put imperial Brazil in a better position than most of Spanish America, it did not imply any *essential* superiority over the neighbors. At the praxeological level he exercised empathy, not estrangement. His was an empathy that seems to have been based on the premise that Brazil's better fortune had been mainly a matter of chance, historical contingency, an outcome

29. "O privilégio de família," p. 394.

of a single event rather than a product of a distinct essence. For the same reason, Brazil could easily fall back at any moment and go through an identical experience. Thus, on the eve of the republic, Joaquim Nabuco started to develop a sense of common past and destiny with Spanish America.

Diagnosing Early Spanish American Symptoms: Eduardo Prado

The two related themes of republicanism and federalism that so heavily preoccupied Nabuco after May 13, 1888 were also singled out by Eduardo Prado in an extended article he published in late 1889 in the *Revista de Portugal*, titled "Political Destinies of Brazil."[30] Watching the events from Europe, free of any formal political obligation or strict identification with any particular party, Prado analyzed the rapid advance of the republican cause and the growing demand for the decentralization of the Empire's institutions in a much more remote tone than Nabuco. In contradistinction with the abolitionist leader, the wealthy wandering *paulista* approached these two issues as an impartial scientific observer. Yet just like the emotionally and ideologically committed Nabuco, he, too, found the Spanish American experience relevant to the questions at stake.

Prado's discussion of the neighboring countries had gone through some changes, even if less dramatic than Nabuco's, since he had last been to Uruguay, Argentina, and Chile some seven years earlier. Most significantly, in his 1882 travel logs he hardly linked these countries' remote or recent experiences, with the exception of isolated comparisons, to the past and present of Brazil. The only connection he drew between these Spanish-speaking nations and his own was the overall *implicit* negation of this connection. The notion of "Latin America" as opposed to "Spanish America" was absent altogether, so that a reader without geographical knowledge could have barely guessed that these nations were situated next door to Brazil. In a telling way, the only explicit reference to the region as a whole did

30. Eduardo Prado, "Destinos políticos do Brasil," *Revista de Portugal* I (1889), pp. 467-491.

not come directly from the traveler-writer himself but through the quotation of a third person, a Chilean leader, who allegedly stated that "there are only two organized countries in South America: the Brazilian Republic and the Chilean Empire."[31]

This implied isolationist approach became much more explicit in Prado's 1889 essay. Analyzing the republicans' weaknesses and strengths, he identified one of their advantages as "the fact that, in reality, we are far away from these neighbors we seek to imitate, driven by a false and artificial feeling of solidarity; further even than from the more civilized nations of Europe. We have no commercial relations with them; we are unfamiliar with their leaders and their affairs; we do not read their newspapers; we do not hear their complaints. Hence, Brazilian politicians have learned nothing from the experience of these republics."[32]

Apparently, republican propaganda–which had a considerable effect on Nabuco's treatment of Spanish America–had also dragged Prado into the developing discussion about Brazil's position in continent. His subterranean isolationism surged to the surface, openly condemning those who participated in the building of "false and artificial solidarity" with Brazil's neighbors. In this regard, his position was at odds with that of Nabuco. At the praxeological level of relation to the Other, the level of rapprochement or distancing, the two opponents of republicanism diverged in their attitudes toward Spanish America. Couching his argument against the republican ideal of a uniform form of government on the continent in a discourse of ethno-cultural distinctiveness, Prado resolutely asserted that "origin and language" set Brazilians apart from "the *other* Americans, Spanish and English."[33]

Unlike his 1882 travel notes, then, "Political Destinies of Brazil" linked the Empire with the Spanish-speaking countries surrounding it through a forceful, *active* denial of similarities with them. In this text, Spanish America surfaced as a significant Other, an important reference point for defining what Brazil *was not* and what it *should not* be. Not only did Prado deny the existence of any grounds for

31. Prado, *Viagens, América, Oceania e Asia*, p. 107.
32. Prado, "Destinos políticos do Brasil," p. 477.
33. Ibid., p. 470;my italics.

Latin American solidarity, he even overtly called for the perpetuation of the Empire's assertive foreign policy in the region, setting Chile's aggressive conduct on the western rim of the continent as a model. For him this was not simply a matter of realpolitik, but of manifest destiny. Achieving hegemony in South America's Atlantic rim should be, according to him, Brazil's main "historical mission" in the external sphere.[34]

Prado's approach to Spanish America appears unequivocal. Excluding its geographical position, nothing united Brazil with these countries, and the only desirable kind of relationship with them, if any at all, was domination. Yet in a somewhat paradoxical way, this "remote" Other found its way into his discussion of Brazil's "political destinies" again and again. This is all the more surprising in view of the essay's much more analytical than programmatic character. If the emotionally involved and politically committed Nabuco was hard-pressed to expose the "dark side" of Spanish America as part of his campaign to save the monarchy, Prado did not have the same kind of motivation. And still he chose to evoke Spanish America repeatedly.

Prado used Spanish America as an interpretive framework right from the beginning of his essay, whose first part concerned the republican form of government. Similarly to most other Brazilian thinkers at the time, he claimed that "the people" was not ready yet for self-government.[35] However, he was referring not only to Brazil. While Europe in the early nineteenth century faced the mission of creating political institutions liberal enough to match the level of highly civilized peoples, asserted Prado, in South America the challenge of the leaders had been the opposite: to form peoples that would equal the liberal stature of the new independent states.[36] Here, the ardent isolationist found something significant in common with Brazil's neighbors.

Farther into the essay, Spanish America serves again as a point of reference when Prado puts his finger on what he sees as both the main strength and weakness of the Brazilian monarchy: namely, the

34. Ibid., p. 480.

35. See, for example, Ângela de Castro Gomes and Marieta de Moraes Ferreira, "Primeira República: Um balanço historiográfico, " *Estudos Históricos* 2.4 (1989), p. 270.

36. Prado, "Destinos politicos do Brasil," p. 469.

lack of any real democratic competition between political parties. In his view, this was also the case in the rest of the hemisphere–excluding Canada and the United States–as no party had been able to attain power by winning an election. Revolution had been the only possible means to achieve a regime change in Spain's former colonies. The sweeping association of Spanish America with political violence had been a central theme in Prado's travel accounts. But whereas in that text it had been treated in its own right as a subject for mockery,[37] here it served to elucidate a flaw in Brazilian politics. Once more we see how central aspects of Spanish American reality are suddenly interwoven into the discussion of Brazil's contemporary problems. Even more importantly, from our perspective, is the fact that in this instance, as in the previous one concerning the political immaturity of the people in Latin America, Prado finds a common denominator–a negative one, to be sure–between Brazil and its tumultuous neighbors. Thus, while at the praxeological level he rules out any association with them, at the axiological level he implicitly places them on an equal plane.[38]

Spanish America makes still another appearance within Prado's text, when he refers to the republicans' encouragement of insubordination among the military. At this point he applies a term of Spanish origin to manifestations of rebelliousness in the Brazilian army: "*caudilhismo*," a word that would soon be widely used in Portuguese. "It is easy to evaluate how dangerous a conflict between the armed troops and the legal regime would be to Brazilian civilization," he writes. "For Brazil that would signify an immeasurable moral decadence, a retrocession of half a century and the loss of the elevated image it enjoys in the world in comparison with the military republics of Spanish America."[39]

Brazil was supposedly far ahead of its neighbors, at a much higher evolutionary stage, but at the same time, Prado's text implies that there was little distance between them. This is because, like Nabuco,

37. For example, he remarked that in the Spanish American republics, with the exception of Argentina and Chile, presidents ended up either in exile or in the grave. Former presidents were therefore "a rare sight" in these countries. Prado, *Viagens*, pp. 106, 123.

38. Prado, "Destinos politicos do Brasil," p. 472.

39. Ibid., p. 478.

he only managed to perceive militarism as a Latin American phenomenon. When he pondered the possible effects of a military intervention in politics, his first vision was that of Brazil's neighbors. He did not perceive such an intervention as an unprecedented phenomenon, but rather as a reproduction of a current one. This perception embodied the assumption that Brazil had something fundamental in common with the Spanish-speaking countries surrounding it. The world (namely Europe), Prado wanted his readers to believe, viewed Brazil far more favorably than it viewed the rest of Latin America. Yet Brazil's uniquely positive image, according to his own analysis, was in fact a very fragile one. Its survival rested solely on the civil character of the country's institutions and its relative political and social peace. Take out these components of Brazil's identity, and it was just like the others.

Our argument, that on the eve of the republic Spanish America remerged as a significant reference point for the construction of both sameness and otherness, receives further support and is best exemplified through the second part of Prado's "Political Destinies of Brazil." In this section of the text, he favorably discusses the second major issue on Brazil's contemporary political agenda: namely, a federalist reform. Once again, Spanish America pervades the text. Prado introduces Argentina into the discussion as an obligatory reference point, and he significantly does so with the conjunction "although": "Although Brazil's circumstances and culture" were different from those of Argentina at the time it adopted a federal structure, writes Prado, "the Brazilian legislators must take into close consideration Argentina's history." Apparently aware of the hidden significance of his call to look across the border, Prado finds it necessary to deny any resemblance between Brazil and its southern neighbor, and he does so more than once. He proceeds to remind his readers about Argentina's long troubled past of fratricidal wars, only to conclude that: "This era of *caudilhismo* in the [Argentine] Republic is over, and while it is improbable that it will ever begin in Brazil, the historical lesson is all the same significant."[40]

There is a remarkable duality in these lines. Prado argues simultaneously both for the relevance of the Argentine experience to the

40. Ibid., p. 486.

Brazilian situation, and for a complete separation between them. One may claim in this regard, of course, that there is no necessary link between *relevance* and *likeness*, that people may perceive any historical case as edifying without assuming a similarity between its circumstances and their own. However, even if this is so, Prado's repeated denials are too suggestive to be ignored, especially when taken together with previous points in the text where we have traced the inherent assumption of significant similarity between Brazil and Spanish America. Especially "suspicious" is Prado's outright rejection of any possibility that Brazil would ever experience an "era of *caudilhismo*," which would come, let us recall, shortly after he described the strengthening republican-military nexus in Brazil and its disastrous potential implications.

A final demonstration of Prado's conflicted attitude toward Spanish America may be found in his conclusive warning against any "servile imitation" of foreign models, even successful ones like those of Canada and the United States. This would be an error that had cost "the other Latin countries of America, who had no tradition of local government or proper education," dearly.[41] Thus, toward the end of the essay, Latin America reappears as an unavoidable conceptual framework. If he previously distinguished between three types of Americans–Brazilian, Spanish and English–Prado now explicitly recognizes the existence of another category, which unites the first two. Furthermore, he fills the Latin American identity with historical content. His Brazil is thus part of a whole, although unique. In his view, if it wishes to preserve its fortunate singularity within this unfortunate whole, then it should avoid the Spanish American path. That is, it should beware of becoming like *Them*. Brazil should distance itself from this Other exactly because it is so dangerously close, and not just in terms of geography.

To conclude, on the eve of the fall of the monarchy, two eloquent Brazilians–one a celebrated statesman of letters, the other about to become the intellectual leader of the monarchist opposition–reacted to the republican challenge by discovering the relevance of the Spanish American experience to Brazil as a negative reference point. Underlying this awakening to the anarchic and authoritarian nature

41. Ibid., p. 487.

of the neighbors' politics was an assumption of innate sameness that Nabuco and Prado reworked and reinforced. In that way, they initiated a negative and pessimistic pattern of identification with Spanish America alongside the positive and optimistic pattern, pattern that would soon acquire both more depth and breadth.

Foreign Minister(!) Bocaiuva Returns to the Plata

It was at that point that the overthrow of the monarchy took place. The impact on men like Nabuco and Prado, notwithstanding their forecasts, was considerable. However, before we move on to discuss monarchist reactions to the seizure of power by the army, it is important to shed some light on the new regime's friendly attitude toward Spanish America, which showed much continuity with republican rhetoric from before November 15, 1889. Here it should be emphasized again that when republicans spoke about America, they were not referring only to the United States, contrary to what is often argued in the historiography.[42] Often cited in this regard is the 1891 constitution, which emulated the U.S. model. Yet contemporary sources indicate that, within this grand northern model, there was a southern one. In a congressional session in 1891, the Brazilian republic's first minister of justice, Senator Manuel Ferraz de Campos Sales, supported his stand on constitutional issues by citing an equivalent Argentine law.[43] In the same vein, a parliamentary commission that examined the demand for new elections upon President Deodoro da Fonseca's resignation in November 1891 issued a report that clearly stated that the republican constitution contained articles borrowed from both the American and the Argentine constitutions.[44]

42. Exceptional in this regard is Clodaldo Bueno, who notes that the "Americanization" of the republic's foreign policy did not always mean "North-Americanization." See Amado Luiz Cervo and Clodoaldo Bueno, *História da política exterior do Brasil* (São Paulo: Editora Atica, 1992), pp. 149-151.

43. A. J. Ribas, *Perfil biographico do Dr. Manoel Ferraz de Campos Salles* (Rio de Janeiro: Typ. Leuzinger, 1896), p. 322.

44. Artur Vieira Peixoto, et al., eds., *Floriano: Memórias e documentos*, 5 vols. (Rio de Janeiro: Serviço Gráfico do Ministério da Educação, 1939-), vol. IV, pp. 105-106.

Five years later, a notable republican leader and one of the country's top law experts, Rodrigo Otávio, published a book that compared the Brazilian constitution with the two aforementioned ones, labeling them as "sources which directly inspired our Constituent Assembly."[45] This is not at all surprising in view of the interest of Rui Barbosa, at this point the republic's first minister of finance and the major author of the 1891 constitution, in Argentine law.[46] But even more significant than the actual borrowing of legislative articles from Brazil's traditional Spanish-speaking rival, from our perspective at least, was the new regime's and its supporters' comfortable, even proud, recognition of this fact.

The case of the constitution illustrates the strengthening of Argentina's elevated status in official or semi-official discourse stressing American and South American solidarity, almost from day one of the republic. As early as December 7, 1889, for example, President Deodoro da Fonseca decreed that the next day would be dedicated to honoring the Argentine Republic with official ceremonies, which were then accompanied by spontaneous demonstrations of friendship.[47] In the next month, the provisional government decreed the conferral of the highest national decoration on the presidents of Uruguay and Argentina. Another decoration was conferred on the Chilean president.[48]

But the Brazilian republic's most dramatic act was the speedy settlement of the Missões boundary dispute with Argentina through

45. Rodrigo Octavio, *Constituições Federaes* (São Paulo/Rio de Janeiro: Livraria Clasica de Alves & C. 1897). The subtitle of this book is *A Comparison of the Federal Constitution of the United States of Brazil with the Constitutions of the Argentine Republic, the United States of America, and Switzerland, Accompanied by their Complete Texts.*

46. See, for example, his elaborate comments on the Argentine Constitution of 1853, in Barbosa, "A imigração na República Argentina," pp. 44-49, and references to Argentina and other South American countries in *O estado de sitio; sua natureza, seus effeitos, seus limites* (Rio de Janeiro: Companhia Impressora, 1892), pp. 28-40.

47. República Argentina, *Tratado de Misiones; Litigio solucionado; Las repúblicas brasilera y argentina; Homenajes; El ministro brasilero Bocayuva en la Plata; Firma del tratado en Montevideo; Resúmen general de las fiestas, 1889-1890*, Buenos Aires (Buenos Aires: A. Sommaruga, 1890), pp. 31-32.

48. Dunshee de Abranches, *Actas e actos do governo provisorio*, 3rd. ed. (Rio de Janeiro: Jornal do Brazil, 1953), pp. 53, 183. This book provides the official protocols of the provisional government's secret sessions, in which many more decrees in this spirit were made.

FIGURE 3.1.
"Argentina and Brazil seal a pact of friendship."
This drawing should be read in conjunction with its 1888 predecessor [Figure 2.2]. Argentina's image remains unchanged, while Brazil is transformed, following the transition from monarchy to republic, from a male Indian into another Marianne. Now it is only the national flags that distinguish the two South American nations, both from one another and from the common French model that unites them. As is evident here, the well-known fascination of the First Republic with North Atlantic models and the growing interest and identification with its next-door neighbors were not contradictory but rather complementary trends. *Revista Illustrada*, Dec. 8, 1889.[49] Courtesy of Arquivo da Casa de Rui Barbosa.

49. My interpretation of this image draws partially from Jens Andermann's analysis in *The Optic of the State: Visuality and Power in Argentina and Brazil* (Pittsburgh: Pittsburgh University Press, 2007), p. 9, and also from our correspondence, for which I thank him.

direct negotiations via telegraph, even though both sides had already agreed to submit the case to arbitration just a few weeks before the fall of the monarchy. In a period when diplomatic visits at the ministerial level were very rare, and with no more that a month in office, Brazilian Foreign Minister Quintino Bocaiuva rushed to Montevideo in order to meet with his Argentine counterpart, Estanislao Zeballos, and to sign on January 25, 1890 a treaty that divided the contested territory equally between the countries. He then proceeded to Buenos Aires and other principal cities in Argentina, where he was welcomed as a hero. In each and every town, there were parades and ceremonial receptions where prominent members of Argentina's political and cultural elites praised the guest and his country for the recent change of regime and of attitude toward America.[50] Indeed, the opening phrase of the Montevideo treaty stated that it had been signed "under the auspices of American constitutional unity and in the name of the fraternal sentiments that should prevail throughout the Continent."[51]

As if that were not enough, another significantly symbolic act occurred on May 25, Argentina's national holiday. That day, President General Deodoro da Fonseca convened his ministers and army units in an open-air ceremony where medals commemorating the Paraguayan War were exchanged with the Argentine minister to Rio, and all government ministers received the rank of general.[52]

Nevertheless, the republic's Americanism did not entail the disappearance of hurt pride, old hatreds, and apprehension about Spanish American expansionism, all mainly associated with Argentina.[53] The promise of a new Latin America, peaceful, ordered and progressive, embedded in the southern neighbor's prosperity, coexisted with jeal-

50. Based on newspaper articles published in the Brazilian and Argentine press during December 1889 and January 1890 and reprinted in *Tratado de Misiones*.

51. *Relatório do Ministério das Relações Exteriores*, for the year 1890 (Rio de Janeiro, 1891), Anexo no. 1, p. 34.

52. "25 de Maio," *Estado de São Paulo*, May 27, 1890, p. 1.

53. About the deep-rooted nature of Brazilian-Argentine hostility, see, for example, Helio Jaguaribe, "Brazil-Argentina. Relações de conflito e cooperação," *Revista Brasileira de Política Internacional* 25 (1982), pp. 132-135; Frank D. McCann, "The Brazilian General Staff and Brazil's Military Situation: 1900-1945," *Journal of Interamerican Studies and World Affairs* 25:3 (1983), pp. 301-305; and Stanley Hilton, "The Argentine Factor in Twentieth-Century Brazilian Foreign Policy Strategy," *Political Science Quarterly* 100:1 (1985), p. 28.

ousy and fear of its might. These were two sides of a constantly flipping coin: competition for white immigrants, power, and prestige could easily translate into identification and a desire to cooperate, or into precisely the opposite positions.

The duality was evident in the public discussion that enveloped the Bocaiuva agreement. While the "*Archi-philo-platino*" minister was celebrating abroad, criticism at home grew. The most vehement assaults came from monarchists, who found it convenient to attack the republican regime on patriotic grounds, but they were not alone. The promptness with which the agreement was negotiated puzzled the French journalist Max Leclerc, who was visiting Brazil at the time. He characterized the foreign policy of the republic as utopian. To his understanding, Brazil had nothing to gain from the act, as relations between the two countries were already cordial. The visitor also noted that public opinion was at best indifferent to Bocaiuva's "theatrical gesture" and that military men did not want to hear anything about ceding even the smallest part of the national territory to Argentina.[54] As a matter of fact, opposition existed within the government itself. In one cabinet session, the navy minister expressed his irritation at the fact that Bocaiuva wandered around the Plata ignoring four different calls to return, while another member reported that a hostile demonstration awaited the foreign minister upon his arrival in Rio's port.[55] Eventually, the Congress voted against the agreement, with Bocaiuva himself asking for its rejection.

The whole episode fits within the framework of José Murilo de Carvalho's argument regarding the republican regime's failure to achieve popular legitimacy due to inner splits and a political culture that was foreign to the majority of Brazilians.[56] At any rate, what

54. Max Leclerc, *Cartas do Brasil*, trans. and annotated by Sérgio Milliet (São Paulo: Companhia Editora Nacional, 1949), pp. 94-97.

55. Abranches, *Actas e actos*, pp. 122-123. On the great amount and intensity of the criticism, see Araujo Jorge, *Ensaios de historia diplomatica do Brasil no regimen republicano. Primeira serie (1889-1912)* (Rio de Janeiro: [n.p.], 1912), pp. 76-77. So severe was the criticism that had been leveled at him, that Bocaiúva dedicated to it 21 out of 36 newspaper articles that he wrote in defense of his conduct as a member of the provisional government, after leaving the Cabinet: "Na defensiva," XV-XXXVI, *O Paiz*, Dec. 13, 1891-Jan. 13, 1892, in Bocaiúva, *Idéias políticas*, vol. 2, pp. 70-145.

56. Carvalho, *A formação das almas*. It is interesting to note that Argentine Foreign Minister Estanislao Zeballos, who signed the agreement with Bocaiúva, explained

made the Americanist component of the regime's identity particularly hard to sell was the great gap between words and reality. While the new rulers of the nation made every rhetorical effort to escape the label of *caudillismo*, the coup itself and the subsequent internal cleavages and authoritarian practices provided all the proof that European and North American observers had needed in order to believe in its validity. Spokesmen for the republic stressed once and again the nonviolent character of the revolution and its adherence to American values of peace and liberty, at the same time that events on the ground increasingly showed the opposite.[57] If Bocaiuva and others had wished for Brazil to look like late-nineteenth-century Argentina, the real picture they produced was, in fact, more reminiscent of Spanish America's age of caudillos. At least this is what the opposing camp felt, thought, and declared.

The Coup and Its Effects: Deodoro da Fonseca = Rosas; Prado = Alberdi

"The Republic is here, and you, who know the history of the South American Republics, can evaluate the crucial road we now have to cross in order to recuperate freedom and perpetuate unity."[58] Thus wrote Joaquim Nabuco to the Baron of Rio Branco, three weeks after General Deodoro da Fonseca had removed Emperor Dom Pedro II from his throne. About six months later, another letter

its eventual rejection in Brazil in similar terms, claiming that the new regime was too weak, due to internal divisions and lack of popular support, to overcome the fierce opposition of monarchist circles. See, Araujo Jorge, *Ensaios de historia diplomatica*, pp. 78-79.

57. On foreign reactions, see, for example, "A revista das revistas," *A Illustração: Revista quinzenal para Portugal e Brazil* (Paris) 6:23 (1889), pp. 363-364; Freyre, *Order and Progress*, pp. 43-44 ; Cervo and Bueno, *História da política exterior*, pp. 141-142. See Cervo and Bueno also for a good illustration of the regime's efforts to counteract the caudillistic image, as well as Brazil, *Mensagem dirigida ao Congresso Nacional pelo Generalíssimo Manuel Deodoro da Fonseca, Chefe do Governo Provisório da República dos Estados Unidos do Brasil, em 15 de novembro de 1890* (Rio de Janeiro: Imprensa Nacional, 1890).

58. Joaquim Nabuco to Rio Branco, Rio de Janeiro, Dec. 7, 1889, in Nabuco, *Cartas a amigos*, vol. 1, p. 184.

from Nabuco arrived, which read, "We enter a series of personalistic military governments that will lead to the degradation of the army, to a bankruptcy resulting from robbery and speculation, as in the other republics of this type, the governments of 'states' of true caudillos, surrounded by a gang of illiterates, and finally to dismemberment, should the national sentiment fail to react in the last moment. What I am writing to you is the same thing that I am writing to [Eduardo] Prado."[59] Sometime in 1891, Rio Branco wrote back in the same vein:

> The news I have of the effect of your writings and your position confirms what you have heard from Sousa Dantas. Nevertheless, I would like you to write a new letter as soon as possible, one in which you appeal to the heart and not only to reason, reminding our people that a constitutional monarchy is a more advanced form of government than the Yankee, Venezuelan or Mexican type of republic, and that it was not on behalf of the Bragança family, but rather on behalf of the country, that the Andrades, the Vasconçelos, the Feijós and the Evaristos aspired to make Brazil an exception within America. [...] History offers countless examples of men who only cared about themselves once they had assumed power. Among these are the *salvadores de la patria americanos* [...] And perhaps it would be worthwhile to show how Canada, Australia, and the English colonies have fared under the parliamentary system. These, like those rampant republics of Spanish America, are also young countries, yet their citizens are free men who do not, and will not, ever suffer the same humiliations inflicted on their subjects by the Santa Annas, Barrios, Rosas, Guzmán Blancos, and *tutti quanti*.[60]

As can be learned from this private correspondence, and as we will see below, the history of Spanish America would serve the core group of the monarchist camp, from the very first moments of the republic, as

59. Joaquim Nabuco to Rio Branco, Rio de Janeiro, July 31, 1890, in ibid., vol. 1, p. 188. Similar views are also expressed in Nabuco's personal diary. See the entry for Feb. 28, 1891 in *Diários*, 2 vols., (Rio de Janeiro/Recife: Bem-Te-Vi/Fundação Joaquim Nabuco, Editora Massangana, 2005), vol. 2, pp. 34-35.

60. Rio Branco to Joaquim Nabuco, n.p., n.d., 1891, AJN 001-74/663. It is interesting to note that this passage is also quoted in Rio Branco's standard biography–written at the invitation of the Brazilian Foreign Office–here, all negative references to North and Spanish America have been expunged. Alvao Lins, *Rio-Branco (o barão do Rio-Branco) biografia pessoal e história política*, 2nd ed. (São Paulo: Companhia Editora Nacional, 1965), p. 172.

a cognitive template as well as an ideological weapon. Here the spatial, chronological, and thematic focus rapidly shifted from the recent advent of "civilization" in South America, to the decades-old "barbarism" of Spanish America as a whole. Although the change of regime occurred without any significant bloodshed, it was immediately perceived and represented as a complete break from a uniquely peaceful past that set Brazil apart from the neighboring nations–and, in turn, as a sign of Hispano-Americanization. In fact, as already shown, this interpretation had been promoted even before November 15, 1889. But, now that the nightmare had come true, tendencies that had already been discernable in earlier forecasts from before the coup would receive much more elaborate and extensive expression, giving rise to outright expressions of belonging to an entity called "Latin America."

Notably, the term itself first started to appear systematically in Joaquim Nabuco's and Eduardo Prado's writings only under the psychological impact of the actual fall of the monarchy.[61] The collapse of the central institution that had separated Brazil, both practically and symbolically, from the surrounding chaos meant the destabilization of one identity and the emergence of another. In a treatise that constituted his first elaborate comment on the new circumstances, published in March 1890, Nabuco repeatedly evoked the anarchic and authoritarian features of Spanish America–where, "despite the growing stability among all these peoples," the rule was still "*Vae Victis*, [...] physical or moral annihilation of the adversary." What may appear to be a regression to the island mentality of the Empire was in reality its breakdown. For political chaos and violence were no longer viewed as a uniquely Spanish American fate, but rather as a common destiny on which basis a Latin American consciousness was forged: "How could we have nurtured the belief," summarized Nabuco, "that we as a republic would not go through the same *via dolorosa* as that along which Latin America is sluggishly dragging herself?"[62]

61. This is in consonance with Lúis Cláudio Villafañe Santos's finding that the term *Latin America* entered the Brazilian diplomatic discourse only after the proclamation of the republic: "A América do sul no discurso diplomático brasileiro," *Revista Brasileira de Política Internacional* 48:2 (2005), p. 187.

62. *Resposta às mensagens do Recife e Nazareth*, pp. 8-15. The same notions were repeated in his *Porque continuo a ser monarchista* (London: Abraham Kingdon & Newnham, 1890).

This birth of Latin American consciousness is best exemplified through Eduardo Prado, who has drawn much scholarly attention as a central exponent of the monarchist stand and an important articulator of Brazilian national identity.[63] Following the fall of the Empire, the hitherto detached Prado joined Nabuco, and immersed himself passionately in the political and identity conflict raging in Brazil, to become the most vehement spokesman of the monarchist camp. Between December 1889 and June 1890, he published a series of articles in the *Revista de Portugal*, in which he abandoned completely the mantle of an outside observer. These articles, which were soon published in Brazil in book form under the title *Fastos da dictadura militar no Brasil* (Annals of the Military Dictatorship in Brazil),[64] are entirely programmatic, and constitute a sarcastic unrelenting attack on the newly established regime. Gone is the scholarly air that characterized the pre-coup "Political Destinies of Brazil," as Spanish America remains heavily present in the texts right from the start, and in a much more explicit form. The previously implicit suggestions of similarity between Brazil and the other former Iberian colonies of the continent turn here into straightforward identifications; self-confidence and feelings of superiority give way to doubt and open declarations of inferiority; hidden concerns and repressed fears rise up to the surface.

Already at the beginning of the first article in the series, written only two weeks after the proclamation of the republic, in which Prado himself confesses that it is still impossible to tell what has actually happened in Brazil for lack of adequate information, the change of regime is presented as a "reprise" of "those dramas [typical of] the

63. Janotti, *Os subversivos*, pp. 30-34, passim; Skidmore, "Eduardo Prado: A Conservative Nationalist Critic"; Carvalho, "Brasil naciones marginadas," p. 412; Freyre, *Order and Progress*, pp. 32-37; José Honório Rodrigues, *História da história do Brasil*, 2 vols. in 3 (São Paulo: Companhia Editora Nacional, 1979-[1988]), vol. 2, tomo 1, *A historiografia conservadora*, pp. 94-97; Ludwig Lauerhass Junior, *Getúlio Vargas e o triunfo do nacionalismo brasileiro* (Belo Horizonte/São Paulo; Itatiaia/Editora da Universidadede São Paulo, 1986), p. 51; Sandra McGee Deutsch, *Las derechas: The Extreme Right in Argentina, Brazil, and Chile, 1890-1939* (Stanford: Stanford University Press, 1999), pp. 38-41.

64. The first edition appeared in Portugal in 1890. The third edition is used here: Eduardo Prado, *Fastos da dictadura militar no brasil* (São Paulo: Escola Typografica Salesiana, 1902).

southern countries."[65] By "southern" here, Prado really means Spain, the mother country, reflecting his view of the Spanish American nations as legitimate heirs of the Metropolis's political culture. At any rate, the focus rapidly shifts from the Peninsula to the former colonies, and remains there throughout the series. Prado's line of argument in this regard is stated clearly and repeatedly: 1) The new regime is militaristic; 2) Military intervention in politics, or caudillism, is a Spanish and more specifically Spanish American phenomenon; and 3) therefore, Brazil now resembles its neighbors, and has become an integral part of Latin America.

As a matter of fact, Prado goes even farther. The Empire, he argues, had managed to establish, already in a very early stage of its existence, the supremacy of the civil element over the military. "And let us remember," he writes, "that it was no easy task to suppress the *caudilhagem* in order to achieve internal peace. And the proof is that half a century later, peace has suddenly disappeared and *caudilhismo* is reemerging in Brazil, whereas in Latin America's most advanced countries it has died out in blood."[66] That is, while Brazil was perceived as marching backward, some of its neighbors were seen as already moving ahead, leaving their barbaric past behind. Not only had Brazil become like them, worse: Brazil had become like what they used to be.

The entire building of Brazil's singularity in Latin America, which Prado constructed in his writings before the advent of the republic, broke down under the impact of the single blow of November 15, 1889. The identity fences that had separated the civilized Luso-American Empire from the Spanish-speaking barbarity collapsed with seemingly stunning ease. Only seemingly because, as already argued before, these fences never stood on solid ground. The instability of the Brazilian identity, as constructed in opposition to the Spanish American Other–simultaneously distant and close–was fully exposed when Prado himself conditioned its entire validity on future developments. If Brazil could not manage to free itself from the "military tyranny," he claimed, then all the positive qualities that had dis-

65. Prado, *Fastos*, p. 2.
66. Ibid., p. 16-17.

tinguished it from its neighbors would be considered "fictitious and transitory, results of an artificial political organization, superior to the real foundation of the Brazilian civilization."[67]

This phrase reflects Prado's loss of confidence in Brazil's singularity in face of the fall of the monarchy. His interpretation of the event is deeply conflictive. On the one hand, he describes the militarization of Brazilian politics as an intentional emulation of an alien model, a disastrous import that contradicted the country's tradition. Thus, for example, the term *pronunciamiento* is introduced time and again in the text in its Spanish spelling, emphasizing the foreign origin of Deodoro da Fonseca's move.[68] On the other hand, by pressing this point, Prado actually conceded that Brazil shared certain innately harmful qualities with its neighbors.

Trapped within the Latin American frame of interpretation, he was unable to explain the political developments, either for himself or for his readers, as a singular product of Brazil's historical development. Throughout his argument, the notion of importation gets mixed up with the concept of reproduction. It is unclear whether Brazil had been infected with *caudillismo* or if the germ always ran in its veins. That is, Prado could not assure that the recent changes at the upper, more visible, political level did not reflect some inherent fundamental flaws of the national character: "Some would say that nations cannot escape the deterministic rules that govern their life. And so the Brazilian military tyranny of today can be regarded as that invincible period of barbarity that is already past in Chile, possibly just ended in Argentina, and in which all other countries in Latin America still lives, to one degree or another."[69]

There are, then, exceptions to the rule. Parts of Spanish America no longer fit the established negative stereotype. As already mentioned, Prado does not sidestep this fact. On the contrary. For the first time, he stresses not only the progress of Chile and Argentina but also–if not mainly–their advantage over Brazil. Somber and threatening comparisons with the country's big southern neighbor abound in this piece. Only several weeks before, Prado assigned

67. Ibid., p. 48.
68. See, for example, ibid., pp. 81, 164, 198.
69. Ibid., p. 48.

Brazil a hegemonic role in the region, while predicting that Argentina would continue to prosper and develop within its own borders.[70] Suddenly, things were turned upside down. Argentina was, according to Prado, aspiring to reconstitute the old Viceroyalty of the River Plate, a goal within its reach thanks to the stream of immigrants it was receiving and the internal political freedom it enjoyed. Brazil, on the other hand, was becoming weaker due to the debilitating effects of militarism. In his warnings, Prado drew of course on a rich past of armed conflicts and mutual hatreds, but something significant had changed. Unlike before, the Argentine threat was not associated with barbarism, but rather with progress. If up until their ascendance to power, the republicans had been the ones who claimed that Brazil was lagging behind its southern neighbor, it was now a leading monarchist who voiced that message–and he did so categorically.

Under the pressure of events, Prado's treatment of Spanish America became much more stereotypical than it had been, albeit not monolithic. His hitherto composite depictions of Argentine and Chilean politics and culture from the early 1880s give way to a reductionist totalizing approach. The anthropological and sociological sensitivity, evident in the earlier texts we have analyzed, disappear under the emotional anxiety and ideological fervor of the traveler-turned-crusader who constructs a dichotomous picture.[71] Latin America is divided into two contrasting spheres, that of civil rule and that of militarism, with only Chile and Argentina in the former and Brazil sliding rapidly into the latter. Prado returns to the familiar civilization/barbarism polarity, only this time the dividing line is drawn elsewhere. The moral border no longer corresponds to the national one

70. Prado, "Destinos políticos do Brasil," p. 480.

71. The emotional drive behind Prado's writing stands out in interpretations by his contemporaries. His close friend and editor of the *Revista de Portugal*, the renowned Portuguese writer Eça de Queirós, explained, for example, that in rushing to denounce the coup of November 15, 1889 Prado had obeyed "a pure instinct [...] an instinct of a fan of art who sights a band of barbarians around a precious monument," Eça de Queirós, "Eduardo Prado," originally published in 1898, reprinted in *Revista do Livro*, 18 (June 1960), p. 121. On the other hand, according to the Brazilian historian Capistrano de Abreu, Prado's monarchism derived from feelings of humiliation caused by the appearance of Spanish American style *pronunciamientos*: shock, indignation and insult. Capistrano de Abreu, "Eduardo Prado," *Jornal do Commercio*, Sep. 5, 1901, reprinted in Rodrigues, *História da história do Brasil*, pp. 95-96.

separating Brazil from its savage surroundings, but, rather, divides the country from within. The barbarians are already inside the house; they are the new masters. What is perceived as an infiltration or awakening of a Spanish American evil, leads Prado eventually to identify himself with former victims and foes of barbarism on the other side of the border.

In the introduction to the compilation of articles, dated September 1890, Prado compared himself to Argentina's Mitre, Sarmiento, Alberdi, and others, who had brought Rosas's despotic rule to the knowledge of the world and fought against the Argentine tyrant from exile. Rosas's newspapers had called them traitors, but history would remember them as heroes, according to the self-proclaimed champion of liberalism in Brazil.[72] The analogy was thus complete. If in the body of the text Deodoro da Fonseca had been identified with Rosas, here in the subsequently written introduction, Prado identified himself with Alberdi. So firm was his Latin American framework of interpretation that the great advocate of Brazilian isolationism, who constantly warned against Argentina's hostile intentions, sought legitimacy through associating himself with one of Brazil's greatest slanderers.

This was not an isolated case. A similar pattern of identification can be found in the private correspondence of Prado's close friend, the Baron of Rio Branco, who secretly aided him in writing the articles. In one of his letters, written shortly after the fall of the monarchy, Rio Branco referred to himself as a "selvagem unitário" (savage Unitarian), also alluding to Rosas's political foes.[73] His adoption of this Spanish American moniker is especially meaningful in view of his deep-rooted animosity toward Argentina, a sentiment that he had expressed in abundant journalistic and historical writings about Luso–Hispano-American armed conflicts in the Plata region since the age of sixteen.[74] Rio Branco's self-definition through the neighboring Other, even more than Prado's, shows how the reluctant and

72. Prado, *Fastos*, p. vii.

73. Rio Branco to Barão Homem de Melo, Liverpool, March 19, 1890, cited in Luís Viana Filho, *A vida do Barão do Rio Branco*, 2nd ed. (São Paulo: Martins, 1967). p. 174.

74. Rio Branco's attitudes toward Spanish America are discussed in chapter 5.

negative type of identification with Spanish America based on the shared experience of *caudillismo* eventually led to a voluntary and positive identification with a specific sector within it.

Caudillistic or Not Caudillistic? Part of Latin America, Either Way

If the fall of the monarchy created a strong sense of a rupture from the past and reinforced the tendency to interpret Brazil within the context of Latin America as a whole, subsequent developments on the ground further fueled this process. In the four years following the coup, actual rule remained in military hands amidst growing political disorder. President Deodoro da Fonseca stayed in power for less than two years. He was pushed out of office due to pressure from the navy and other military circles, and replaced by another officer, Floriano Peixoto (1891-94). The Iron Marshall, as Peixoto was widely known, had to contend with an uprising in Rio Grande do Sul (1893-95)–possibly the bloodiest civil war in Brazil's history–and with a rebellion in the navy (1893-94) that at some point merged to a joint struggle with monarchical characteristics against his government. At this time Peixoto ruled by decree, thus eliminating freedom of speech and repressing rival political activities. Meanwhile, Rio de Janeiro, the capital, experienced a surge of popular agitation and political violence that reached its peak with an assassination attempt on the president in 1897. Instability also characterized the economy. After a period of intense speculative activity, the stock market crashed in 1891, leading to several years of high inflation.[75]

The strong military presence in power, political instability, violence, repression, and financial collapse were all perceived and repre-

75. For a general overview, consult Ronald M. Schneider, *"Order and Progress," A Political History of Brazil*, (Boulder; Westview Press, 1991), pp. 70-81. On the civil war in Rio Grande do Sul, see Joseph Love, *Rio Grande do Sul and Brazilian Regionalism, 1882-1930* (Stanford: Stanford University Press, 1971), chap. 3, meaningfully titled "Terror and War." For Rio de Janeiro, see Carvalho, *Os bestializados*, pp. 70-71, passim; June E. Hahner, "Jacobinos versus Galegos: Urban Radicals versus Portuguese Immigrants in Rio de Janeiro in the 1890s," *Journal of Interamerican Studies and World Affairs* 18:2 (May 1976), pp. 125-154.

sented as signs of Hispano-Americanization, by this time not only by monarchists but also by disillusioned republicans. Leaders from both camps thus further contributed to the identification of Brazil as a Latin American country.

Eduardo Prado published a second anti-republican treatise in 1893, a text that was widely discussed during the period and that became a milestone in the Brazilian process of self-definition.[76] This time Prado focused his attack on the new regime's political and cultural rapprochement with the United States, which provided the model for the new 1891 federalist constitution. *A ilusão americana* was a fierce attack against what Prado saw as the northern country's unhealthy influence–political, economic and moral–not only over Brazil, but over the rest of the continent as well. Significantly, the term "Latin America," only sporadically used in Prado's earlier texts, was repeatedly employed here to designate a group of nations that were essentially different from the United States. It is with a good reason that *A ilusão* has been mentioned in the same breath as José Enrique Rodó's more celebrated *Ariel* (1900), which is remembered for establishing the antithesis between a materialistic United States and a spiritual Latin America.[77] Yet, little attention has been given to the *intra*–Latin American dimension of Prado's book.

To a large degree, *A ilusão americana* constituted, both implicitly and explicitly, yet another interpretation of Brazil through the Spanish American Other. This was strongly evident already in the opening section of the text, dedicated to the "the Iberian nations of America" rather than to the United States, as one might expect. Here, Prado described the history of the relationships among these countries as full of hatreds and aggressions, and then moved to make the bold isolationist statement, which is also cited in the beginning of this work, totally negating the idea that Brazil belonged in this group of nations: "Geologists say that the River Plate and the Amazon were once two long, connected seas. Brazil, an immense island, was then a continent in its own right," he wrote, and added, "the Brazilian massif has profound roots and eternal foundations that are uniquely its

76. Skidmore. "Eduardo Prado: A Conservative Nationalist Critic," p. 153.

77. Darrel Levi, *The Prados of São Paulo*, p. 128; Carvalho, "The Force of Tradition," p. 159.

own. This is why the volcanic eruptions of the other system do not reach the Brazilian shores."[78]

The use of the present tense in the last sentence draws attention. Obviously the "volcanic eruptions" *did* reach the Brazilian shores. Indeed, Prado was quick to correct himself and acknowledge their impact on Brazilian politics–albeit not on the deeper layers of the nation's character, which supposedly remained stable and quiet in the midst of Spanish American revolutions and bloodshed. These opening phrases of *A ilusão americana* represent an effort to reconstruct Brazil's singular identity after its near collapse in the immediate aftermath of the coup. Prado now redrew the separating line between civilization and barbarism, stability and turmoil, peace and violence, along the national borders and in much bolder strokes than during the last days of the Empire. Furthermore, the geological metaphor removed these dichotomies from human time, transforming Brazil's peaceful evolution from a distinguishing mark of its history into a defining feature of its essence.

Yet paradoxically, the total negation of any affinity with the neighboring countries gave way, toward the end of the text, to an almost straightforward identification on the basis of the very same violent/nonviolent polarity. In the last section of the book, dedicated to North American moral and intellectual influences, Prado set "the respect for human life and liberty" as the true measure of a given people's level of civilization. According to this criterion, he maintained, the United States was inferior to Brazil: whereas the spirit of the first was "violent," "the Latin spirit" of Iberian origins of the latter was "juridical."[79] With this, Prado came very close to defining Brazil's Spanish-speaking neighbors as peaceful, thus completely obliterating the dividing line between Them and Us that he himself had just drawn.

Apparently, as far as Prado was concerned, there were two Spanish Americas, the one violent, the other not, and Brazil, in a very confusing manner, was identified with both. For in fact, there were also two Brazils. Allegedly peaceful in essence, Portuguese America came to suffer from the same predicament of chronic disorder as Spanish

78. Prado, *A ilusão americana*, p. 10.
79. Ibid., pp. 173-175.

America and from similar reasons, namely the copying of institutions that were alien to both its history and race. This was a mainstay of *A ilusão americana*.[80] It should be noted that in Prado's interpretation, the eruption and the perpetuation of violence in Brazil were not a mere accident of history, but rather an outcome–as well as further proof–of its belonging to Latin America due to shared historical experiences and racial/cultural origins. In short, the immediate circumstances led Prado to conflicting interpretations of Spanish America and Brazil, interpretations which in turn produced contradictory conclusions with regard to Brazil's place in Latin America. Brazil did *not* belong because it was peaceful, this Prado stated very clearly. But at the same it *did* belong–an idea he expressed more implicitly–for exactly the same reason, or for the opposite one. That is, violent or nonviolent, ordered or disordered, Brazil was part of Latin America either way.

In fact, with the fast-increasing militarization and brutalization of Brazil's political life, this composite view of the Self and of the Other soon engulfed republican leaders as well. This can be seen in the person of Rui Barbosa, who became a leading critic of the regime during the rule of Floriano Peixoto.[81] Persecuted by the government for alleged involvement in the 1893 Naval Revolt, senator Barbosa fled to Buenos Aires–a city "immeasurably superior" to Rio de Janeiro, he wrote to his wife[82]–where he stayed for several months. During this period of exile, he published a series of programmatic articles destined for Brazilian readership in the city's prestigious newspaper *La Nación*, an act which he defended by placing it in an explicitly defined Latin American context. To take advantage of the freedom of speech in Argentina, according to Rui, was to take advantage of "a right that is as old as the history of the military tyrannies in America, a right invoked, throughout the ages, by all those shipwrecked in the stormy seas of caudillism in this continent." Along this line, the main

80. Ibid., esp. pp. 143-146.

81. Curiously, even Peixoto himself, following a coup attempt against him, warned against "anarchy and *caudillismo*." Hahner, *Civilian-Military Relations in Brazil*, p. 77.

82. Letter dated Sep. 25, 1893, Rui Barbosa, *Mocidade e exílio* (São Paulo: Companhia Editora Nacional, 1934), p. 210.

advocate of civil liberties in Brazil further identified himself with prominent leaders of Argentine liberalism who had campaigned against Rosas from exile. In particular, he singled out the writings of Argentina's leading jurist, Juan Bautista Alberdi, held "dear by all the friends of free institutions in Latin America."[83] Like Prado and Nabuco, Rui evoked a vision of Spanish America and Brazil as comprising a single battlefield between two major forces.

Sparse and poorly articulated at first, this new-born vision of Brazil as forming part of a Janus-faced Latin America, associated with North Atlantic order and progress as much as with autochthonous *caudillismo*, would henceforth be given much fuller expression. Two lengthy essays published in 1895, "Duas glórias da humanidade" by Rui Barbosa and *Balmaceda* by Joaquim Nabuco, showed the way. Both works constituted a criticism of Floriano Peixoto's despotic rule through a discussion of Spanish American leaders, Paraguay's José Gaspar Francia and Argentina's Rosas in the first, and Chile's José Manuel Balmaceda in the second. The examples were typically drawn from Brazil's southern neighbors but stood for a broader phenomenon, as was made explicit in the concluding pages of the two texts, in which both authors diagnosed "Latin America" as suffering from chronic disorder and authoritarianism. Nabuco even prescribed a remedy. This should be sought, he wrote in the first-person plural, "inside each and every one of our countries [...] in all of them there are men whose cultural stature equals that of Europe's best, and who can form the Liberal League of the Continent. The cause is, in fact, a shared one."[84]

* * *

The growing threat to the existence of the monarchy in the late 1880s led Brazilian intellectuals to rediscover the relevance of the

83. "Quarta carta a *La Nación*," Nov. 13, 1893, in *Obras completas*, vol. XX, t. I, pp. 354-359.

84. Both texts first appeared as serialized articles in *Jornal do Commercio* and then in book form. See Joaquim Nabuco, *Balmaceda* (São Paulo: Instituto Progresso Editorial, 1949[1895]), p. 142; and Rui Barbosa, "Duas glories da humanidade," in *Cartas de Inglaterra* [1896], *Obras completas*, vol. XXIII, t. I, p. 254.

Spanish American experience as a negative reference point for assessing and influencing their own circumstances. Underlying this awakening to the anarchic and authoritarian nature of the neighbors' politics had been a notion of common essence that was now reworked and reinforced. In that way, a negative and pessimistic course of identification with Spanish America, based on the specter of caudillistic violence, opened up alongside the optimistic one. After the 1889 military coup, this course was deepened and broadened as monarchist leaders were thrown into an unfamiliar reality that shattered some vital components of the their national identity. Facing a sudden break from the old order, an abrupt eruption of what for them had been unknown or repressed qualities of the nation, these men had to make sense of their new circumstances. They had to give meaning to a radically different sociopolitical context and redefine themselves and their nation. In doing so, they continued to turn their eyes to the neighbors, focusing mainly on the less-promising aspects of nineteenth-century Spanish American political life.

During the first years of the republic, neither Brazil's portrait of its neighbors nor of itself were fixed. A combination of conscious manipulations and psychological reactions, pessimism and optimism, gave rise to varying interpretations of Spanish America and Brazil, past, present and future. Caudillistic or not caudillistic? Part of Latin America or not? These questions received no decisive answers, but their very discussion reflected and, in turn, contributed to the formation of a new Latin American consciousness among Brazilians; a consciousness that would become ideologized with the change of circumstances at around the turn of the century, both inside and outside of the national borders.

Chapter 4
Close Encounters of the Peripheral Kind: Luso-Hispano-American Interaction in the Age of Empire and the Ideologization of "Latin America"

> I have followed with curiosity and interest the manifestations of your Monroeism or, better said, your Rooseveltianism, and although I know how enthusiastically you always apply yourself to those issues with which you have become infatuated, I could not believe that you would go that far with your Americanism ...North Americanism [*Americanismo... do norte*]. I cannot say that I unreservedly applaud this, because my Monroeism is less passionate and my Rooseveltianism is even less so. [...] Besides, you, Sir, were right when you once wrote to me that I should go to South America in order to become fully acquainted with the mappa mundi of our diplomacy. My knowledge of this realm [...] would not be complete without this spectacle, and it turns out that it was a good moment to arrive [in Venezuela] since the comedy is now approaching the climax of the plot .... In Japan and in China I had the chance to learn how vulgar Europeans can be, and in Venezuela I now see how Europeans and Americans can also be thieves and speculators. I do not turn a blind eye to the flaws, the crimes even, of this country, of the people here. But the other side is by no means morally superior or more edifying.[1]

Thus wrote Oliveira Lima from Caracas, where he served as Brazil's minister to Venezuela, to the recently appointed ambassador to Washington, Joaquim Nabuco, in late 1905. About a year and a

1. Oliveira Lima to Joaquim Nabuco, Oct. 23, 1905, excerpted in Fernando da Cruz Gouvêa, *Oliveira Lima, uma biografia*, 3 vols. (Recife: Instituto Arqueológico, Histórico e Geográfico Pernambucano, 1976), vol. 2, p. 690.

half later, Oliveira Lima received a letter from Euclides da Cunha, then serving as an aide to Foreign Minister Baron of Rio Branco, in which the already consecrated author of the instant classic *Os Sertões* (1902) recounted to Lima some of his impressions of the visit of Argentina's former President Julio Argentino Roca (1880-1886; 1898-1904) to the Brazilian capital in March 1907. Da Cunha lamented the recent change of Rio de Janeiro's urban face and social climate. He regretted the rapid disappearance of the city's "beautiful old attributes, prudent reserve, disciplined sentiments and modest pride." In his view, the celebrations in Roca's honor reflected this trend:

> The festivities exceeded by far what Rio Branco, whose original initiative and intentions were comprehensible and justified, had envisaged. Our people went beyond the norm, and thus, during eight days, the *gringo* (with whom tomorrow we would inevitably have to fight) received flatteries that were enough for his entire life. In the end, the representative of the Military Club sang for him a moving hymn for peace ... and made an apology of a woman!! Very curious and eloquent. But I am scared of what the cunning caudillo would think about our virility and our courage in view of the pretentious lyricism of our sword bearers.[2]

These passages by Oliveira Lima and da Cunha reflect several important features of what I call close encounters of the peripheral kind–encounters between Portuguese– and Spanish–speaking Americans, which grew in number and visibility during the first decade of the 1900s. In his letter to Nabuco, Oliveira Lima refers to Europeans and Americans as "the other side," the other side of the Venezuelans and, by extension, of Spanish America as a whole–which, both Brazilians agreed, it was crucial to know firsthand. Europe and the United States on the one hand, and Spanish America on the other, these were indeed the twin poles, the two significant external Others, in between which the Brazilian elite's identity was being formed, the third one being internal, the *povo*. But fin-de-siècle encounters between upper class Brazilians and Spanish America(ns) were differ-

2. Letter dated March 20, 1907, transcribed in Thomas Skidmore and Thomas Holloway, "New Light on Euclides da Cunha: Letters to Oliveira Lima, 1903-1909," *Luso-Brazilian Review* 8:1 (1971), pp. 39-40.

ent from, though surely related to, the encounters at the so-called "contact zones" between Western and non-Western societies, colonizers and colonized, whites and non-whites, modernizing elites and traditionalist populations, so widely explored in modern scholarship. Unlike colonial and neocolonial engagements, whether external or internal, between "*disparate* cultures" that took place in contexts of "radically asymmetrical relations of power," the interaction to be described here occurred on the basis of cultural similarity and relative equality.[3]

In order to perfect our understanding of the dynamics of Brazilian national identity, we should then follow in the footsteps of Oliveira Lima and other Brazilian literati. In the same way that he had to familiarize himself with Spanish America in order to complete the map of Brazilian diplomacy, so must we explore this lesser-known interaction within and across Latin America. As will be revealed, horizontal encounters of this kind did *not* entail the obliteration of either side's identity (as often happens in highly hierarchical and conflictual relations of the previous type), but rather endowed it with a new supranational facet through the discovery and construction of sameness.[4]

Direct, unmediated meetings between educated elite members of both sides, the Brazilian and the Spanish American, were not in themselves new, of course. As we have seen in the previous chapters, Eduardo Prado, Quintino Bocaiuva, Rio Branco, Joaquim Nabuco, Rui Barbosa, and Oliveira Lima, as well as some other Brazilian men

3. The quoted terms are from Pratt, *Imperial Eyes*, p. 7. For a similar emphasis, see Gilbert M. Joseph, "Close Encounters: Toward a New Cultural History of U.S.–Latin American Relations," in Gilbert M. Joseph, Catherine C. LeGrand, and Ricardo D. Salvatore, eds., *Close Encounters of Empire: Writing the Cultural History of U.S.-Latin American Relations* (Durham: Duke University Press, 1998), pp. 3-46, and other contributions in the same volume.

4. Here we may return to Tzvetan Todorov's typology, utilized as an analytical framework in the previous chapters. Drawing on the sanguinary case of the Spanish conquest of America, the model he presents (as a historian, not as a moralist) does not make room for these kinds of developments at the praxeological level of rapprochement or distancing in relation to the other. It is either we identify ourselves with the other, he observes, or else we identify the other with ourselves. Submission to the other or the other's submission are the only two possible modes of action (the third mode being indifference). *The Conquest of America*, p. 185.

of state and/or letters, had all spent time with Spanish-speaking peers in various contexts during the last quarter of the nineteenth century. Some of these encounters were product of routine diplomatic service abroad, on the one hand, or unique personal circumstances, on the other. In general, though, increasing contacts between members of the Latin American elites should be understood in the context of the economic, intellectual, and juridical internationalization of the world that was then reaching its apogee.

At the threshold of the twentieth century, the world was becoming ever "more conscious of its one-ness," seeking institutionalization of individual and national rights as a counterbalance to intensifying imperialism and arms races. International associations and organizations, which convened regularly and brought together delegates from around the globe proliferated, in a scene dominated by the law of the powerful.[5] The two peace conferences at The Hague in 1899 and 1907 are a notable example. Brazil's recently elected president, Manuel Ferraz de Campos Sales's (1898-1902) public reference to the invitation from the Russian tsar to his country to participate in the first conference, illustrates well the spread of this ideational climate to Latin America. In his first yearly message to the Congress, Campos Sales depicted the activity surrounding the idea of disarmament and on behalf of universal peace as "highly humanitarian and civilizing, the supreme factor of international politics."[6] In spite of

5. Geoffrey Best, "Peace Conferences and the Age of Total War: The 1899 Hague Peace Conference and What Came After," *International Affairs* 75:3 (1999), p. 620. On the rise of international peace activism and spread of arbitration treaties during the late nineteenth and early twentieth century, see Sandi E. Cooper, *Patriotic Pacifism: Waging War on War in Europe, 1815-1914* (New York: Oxford, 1991), esp. part 2. The duality of imperialism/internationalism was also imbedded in the world fairs that burgeoned during this period. See Alvaro Fernández Bravo, "Ambivalent Argentina, Nationalism, Exoticism, and Latin Americanism, at the 1889 Paris Universal Exposition," *Nepantla: Views from South* 2:1 (2001), p. 116. On the proliferation of international congresses and societies and Brazilian participation, see Love, *São Paulo*, p. 220.

6. Brazil, *Mensagem apresentada ao Congresso Nacional na abertuta da terceira sessão da terceira legislatura pelo presidente da republica M. Ferraz de Campos Salles* (Rio de Janeiro, 1899), May 3, 1899, p. 10. For academic activities and publications in the field of international law in Brazil during this time, see Vicente Marrota Rangel, "Direito internacional e relações internacionais: A teoria tridimensionalista no contexto brasileiro," in Universidad Simón Bolívar, Instituto de Altos Estudios de Améri-

the elevated rhetoric, Brazil did not participate in this specific international event, but it would soon do so in others.

The 1882 Continental Exposition in Buenos Aires, the 1888 South American Congress of International Private Law in Montevideo, the 1889 First International American Conference in Washington, and the arbitration agreement between Brazil and Argentina over the Missões territory, also in 1889, can all be seen as incipient indications of the aforementioned global trends. The 1890s did not see much continuation of such activity in the Americas, possibly due–at least in part–to the internal political and economic troubles experienced by Argentina, a major player in the South American sphere. This was also certainly true for Brazil which plunged into the turmoil of the republic's early years. Yet, by the turn of the century, things had changed on both sides of the River Plate.

Argentina was now back on track. In 1900, writes historian Thomas McGann, "the Oligarchy was confident [...] the nation at peace and richer than at any previous time in its history. The country entered its *novecientos*–the 'nineteen hundreds'–her postponed gay nineties, her halcyon decade or so."[7] Brazil entered the new century in a less privileged position, at least in the eyes of its contemporaries,[8] but soon followed in the footsteps of its southern neighbor, securing its own oligarchic political arrangement. In Portuguese America, too, "triumphalist liberalism," to use Tulio Halperin Donghi's terms, evolved into "authoritarian developmentalism." The *Ordem e Progresso* emblem on the Brazilian flag, corresponding in spirit to the Argentine motto of *Paz y Administración*, had come to better resemble reality, as far as the elites were concerned. After the remodeling project of Rio de Janeiro (1902-1906) along French lines, which symbolized the elites' prosperity, the Brazilian capital could compete with Buenos Aires over the coveted title of "Paris in America."[9]

ca Latina, *Teorías de relaciones internacionales y de derecho internacional en América Latina* (Bogotá: Fundación Simón Bolívar: Departamento de Asuntos Culturales de la OEA, 1989), pp. 467-471.

7. McGann, *Argentina*, pp. 188, 192.

8. Skidmore, *Black into White*, pp. 136, 145.

9. Quote from Tulio Halperín Donghi, *The Contemporary History of Latin America*, trans. and ed. by John Charles Chasteen (Durham: Duke University Press, 1993), p. 136. Jeffrey Needell makes direct reference to the convergence of Brazilian

A major expression of the improvement of internal conditions in both countries, and of the desire of the governing elites to secure order and progress, was the exchange of presidential visits in 1899 and 1900, on Argentina's initiative. This first visit ever of a head of state to Brazil would be followed in the next years by several other visits by high-level Spanish American statesmen, in which the initiative had been taken by Brazil, as in the case of Roca's second visit in 1907 (described in Da Cunha's letter cited above). Under the guidance of Rio Branco, who was named foreign minister in 1902 and who remained in office for the next ten years, Brazilian foreign policy became much more consistent and assertive than it had been during the republic's first decade, now targeted at achieving supremacy in South America.[10]

This pattern was also manifested in Brazil's approach to international activities at the subcontinental and continental levels, which were gathering new steam at about the same time as bilateral activities. In 1898, the First Latin American Scientific Congress convened in Buenos Aires, followed by a second one in Montevideo three years later. Brazil did not send official delegates to these two meetings–although Brazilian scholars did take part–yet, in 1905, the country not only participated but also hosted the third congress.[11] At the con-

and Argentine points of view at this particular moment. According to him, the elites of the two countries "conceived the paths of their nations as lying in the same direction [... and] thought they were about to cross the universal threshold of civilization." Significantly, Needell also mentions that the urban reform of Rio de Janeiro was carried out "in conscious competition with the earlier reform of Buenos Aires," but he does not ponder the meaning of this instance of inter–Latin American interaction. See "Rio de Janeiro and Buenos Aires," p. 524. More or less along the same lines, Bradford Burns extends this argument to Latin America as a whole, again without discussing intellectual exchanges within the continent. See Burns, *The Poverty of Progress*, esp. chap. 2.

10. E. Bradford Burns, *The Unwritten Alliance: Rio-Branco and Brazilian-American Relations* (New York: Columbia University Press, 1966), pp. 37-38, 126, passim. This book is still the standard work on Brazilian diplomacy during Rio Branco's term. For a more recent account, see Joseph Smith, *Unequal Giants: Diplomatic Relations Between the United States and Brazil, 1889-1930* (Pittsburgh: University of Pittsburgh Press, 1991), chap. 2, esp. pp. 37-38, 48-49.

11. "Congreso científico latino americano: Segunda comunicación," *Anales de la Sociedad Científica Argentina*, entry II, no. XLV (Feb. 1898), pp. 113-119; *Segunda reunión del Congreso científico latino americano celebrada en Montevideo del 20 al 31 de marzo de 1901* (Montevideo, Tip. y enc. "Al libro inglés," 1901), pp. IIV-40.

tinental level, the United States started pushing in early 1900 for a second Pan-American meeting, which eventually convened in Mexico in October 1901. Brazil's participation began low key, but, as in the case of its strictly Latin American activities, it rapidly moved to play a major role.[12] In 1906, the Brazilian Foreign Office went out of its way to accord a warm and extravagant welcome to a group of notable delegates from around the continent, including U.S. Secretary of State Elihu Root, who arrived for the Third Pan-American Conference.

Out of the many inter-American encounters of the first decade of the twentieth century, it is the exchange of presidential visits between Brazil and Argentina mentioned above and the Third Pan-American Conference that stand at the center of this chapter. These two bilateral and international events have mainly been studied from a realist perspective, thus leaving their rich cultural content almost untouched.[13] Embedded worldviews, values, ideologies, and senti-

12. The single Brazilian representative to the Mexico conference died during the meeting, and was not replaced. See "Pereira, José Hygino Duarte," in Argeu Guimaraes, *Diccionario bio-bibliographico brasileiro, de diplomacia, politica externa e direito internacional* (Rio de Janeiro: Published by the author, 1938), p. 353.

13. The only extensive treatments of the two presidential visits are Rosendo Fraga, "La visita de Roca a Rio de Janeiro," and Luiz Felipe de Seixas Corrêa, "La visita de Campos Salles a la Argentina," in Fraga and de Seixas Corrêa, eds., *Argentina Brasil: Centenario de 2 visitas: Historia fotográfica* (Buenos Aires: Editorial Centro de Estudios Unión para la Nueva Mayoría, 1998). Luiz Alberto Moniz Bandeira, an authority on Brazil's hemispheric relations, mentions the visits only in passing in his recent comprehensive study, *Brasil, Argentina e Estados Unidos: Conflito e integração na América do Sul (Da Triplice Aliança ao Mercosul, 1870-2003)* 2nd revised and extended ed. (Rio de Janeiro: Revan, 2003), p. 57. More elaborate discussions can be found in Clodoaldo Bueno, *A república e sua política exterior (1889 a 1902)*, (São Paulo/Brasília: Editora UNESP/IPRI, 1995), pp. 249-254; and Sérgio Danese, *Diplomacia presidencial: História e crítica* (Rio de Janeiro: Topbooks, 1999), pp. 263-274. Stanley Hilton significantly notes that "frequent protestations of historic fraternity and solidarity by Brazilian spokesmen" should not be treated as "insignificant rhetoric of the moment." See Hilton, "The Argentine Factor," p. 36. The reason he gives, though, is "their strategic character and the importance of diplomacy to a military weak country," not their cultural weight. About the Third Pan-American Conference from the diplomatic perspective, see A. Curtis Wilgus, "The Third International American Conference at Rio de Janeiro, 1906," *Hispanic American Historical Review* 12:4 (Nov., 1932), pp. 420-456; Burns, *The Unwritten Alliance*, pp. 108-114; Smith, *Unequal Giants*, pp. 53-57. Brief allusions to the cultural significance of the event as a public display of a Europeanized Brazil are found in Skidmore, *Black into White*, pp.

ments have received attention–if at all–only inasmuch as they shaped foreign policy making. That is, they are addressed in terms of cause and effect, but are not dealt with in and of themselves. The following pages provide, instead, an examination of the symbolic interaction between Brazilians and Spanish Americans–practiced through verbal and visual representations alike–as a window to the interplay between Self-Other perceptions.

In the first decade of twentieth-century, Brazilians' views of Spanish America, and of Brazil itself within the Latin American context, had grown–as was also happening in the United States–more complex. Still, several common denominators can be discerned. If the abolition of slavery marked the opening of what I have called a positive path of identification with Spanish America, and if the initially caudillistic nature of the republic opened a negative path of this kind, the 1900s witnessed the emergence of more synthetic perceptions. Spanish America was neither entirely disordered, weak, and backward, nor fully stable, vigorous, and advanced. The latter adjectives were principally associated with Argentina, Chile, and Porfirio Díaz's Mexico, while the other Spanish-American countries usually were ascribed the first kind of labels.[14]

However, negative or positive moral judgments did not necessarily correspond, to national divisions. For instance, Oliveira Lima developed, as can be learned from his letter, a considerably mixed approach to Venezuela, a country generally viewed with contempt. In like manner, even Argentina–admired to the point of being feared–was sometimes seen through a pejorative European/North American lens. All in all, by now Brazilian elites had come to perceive themselves, to one extent or another, willingly or unwillingly,

136-137; and Jeffrey Needell, "The Domestic Civilizing Mission: The Cultural Role of the State in Brazil, 1808-1930," *Luso-Brazilian Review* 36:1 (Summer 1999), p. 7.

14. A clear, concise statement of this vision appears in Euclides da Cunha, "Solidariedade Sul-Americana," *O Paiz*, May 31, 1904, in *Contrastes e confrontos* (São Paulo: Editora Cultrix, 1975 [1907]), pp. 108-109. For an interesting discussion of da Cunha's dual approach toward Spanish America, see Kátia Gerab Baggio, "A América Latina e os Estados Unidos na visão de Euclides da Cunha," *Estudos de História* 7:2 (2000), pp. 55-68. On the disintegration of U.S. stereotypes concerning Latin America during this period, see Ricardo Salvatore, "The Enterprise of Knowledge: Representational Machines of Informal Empire," in Joseph, et al., eds., *Close Encounters of Empire*, p. 83.

as Latin Americans. This shared consciousness was infused with varying combinations of pessimism and optimism, and engendered differing ideological formulas. But before we move to examine these dynamics as reflected in encounters between Latin Americans themselves, we must first direct our attention to a dramatic historical development at the contact zone between Latin Americans and North Americans.

PART 1
1898, Enter the United States: Brazilian Reactions

Arielismo in Brazil: Before and after Rodó

"'Ninety-eight' is not only a Spanish date, it is also, and perhaps most importantly, a Latin American date that should serve to designate a no less complex group of writers and thinkers on this side of the Atlantic, generally known by the vague name *modernistas*. It is 'ninety-eight'–the visible presence of the North American imperialism in Latin America–already foretold by Martí, which informs the later work of someone like Darío or Rodó."[15] The works of both figures to whom the Cuban Roberto Fernández Retamar refers–the Nicaraguan poet, who would visit Rio de Janeiro in 1906 as the secretary of his country's delegation to the Pan-American Conference, and the Uruguayan thinker–were not completely unknown in Brazil. Rodó's essay *Ariel* (1900) was reviewed the year of its publication in Rio de Janeiro's *Jornal do Comércio*, together with *Peligros americanos* (1898) by the Argentine Rodríguez del Busto. José Veríssimo, a leading literary critic, discussed the two books in a joint review article titled "The Regeneration of Latin America." He opened his review by singling out the existence "in Latin America, or more accurately in Spanish America, [of] a favorable trend of opinion toward a more conscious and expressive racial and national sentiment, and a systematic affirmation of the ethnic and national [*pátrio*] self."[16]

Veríssimo, a founding member of The Brazilian Academy of Letters like Nabuco, Rui Barbosa, and Oliveira Lima, with whom he

15. Roberto Fernández Retamar, *Caliban and other Essays*, trans. by Edward Baker (Minneapolis: University of Minnesota Press, 1989), p. 10.

16. José Veríssimo, "A regeneração da América Latina," in *José Veríssimo, teoria, crítica e história literária*, compilation and introduction by João Alexandre Barbosa (São Paulo: Brasiliense, 1986), p. 17. This article also appeared in book form: Veríssimo, *Homens e cousas estrangeiras*, 3 vols. (Rio de Janeiro: Garnier, 1902, 1905, 1910), vol. I (1899-1900). Rubén Darío's Arielism was noticed by another prominent literary critic: Araripe Júnior, "Os raros," *Gazeta de Notícias*, Oct. 2, 1900, in *Obra crítica de Araripe Júnior*, 5 vols. (Rio de Janeiro: Ministério da Educação e Cultura, Casa de Rui Barbosa, 1958-1970), vol. 3, p. 465.

maintained close relationships, endorsed the two Spanish American authors' preoccupations with U.S. expansionism in face of the Spanish-American War. Veríssimo's critical stand contrasted with the official policy of his government, the only one in Latin America alongside Mexico, as he himself acknowledged, to adopt a sympathetic neutrality toward the North American superpower.[17] The official Brazilian stand expressed a gradual improvement in the relationships with the latter since the establishment of the republic. As already mentioned, the friendly approach of historical republicans toward their Spanish American neighbors went hand in hand with their Americanism and North Americanism. Quintino Bocaiuva, the champion of Brazilian-Argentine rapprochement, was also an old admirer of the United States. Pro-American sentiments were especially dominant among the Jacobin faction of the republican camp, and received their greatest expression during Floriano Peixoto's years in power. It was in that context that Eduardo Prado wrote his famous anti-Yankee treatise, *A ilusão americana* (1893) which Veríssimo did not fail to mention in his article.[18]

Brazilian thinkers and statesmen were in general less prone to hostile attitudes toward the United States than their Spanish American counterparts. Nonetheless, as Fernández Retamar himself has noted–what may be called anachronistically, after Rodó's essay–Arielist stances had appeared in Brazil earlier than in other parts of the continent. Retamar, and also literary critic Jean Franco, mention in this regard José Veríssimo's own *A educação nacional*, published as early as 1890.[19] This book preceded Prado's *A ilusão americana* in warning against the blind importation of cultural elements from

17. According to Moniz Bandeira, *Presença dos Estados Unidos*, p. 150, Brazil was the only country in Latin American who showed sympathy to the U.S. during this war.

18. Bandeira, *Presença dos Estados Unidos*, p. 145; Topik, *Trade and Gunboats*, pp. 102-103, 176-177; Suely Robles Reis de Queiroz, *Os radicais da república. Jacobinismo: Ideologia e ação, 1893-1897* (São Paulo: Brasiliense, 1986), pp. 106-107, 222.

19. Jean Franco, *The Modern Culture of Latin America: Society and the Artist* (Harmondsworth, Middlesex: Penguin, 1970), p. 62; and João Alexandre Barbosa, "Apresentação," in *José Veríssimo*, p. 10. In his presentation, Barbosa explains that one of his motives for organizing this compilation of articles by Veríssimo was "to question the *fable convenue* that Brazilian intellectuals are unfamiliar with or undervalue the work of their Spanish American neighbors," pp. 10-11.

North America. "Deep in my Brazilian heart," wrote Veríssimo in regard to the United States, "there is something that disdains this nation which is so excessively practical, so colossally egoist, and so immanently, forgive me the expression, *strugforlifista*... I admire it but I do not esteem it."[20] A decade would pass before Rodó would make public his own complicated feelings about North Americans, drawing a similar distinction: "although I do not love them, I admire them."[21]

As a matter of fact, the Brazilian origins of the concept that stresses an opposition between the materialism and utilitarianism of the "Anglo-Saxon" country on the one hand, and Latin spirituality on the other hand–which is at the core of all of the above mentioned texts–may be traced to at least as far back as the mid-1870s. The following quote from the editors of *O Novo Mundo*, a Portuguese-language journal of republican inclination, basically favorable to the United States, that was published in New York and designed for Brazilian readership in Brazil, is telling: "Nothing gives us more pleasure, for example, than to attend to the presumptuous vanity with which some of our 'statesmen' and carpet-baggers speak about this disgusting mass of Americans who spend their life kneeling before the god of the dollar and reciting their kyrie: *Time is money*. We do not strive, and never have, to Americanize Brazil."[22] Said vanity clearly characterized the young Joaquim Nabuco who in 1877, while serving as an attaché to the Brazilian legation in the United States, noted in his diary that "man here is a money-making machine, humanity's clear goal is to get rich, the dollar is the god of this plutocracy of forty million men."[23]

20. *Strugforlifista* comes from the English language: "Struggle for life." José Veríssimo, *A educação nacional*, p. 132.

21. José Enrique Rodó, *Ariel*, trans. by Margaret Sayers Peden (Austin: University of Texas Press, 1988), p. 77.

22. "Um contraste," *O Novo Mundo*, vol. 56 (May 23, 1875), p. 190. About this journal, see George C. A. Boehrer, "José Carlos Rodrigues and *O Novo Mundo*, 1870-1879," *Journal of Inter-American Studies* 9:1 (Jan., 1967), pp. 127-144.

23. Entry for March 10, 1877, Nabuco, *Diários*, vol. 1, p. 124. In his preface to this section of Nabuco's diaries, Evaldo Cabral de Mello suggests that these condescending remarks can be attributed to European stereotypes of U.S. society. See Ibid., p. 88.

A more detailed genealogy or internal analysis of *arielismo* in Brazil and elsewhere is beyond the scope of this work. Let it suffice to point that the entire range of diplomatic activity and intellectual production to be discussed henceforth should be understood in a twofold context of 1) a long tradition of Arielist North-South polarities in Brazil, and 2) what José Verrísimo depicted in his 1900 review of Rodó's book as the "old racial hatred" and "racial sentiment" that the 1898 war had aroused throughout Spanish America. In other words, when Brazilian men-of-state-and-letters came to interpret the new hemispheric circumstances, they did not start from scratch. Nor were they working in a vacuum. Their interpretations were informed by established images of the United States and by the rise of Pan–Latin American sentiments and politics that stressed the conflict of character and interests between the so-called Anglo-Saxon and Latin parts of the continent.

"Like Cuba and the Philippines, Mexico and Nicaragua": Joaquim Nabuco

In 1897, the Academia Brasileira de Letras was founded, bringing together Joaquim Nabuco and Rui Barbosa, Eduardo Prado and Oliveira Lima, monarchists and republicans. Patterned on the Académie Française, the institution and its rituals may well be interpreted as yet another expression of the Carioca upper class's desperate identification with European culture, an identification not free from ambivalence and self-criticism. The founders of the Brazilian Academy were no exception to the well-documented discontent of fin-de-siècle Latin American literati with "the artificial, inauthentic, and imitative nature" of their cultural life.[24] This was made manifest in Joaquim Nabuco's inaugural address as the newly nominated general secretary of the Academy, an address often cited for its emphasis on the need to produce an authentically Brazilian literature.[25] But what should interest us more particularly is that the sense of cultural

24. Schwarz, "Nationalism by Elimination," p. 77, passim.

25. Needell, *A Tropical Belle Époque*, pp. 194-195; Skidmore, *Black into White*, pp. 91-92.

artificiality and the concomitant romantic quest for genuinely national literature take Nabuco back in time to the Library of Buenos Aires. There, he recounted, "I read a few pages written by General Mitre whom I truly admire; the idea is that Spanish American literature has not yet produced its one [great] book." Brazil, continued Nabuco, fit within this verdict. "The Brazilian soul" had already been defined, delineated and expressed in diverse works of literature, but it had not, as of yet, been condensed into a single book, "our national book." It was the mission of the Academy to provide the right milieu for the emergence of "the kind of work in which General Mitre sees the sign of strength, of literary sinew."[26]

Once more we witness the pattern of a model-within-a-model. If in a previous instance it was the *concrete* city of Buenos Aires that served as an example of how to create a "civilized" urban space in a peripheral setting, here it is the *lettered* city of Buenos Aires that shows the way toward the "universal norm" of an organic national literature.

In his diagnosis of Brazil's cultural deficiency Nabuco draws, then, on the reflections of an Argentine writer concerning Spanish America as a whole, an act which simultaneously presupposes and creates sameness. Apparent is his pessimistic Latin American consciousness, a consciousness which continues to deepen. The year afterward he writes an obituary for his friend, the Chilean politician and publicist Guillermo Puelma-Tupper, that reads like an obituary for an entire subcontinent. Here again he contemplates the imitative nature of Brazil's intellectual life within a wider Latin American framework, describing the deceased as an example of the kind of vigorous intellectual leader "our countries" need in order to stir up their "indolent, stagnant social setting." America may one day surpass the old continent intellectually, yet, in the meantime, it is only capable of reflection on European ideas. Interweaving biological essentialist notions with awareness of historical contingencies, determinism with recognition of human agency, and featuring the trope of juvenility, Nabuco's indictment is severe: "Unfortunately, there is always a certain lacuna in *our* organizations, a vice, an error, in *our* formula. It

26. Speech delivered on July 20, 1897, in Nabuco, *Escritos e Discursos Literários*, pp. 186-187.

takes centuries for the races to be formed; *we*, South Americans, who strived for a better life in the nineteenth century, had wanted to be born too early, and therefore *we* all failed."[27]

These preoccupations with Latin American spiritual feebleness were soon joined and reinforced by external factors. In an interview he gave to the *Estado de São Paulo*, and which was reprinted in Rio de Janeiro's *Jornal do Comércio* in September 1898, Nabuco emphasized the importance of international circumstances for Brazil's and Latin America's future. The interviewer's last question focused, like the previous ones, on Brazil's domestic politics and economic condition. However, the answer went interestingly in another direction: "Today we are one of the many unknown factors of a vast problem, namely the American problem. Europe, Africa, and Asia now form a single political unit. Confronted by this colossal mass, which should be called the European mass, what is South America's destiny? Is it to form a whole with the United States? Or perhaps enter the European sphere of influence, with the United States or against it? Nobody knows. [...] How do you expect me to predict what would be our internal situation four years from now, when it is, at least to a certain extent, a reflection of the general external situation."[28]

Nabuco's expansion of the topic is noteworthy but hardly surprising. The international sphere always attracted his attention in a double way. He looked abroad not only for ideational and political guidance, but also as a way to understand Brazil's circumstances as parts and products of international events and processes. External developments were relevant to the situation at home both as a frame of interpretation and as a direct influence. The reader might recall Nabuco's linkage of internal issues to foreign policy in his triple plan of abolition, federation, and peace, destined to save the monarchy, and in his articles about the Latin American crisis from the early 1890s, a linkage also present in his monumental historical work, *Um estadista do império*, documenting the career of his father. At once a

27. Joaquim Nabuco, "Guilherme Puelma-Tupper," in *Escritos e Discursos Literários*, pp. 192, 199; my italics. Similar views are found in his private correspondence from this time. See, for example, Joaquim Nabuco to Hilário de Gouvêa, Rio de Janeiro, Aug. 19, 1898, in *Cartas a amigos*, vol. 1, p. 287.

28. *Jornal do Commercio*, Sep. 26, 1898, n.pag., clipping 001.16-74/188, AJN.

biography and a thorough political history of Brazil under Dom Pedro II written during Nabuco's self-exile from politics, it included extensive treatment of the Paraguayan War, singling this international conflagration as a turning point in the nation's domestic evolution. In Nabuco's analysis, the War of the Triple Alliance signified the beginning of the Empire's end, an interpretation which has become very influential in Brazilian historiography.[29]

His already mentioned essay *Balmaceda*, written roughly in the same period, again exemplified this broad outlook, dealing with the issue of political instability and authoritarianism in Brazil through comparison to Chile. So strong was this tendency to look beyond the national borders, that the book's concluding discussion of alternative outcomes or answers to "the Latin American Question" began with a detailed speculation on the chances for European or North American interference in the region just in order to eventually rule them out. At that time, Nabuco identified chronic misgovernment as Latin America's central problem. The internal conditions of each and every country represented his main preoccupation, and his response was also to emerge from within the subcontinent. He discarded categorically any possibility of external intervention that might change the face of things. Latin Americans should redeem themselves, no one else would do it for them; thus stated Nabuco in 1895.[30]

But by 1899, this view had radically changed. The preoccupations with the changing world order, already hinted at in the aforementioned interview, were now identified more clearly and took center stage. In a private letter he wrote at the beginning of that year, just a very short time before accepting President Campos Sales's invitation to represent Brazil in the arbitration case concerning the border with British Guiana, which marked his return to active public life, Nabuco pinpointed a new major source of concern:

29. Richard Graham, "Joaquim Nabuco, Conservative Historian," *Luso-Brazilian Review*, 17:1 (1980), p. 2; Whigham and Kraay, "War, Politics, and Society," p. 17. So extensive was Nabuco's treatment of the Paraguayan War that the sections dealing with it were translated into Spanish and published as a separate book under the title *La guerra del Paraguay* (Paris: Garnier Hermanos, 1901).

30. Joaquim Nabuco, *Balmaceda*, pp. 137-143.

> I am among those who think, that our national decay has begun; that we are entering the [North] American orbit, like Cuba and the Philippines, Mexico and Nicaragua; that our evolution will follow the same path as the other satellites of Washington, and that the only way we can achieve some dignity and lead an independent life–intellectually, that is–is to produce several brilliant spirits who will elevate our literature beyond the contingencies of political and material absorption or elimination.[31]

This sentence is of double significance. First, it shows the heretofore overlooked magnitude, as well as the exact nature of the effect of the Spanish-American War on Nabuco's mind. Secondly, it reveals an interesting linking of the earthly dangers of the North to the Latin American, and more specifically Brazilian, spiritual crisis diagnosed the year before. Nabuco thus assumes an escapist, idealistic approach, positing literary creation as an answer to material extermination. The former abolitionist leader, the champion of state reform and social transformation, abandons all worldly projects and suggests instead a spiritual regeneration, with what may be called anachronistically Arielist overtones.[32]

A short time after he had communicated his understanding that hemispheric politics would never be the same after the Spanish–American War, Nabuco also pronounced it in public. He did so in an open letter to Rui Barbosa, who had praised the republic's decision to call the stanch monarchist leader to the flag. Here, Nabuco justified his acceptance of President Campos Sales's invitation in terms that are worthwhile quoting:

> Nobody can say that Brazilian policy and diplomacy today can continue to be the same as before, when the American federation still followed the advice of its founding fathers not to have any colonies or seek allies. Therefore, all important political positions and offices, both in the government as well as in the opposition and the press, should from now on be

31. Joaquim Nabuco to Carlos Magalhães de Azeredo, Rio de Janeiro, Feb. 14, 1899, in *Cartas a amigos*, vol. 2, p. 5.

32. As Nabuco himself explained in the conclusion of his autobiography, written during this time, "During the last ten years, then, my political interest has gradually given way to religious and literary interests, to the point of being reduced to, almost only, what it has in common with them." *Minha formação*, 9th ed. (Rio de Janeiro: Livraria J. Olympio Editora, 1976 [1900]), p. 167.

taken up bearing in mind the sacred horror that accompanies those responsible for the fate of the nation in times of crisis and change.[33]

If in the private letter he posited Brazilian spiritual revival as a response to North American imperialism, here Nabuco suggests a second kind of reply, in agreement with his renewed status as a man of state. Indeed, within a few years, Nabuco would combine these two modes of action. As the Brazilian ambassador to the United States, he would pursue an idealistic Pan-American project, to be discussed later on. For the time being, it is important to emphasize the background against which Nabuco's incorporation into the republic's diplomatic service took place. From 1898 on, all thinking about Brazil's continental insertion would take place under the shadow of U.S. imperialism.

"American Chinas": Rui Barbosa

Nabuco was not the only prominent Brazilian man–of–state–and–letters to point out the far-reaching significance of the Spanish-American War. The implications of the Caribbean-Pacific campaign were also discussed, and in much greater detail, in the journalistic writing of Rui Barbosa, now a senator and editor of the daily *A Imprensa*. In April through May 1899, he penned in this newspaper several articles about the new danger that the United States' growing power and aggression represented for Brazil.[34] Unlike his fellow abolitionist, Rui did not come to pursue a steady diplomatic career,

33. Nabuco's letter, dated March 14, 1899, was published two days later by Rui Barbosa in the newspaper he edited, *A Imprensa*, under the title "Entre velhos amigos." Rui Barbosa, *Obras Completas*, vol. XXVI (1899), t. IV, pp. 97-99.

34. Rui Barbosa, "A nova potência militar," April 9, 1899, "A higiene e a expansão americana," April 11, 1899, "Chinas americanas," 18 de abril de 1899, "O futuro dos Estados Unidos," April 18, 1899, in Barbosa, *Obras Completas*, vol. XXVI, t. IV, pp. 249-262, 269-274, 315-320, 321-326; "O continente enfêrmo," May 3, 1899, "O deleixo latino-americano," May 4, 1899, "Vã confiança – A ilusão americana," May 29, 1899, "Vã confiança – A doutrina de Monroe: sua origem," May 30, 1899; "A história repete-se," June 9, 1899, in ibid., vol. XXVI, t. V, pp. 15-18, 19-22, 151-154, 155-162, 217-226.

although his rhetorical and legal skills would lead him to assume several diplomatic assignments during the 1900s, including a high-profile leadership of the Brazilian legation to the Second Peace Conference at The Hague in 1907. Inflating his public image at the time as a defender of the nation's rights and honor against the encroachment of external powers, this mission has drawn some scholarly attention. Yet, otherwise, Rui is usually remembered as the main liberal advocate of the rule of law and individual rights in Brazilian domestic politics, leaving his writings on world and hemispheric affairs largely untouched.[35]

A close reading of these writings reveals an inconsistent attitude toward the United States and its conduct in the continent. According to Rui's own account in a private letter to Joaquim Nabuco from 1906, the United States had attracted his attention and sympathy already when he was a student in the 1860s, then giving way to fascination with England, only to become a central source of inspiration again with the proclamation of the republic.[36] Yet following his breakup with the Peixoto regime, he came to express some very critical views of the northern power that do not fit well with his self-portrayal as a great admirer of it and champion of Brazil-U.S. rapprochement. Writing in 1895 to a friend from exile in London, he ridiculed Floriano's "monomania of adulation for the United States, a country that so openly scorns us and whose policy toward the other republics of the hemisphere is so scandalously oppressive."[37] Later that year, he composed a short declaration against the Brazilian Senate's

35. See, for example, Luís Viana Filho, *A vida de Rui Barbosa*, 8th ed. revised (Rio de Janeiro: Livraria J. Olympio Editora, 1977); R. Magalhães Júnior, *Rui, o homem e o mito*, 2nd revised and expanded ed. (Rio de Janeiro: Editôra Civilização Brasileira, 1965); João Felipe Gonçalves, *Rui Barbosa: Pondo as idéias no lugar* (Rio de Janeiro: FGV Editora, 2000).

36. Rui Barbosa to Joaquim Nabuco, Rio de Janeiro, July 26, 1906, in Rui Barbosa, *Meu caro Rui, meu caro Nabuco*, José Almino de Alencar and Ana Maria Pessoa dos Santos, eds. (Rio de Janeiro: Casa de Rui Barbosa, 1999), pp. 38-39.

37. Rui Barbosa to Carlos Aguiar, London, March 12, 1895, excerpted in Viana Filho, *A vida de Rui Barbosa*, p. 238. According to Richard Graham [*Britain*, pp. 313-314], Barbosa's views of the United States itself and its foreign policy changed from negative circa 1895, to positive by 1906, as part of the overall reorientation of Brazilian foreign policy away from Britain and toward North America, but partially also because of personal interests.

endorsement of President Grover Cleveland's message to Congress asserting the claim of the United States to intervene in the dispute between Venezuela and England. Destined for publication in *La Prensa* of Buenos Aires and in the *New York Herald*, Rui's statement censured this recent application of the Monroe Doctrine as an expression of U.S. hegemony over "the two Americas," and called for a trustful relationship with Europe, "to which we owe our civilization," reasoning that "the ambitions that today threaten us are located in this continent rather than in the Old."[38]

These short lines should be read as the continuation of Rui's earlier discovery and construction, when in exile in Buenos Aires, of a shared Latin American fate, and as a harbinger of his later thoughts on hemispheric politics. Born out of Brazil's recent experience with caudillism, the concept of "Latin America" was now applied to the realm of international relations, a move which would be greatly reinforced in the aftermath of 1898.

Rui Barbosa cast a wide net in his 1899 discussion of North American expansionism, both historically and geographically. The first of his articles traced the "unprecedented phenomenon" of growing U.S. military power back to the beginning of the Civil War, and set it within the context of recent European theories distinguishing between moribund and vigorous nations, also alluding to the recent European takeover of China. Evoking Nabuco's view of the matter as expressed in the aforementioned open correspondence between them, Rui described the advent of the United States into the group of the "hunting nations," as "the most important novelty of this era."[39] The notion of 1898 as a high point of long-term moral and political developments, both within the United States and in Europe, dominated the entire series. There was an emphasis throughout on the fact that "positive theories about the origin of the species and man, with the principle of survival of the fittest and the elimination of the infe-

38. "Declaração de Rui Brabosa desfavorável a moção de aplausos enviada pelo Senado brasileiro ao senado americano por ocasião da mensagem do presidente Cleveland ao Congresso dos Estados Unidos, assumindo o patrocínio da Venezuela na questão com a Inglaterra," n.d., 1895, RB PI 23, Arquivo da Casa de Rui Barbosa [Henceforth ACRB]. I was not able to verify whether it was actually published in the mentioned newspapers as planned.

39. Barbosa, "A nova potência militar," p. 249.

rior ones, the incompetents, the useless, had destroyed, in individual and public life alike, the old philosophical, idealistic, Christian, notions of justice that taught respect for the weak and restrain on the part of the strong. [On the fact] in short, that the law of the cannon have replaced the law of nations."[40]

Of special interest here is Rui's positioning of Brazil within this hostile international environment. In the same way that he portrays the growing might and aggression of the U.S. as part of a worldwide trend, so he discusses Brazilian weakness as part of a more general Latin American predicament, a perspective that becomes more and more pronounced as the series advances. While the first three articles concentrated on the United States, carrying the telling titles "The New Military Power," "Hygiene and American Expansion," and "The Future of the United States," the fourth one bore the title "American Chinas," shifting focus to the countries lying south of the Rio Grande. According to Rui, only Paraguay, isolated under López's rule, had acquired this derogative label in the past, while now it was being applied to the entire "non-English part of the hemisphere." This formula, defining Latin America through negation, exemplifies the reinforcement of an Us-versus-Them sentiment in face of growing U.S. pressure. Rui called upon Brazilians to abandon any illusions of North American protection. There would be no exceptions to the rule: "Together with Indians and half-breeds, so will each and every descendant of Spain and Portugal beneath this sky and, together with the most infamous and weakest republics of this continent, also the best and the strongest, such as Mexico, Argentina, and Chile, be thrown into the cauldron that awaits the arrival of the Pantagruelian invaders."[41]

There are then the infamous and the weak, and there are the best and strong. The division of Latin America into these two discrete categories reveals an ambivalent attitude toward the dominant social-Darwinist logic of the day, an attitude deriving from Rui's double location in a country he himself perceives as at once powerful and helpless. He condemns the "survival of the fittest" mandate in international relations but at the same time adopts it, applying terminolo-

40. Barbosa, "O deleixo latino-americano," p. 20.
41. Barbosa, "Chinas americanas," p. 317.

gy and moral standards from the North-South context to South-South relationships. Here is one type of reaction to the European and North American tendency to lump the countries of Latin America together as potential prey. However, these outside threats could simultaneously produce, as Rui's case exemplifies, an opposite type of response as well. Thus, notwithstanding the distinction between weak and strong inside the periphery, the fifth and sixth articles of the series gave full-blown expression to the concept of "Latin America" as a unified whole. Both texts relied heavily on a recently published pamphlet titled *El continente enfermo* (*The Sick Continent*, 1899) by the Venezuelan César Zumeta. Rui borrowed this diagnostic caption for one of his own articles, endorsing fully the latter's observations regarding the hostile intentions of the United States and the unpreparedness of the Latin American countries–"the threatened peoples," was one of Zumeta's cited monikers–in the face of the danger.[42] The reliance on a Spanish American text is all the more intriguing in view of Rui's own opening remark that Zumeta's pamphlet plants the same questions that he, Rui, had already presented several times to the readers of *A Imprensa*. We may conclude, then, that the only function of the dialogue with the Venezuelan intellectual had been to emphasize the shared nature of the threat, the common fate.

This emphasis reached its apex in the second of Rui's two Luso–Hispano-American duets with Zumeta, in which he had moved to refer to Latin America in the first-person plural. Not only that, but he also listed some typical traits of the Latin "race"–"vanity, improvidence, and imagination"–that, together with the glorious memories of the independence period, bring Latin Americans to falsely believe that they can perpetuate their freedom, turning a blind eye to the change of circumstances around them.[43] The construction of "Latin America" on the twofold basis of fixed ethnic attributes and historical specificities is reminiscent of Nabuco, and so is the somber view of the region's future. However, although the two Brazilians share similar preoccupations, they differ on cures. A much more realistic Rui, for whom "imagination" is a dangerous trait, does

42. Barbosa, "O continente enfêrmo," p. 15.
43. Barbosa, "O deleixo latino-americano," p. 19.

not seek salvation in the spiritual realm, proposing instead, as we shall see ahead, more mundane measures.

Having drawn the Latin American contours of the question, Rui continued the series with two articles about the Monroe Doctrine, both bearing the headline "Vain Confidence." Here he claimed–following Eduardo Prado, from whose *A ilusão americana* he borrowed the subtitle of the first text–that the United States' hemispheric policy had always been guided by selfish calculations. Therefore, there was no reason to perceive the ultimate occupation of Cuba as a deviation from the original Monroeist principles, nor to trust North American goodwill, as Floriano Peixoto and his followers wrongly did. This argument was further supported by references to Spanish American thinkers (in this case, writings by Argentines Alberdi and Mitre from around the middle of the nineteenth century), calling upon those Brazilians who still stuck to the American illusion despite the recent unequivocal proof of the Yankees' true motivations to finally comprehend that which had been understood long ago on the other side of the River Plate.[44]

This continuous show of respect for and solidarity with Spanish-speaking neighbors to the north and to the south of Brazil did not prevent Rui from marking some of them as a menace. The twin articles about the Monroe Doctrine were shortly followed by another pair, which focused on the need to build Brazil's military power as a counterweight to Argentina's strength. Although relationships between the two countries were excellent, so went the argument, they could not rely on goodwill. Stable friendship could only be based on mutual respect of each side's "vigor" and on a common understanding that each side might violate the rights of the other. In this regard, Latin America was no different from any other part of the world. Brute force and selfish interests were the sole principles that governed international relations, no matter where.[45] Stated in such a blunt manner, these points by Rui remind us that Brazilian

44. Barbosa, "Vã confiança–A ilusão americana," p. 152; and Barbosa "Vã confiança–A doutrina de Monroe: sua origem," p. 161.

45. Rui Barbosa, "O perigo imediato," June 10, 1899, *Obras Completas*, vol. XXVI, t. V, pp. 227-234; "Três exércitos ," July 13, 1899, ibid., vol. XXVI, t. VI, pp. 75-82.

identification with its Spanish American neighbors vis-à-vis North America had its limits. It could certainly not obliterate an old rivalry such as the Argentine-Brazilian one, especially in an age of Jingoistic rhetoric and arms races both in the world at large and within South America itself.[46] As we have already seen in the case of the monarchist attack on the Bocaiuva-Zeballos agreement, and as will be further shown ahead, nationalist appeals like Rui's could affect public opinion and bring personal political gains. The target might equally be the United States or any Spanish American country, most likely Argentina.

However, no matter how feared or despised, Argentina's status as an enviable model was by now tightly secured, alongside that of Chile, the more remote traditional ally from across the Andes. In accordance with the rising nationalist-imperialist atmosphere of the period, these two countries won positive value judgments not only for their political stability, economic conditions, or intellectual life, but also for their military strength, closely associated with national honor and virility.[47] In his second article of the set about military power mentioned in the previous paragraph, titled "Three Armies," Rui quoted extensively from a recent report about the Chilean armed forces, published in the Brazilian Army's *Revista Militar.* The focus was on the great contribution of foreign German instruction to the quality of the national army; on "Germanic reproduction [...] which characterizes all aspects of military life there, and is evident both in appearance and practice. The Chilean serviceman is German from head to toes."[48]

Again we see how Spanish American countries win admiration for being a successful copy of North Atlantic models, external manifestations being no less important than substance. Moreover, Chile in

46. Bueno, *A república e sua política exterior,* pp. 246-247; Bandeira, *Brasil, Argentina e Estados Unidos*, pp. 59, 94-111.

47. On the association of military power with honor and masculinity in the world of that time, see John Horne, "Masculinity in Politics and War in the Age of Nation-States and World Wars, 1850-1950," in Stefan Dudink, Karen Hagemann and John Tosh, eds., *Masculinities in Politics and War: Gendering Modern History* (Manchester: Manchester University Press, 2004), pp. 22-40; For the Brazilian case, see Beattie, *The Tribute of Blood*, pp. 11, 120-121, 273.

48. Barbosa, "Três exércitos," p. 81.

general, as described in this article, and not only its army, did not exhibit any Latin characteristics such as those that Rui himself had previously attributed to it. Quite the contrary, Chileans now seemed to have qualities typical of the northern races.

The same also applies to Argentina, to which Rui turned toward the conclusion of the text. He recalled imposing images of the Argentine military marching through the streets of "the imperious capital," from the time of his stay in Buenos Aires. Singing the praise of yet another "truly European" army, Rui reminded his Brazilian readers of the coming visit of one of its generals. "It is therefore a formidable judge who is going to receive the welcome of our military forces," he wrote in reference to Argentina's president Julio Argentino Roca scheduled to arrive soon in Rio de Janeiro. "I truly hope we will be able to withstand this test courageously and come out of it with honor. *Noblesse oblige*," he continued, in a manner which may remind the reader of Euclides da Cunha's concerns about Brazilian courage and "virility" in the context of Roca's second visit. "We must show our old [Argentine] allies, that our generation is no less worthy of the laurels we won together with Mitre's soldiers, and at the same time prove that we did not need to attend the German school, together with Argentina and Chile, in order to make a good impression before the Andes and the River Plate."[49] Indeed, as we are about to witness, Brazilians went to great length in order to demonstrate their masculinity and appear strong before their respected visitor.

49. Ibid.

PART 2
Two Visits, One Message: Virility, Order, and Progress

Orderly Arrival

On August 8, 1899, at around noon, some ten years after it had carried Foreign Minister Quintino Bocaiuva to the Plata to convene with his Argentine peer Estanislao Zeballos and sign the Montevideo agreement, the Brazilian navy's flagship *Riachuelo* was about to serve as platform for another Luso–Hispano-American encounter. This time, the location was the home waters of Guanabara Bay, and the ranking of the representatives of both sides one level higher. On board stood the president of the republic, Manuel Ferraz de Campos Sales, ready to meet his Argentine counterpart, Julio Argentino Roca. The latter approached the Brazilian shore aboard his navy's most modern battleship, the dreadnought *San Martin*, accompanied by the cruiser *Buenos Aires* and the torpedo boat *Patria*. Three Brazilian vessels, corresponding in size, welcomed the Argentine squadron outside the bay and escorted it on its way past the fortresses guarding the entrance.[50] It was a well choreographed spectacle of equal military force–which, in truth, was not equal–on an occasion meant to signify peaceful intentions and rapprochement. Indeed, these supposedly conflicting messages would dominate Roca's visit to Rio de Janeiro and Campos Sales's reciprocal visit to Buenos Aires the following year.

The war/peace and military/civil dualities were also evident in the presence of four more local boats, which joined the triumphal cruise into the bay. One, chartered by a joint committee of Rio de Janeiro's press, waved the flags of the city's major newspapers and carried a group of upper-class women. The second carried faculty and students

50. The henceforth description of the arrival and first welcome is based on Luis Vicente Varela, *El Brasil y la Argentina: confraternidad sud-americana; obra descriptiva, ilustrada con fotograbados de las más importantes festividades; Pub. por la Intendencia municipal de la capital de la República Argentina* (Buenos Aires: Impr. de J. Peuser, 1901), pp. 29-36; and Carlos Bustos, "El viaje del presidente," *Caras y Caretas*, Aug. 26, 1899, n.pag.

from the Rio de Janeiro Medical School. The third had war veterans. The fourth transported staff members of the daily newspaper *Jornal do Brasil*. This composition again reflected various motifs that would be repeated throughout the ten-day visit.

A clear effort had been made to give the event a public mold. It was almost all about external appearances, not indoor deliberations. Evidently, in South America, like in other parts of the world, eighteenth-century-style cabinet diplomacy was withering.[51] As we have already seen in previous chapters, public opinion could play an important role in international relations in the region. Such was the case in the aftermath of abolition, when an outburst of friendly symbolic acts and rhetoric in Argentina ignited a similar response in Brazil, and such was also the case with the ill-fated 1890 Missões agreement. The press on both sides of the River Plate played a major part in this process, and during the first decade of the 1900s it would contribute more and more significantly to the creation of an either warlike or amicable climate in the region, as it did now.[52] As Joaquim Nabuco explained in a letter to President Afonso Pena several years afterwards by quoting Secretary of State Elihu Root, "the statesmen of today operate in an explosive environment."[53] For a matter of fact, journalists did not only cover the continuous heavy stream of parades, banquettes, speeches and excursions that characterized the two presidential visits under discussion, they also actively participated in such events. Sailing to welcome the Argentine guests, the vessels hired by Rio de Janeiro newspapers symbolized the notion of reconciliation between two societies, not just governments.[54]

51. Cassels, *Ideology and International Relations,* p. 93; Danese, *Diplomacia presidencial,* p. 257; Bloom, *Identity and International Relations*, p. 88.

52. See, for example, Minister of Foreign Relations Barão do Rio Branco, Rio de Janeiro, to Brazilian Minister Cyro de Azevedo, Buenos Aires, 2/4 reservado, Dec. 12, 1903, AHI; Brazilian Minister Cyro de Azevedo, Buenos Aires, to Minister of Foreign Relations Barão do Rio Branco, Rio de Janeiro, 2/6, Feb. 9, 1905, AHI; Oliveira Lima, *Pan-americanismo: Monroe, Bolivar, Roosevelt* (Brasília/Rio de Janeiro: Senado Federal/Fundação Casa de Rui Barbosa, 1980 [1907]), p. 112.

53. Joaquim Nabuco to Afonso Pena, Washington, Jan. 19, 1908, AJN 999.

54. This notion was expressed by many at the time, including President Campos Sales himself in his annual message to the Congress. Brazil, *Mensagem apresentada ao Congresso Nacional na abertura da primeira sessão da quarta legislatura pelo presidente da republica M. Ferraz de Campos Salles* (Rio de Janeiro, 1900), May 3, 1900, p.

The same applies to the maritime representation of the Medical School. Like a vibrant patriotic press, education–and, especially, scientific education–was perceived as a sign and agent of progress. And progress was what the two-sided diplomatic drama was meant to facilitate through securing regional stability, and what both participating sides were eager to demonstrate. As for the war veterans, they were there in the bay to recall a past brotherhood in arms. The memory of the Paraguayan War would be evoked time and again by Brazilians and Argentines alike during the coming days in Rio de Janeiro, and the following year in Buenos Aires. This was the relevant past they selected in order to fortify their interest-driven rapprochement, a common choice that bespoke identical worldviews and ideals. Last, the noticeable presence of the "gentle sex" on board the *Itaituba* functioned as a counterpoint to the masculine and military elements of the spectacle, evoking contemporary conceptions of "respectable" women as dedicated patriotic companions, albeit subordinate, in the national pursuit of progress.[55]

Escorted, then, by this complex symbolism of peace and war, civil rule and military strength, past and future, the Argentine flagship *San Martín* approached the shore and was anchored. At this point a unique vessel, standing out from among numerous small boats that now surrounded the *San Martin*, sailed toward it and came along its broadside. It was a barge that had been originally constructed for the Portuguese king, João VI, and especially renovated for this occasion in order to transport the distinguished Spanish-speaking guest. Here was a clear sign that the republic had come to terms with its European origins and monarchical past. The Americanism of the so-called Old Republic, that oligarchic conservative structure that took shape during Campos Sales's term (1898-1902), lacked the anti-European sentiments that typified Floriano Peixoto's rule and his supporters. The principal champion of American solidarity during the 1900s, and even accepting of the United States' continental hegemony, would be

6. See also, Rui Barbosa, "Não desafinemos," *A Imprensa*, Aug. 2, 1899, in *Obras Completas*, vol. XXVI, t. VI, pp. 193-194.

55. June E. Hahner, *Emancipating the Female Sex: The Struggle for Women's Rights in Brazil, 1850-1940* (Durham: Duke University Press, 1990), pp. 47-50, 113-119.

FIGURE 4.1
Benjamin Parlagreco, *Visita do General Roca*, 1900(?).
Museu Histórico e Diplomático do Itamaraty, Rio de Janeiro.

no other than–as is hinted in Oliveira Lima's letter quoted above–Joaquim Nabuco, the great worshipper of imperial Brazil and European culture.

But it is too early to speak about Nabuco the Monroeist. Let us return to the Argentine president, who descended into the historic state barge that took him and his entourage a short distance to the *Riachuelo*, where his Brazilian counterpart received him. The scene was immortalized by the artist Benjamin Parlagreco in a large painting that soon found its way to one of the walls of the Itamaraty Palace, home of the Brazilian Foreign Office [Figure 4.1]. The overall atmosphere of the painting is bright and serene. The *Riachuelo*, situated at forefront to the left, standing out with its dark color, looks quite harmless. The Argentine warships are far in the background, their menacing aspects thus also lessened, although not fully undone. In like manner, most of the human figures are dressed as civilians. The more popular, spontaneous components of this maritime reception are manifested in the smaller boats, which break the rigid organization of the larger vessels. Ultimately, though, there is a strong sense of order, conveyed through the composition of both the larger details and the smaller ones that pertain to the well-organized ceremony aboard the *Riachuelo*, where most of the participants are stretched upright in harmony with the ships' masts.

FIGURE 4.2
Roca's arrival in Rio de Janeiro.
The orderly atmosphere of Parlagreco's painting becomes even more pronounced when compared to this drawing, which appeared in a special issue of the popular *Don Quixote* magazine (Aug. 10, 1899) and describes the same scene.

TRIPLE ALLIANCES, PAST AND PRESENT

"A Historic Day" declared the headline of an article by Rui Barbosa which the *Diário de Notícias* published on the same morning. Less than a month had passed since the senator and newspaper editor called attention to the military weakness of Brazil compared to its southern neighbor, and the focus shifted back from potential aggression to solidarity, this time with a much more assertive tone. While his April–May articles had revealed a Latin American consciousness by way of references to Spanish American writers and an emphasis on Latin American vulnerability, here we witness its ideologization–or, in other words, the emergence of Latin American*ism*. The most Rui had previously suggested in terms of response to the common North American menace was disillusionment, whereas now he raised the notion of active cooperation between "the three grand nations of South America." A process of approximation between

Brazil, Chile, and Argentina had started long ago, thanks to a growing shared awareness of a common interest: "to vigorously safeguard the Latin contingent in America's evolution." In reference to the Argentine President's current visit to Rio de Janeiro and preceding meeting with his Chilean counterpart Federico Errázuriz in January at the Straits of Magellan, Rui supportively concluded that Roca was laying the basis for "southern peace and Latin security in the continent of Columbus."[56]

This idea of joining forces was pronounced even more bluntly the day afterward, in a detailed comment on a recent interview with the Brazilian minister to the United States, Joaquim Francisco de Assis Brasil, that had been published in the New York press. Here Rui supported Assis Brasil's allusions in the interview to a South American alliance and North American expansionism, but criticized him for being too open.[57] Assis Brasil's statements indeed deviated from the official Brazilian line on this issue, yet Rui's visibly anti-Yankee stand was by no means isolated,[58] nor was his vision of "Latin" cooperation a matter of wishful thinking. The possibility of a triple South American league between Argentina, Brazil, and Chile was widely discussed during that time, especially in Argentina, where it reflected the policy of the Roca administration.[59]

Eventually, the mutual visits did not yield any such kind of agreement. From our perspective, however, it is not the fact that the Argentine initiative did not materialize that matters, but rather the birth of the idea itself and the spiritual climate, both south and north of the River Plate, from which it emerged. The notion of an Argentine-

56. Rui Barbosa, "Um dia histórico," *A Imprensa*, Aug. 8, 1899, in *Obras Completas*, vol. XXVI, t. VI, pp. 197-200.

57. Rui Barbosa, "Frutas do Tempo," *A Imprensa*, Aug. 9, 1899, in ibid., pp. 201-206.

58. At the end of May 1899, the Argentine minister to Rio de Janeiro, Manuel Gorostiaga, reported to the Foreign Ministry in Buenos Aires about Brazilian fears of prospective conflict with the United States. He mentioned Rui Barbosa's recent writings on this issue in *A Imprensa,* and added that Barbosa's position could not be ascribed to his opposition to the Campos Sales administration, since Quintnio Bocaiuva's *O Paiz*, which favored the current administration, had manifested similar preoccupations. Mentioned in Fraga, "La visita de Roca," p. 24; Bandeira, *Brasil, Argentina e Estados Unidos*, chap. 2; Smith, *Unequal Giants*, pp. 39-40.

59. Fraga, "La visita de Roca," p. 19.

Brazilian-Chilean (ABC) alliance embodied feelings, values, and perceptions, which were strongly evident in other discursive components of the two presidential visits. It reflected intensifying anxieties over external aggression, together with varying degrees of self-confidence and mutual appreciation. Here was a celebration of force and, at the same time, a desire to restrain it, nationalism and internationalism.

Yet it is also important to note what was *not* there: namely, idealism à la Rodó. If 1898 encouraged the emergence of an anti-materialist intellectual movement in Latin America, it was hardly evident in the 1899/1900 representations of Brazilian-Argentine rapprochement. If *arielismo* was rooted in the powerlessness of Latin American intellectuals "to act or to affect the destiny of their continent except in the realm of ideas,"[60] then the exchange of visits and the plan of an ABC alliance revealed a very different response to shared Luso–Hispano-American preoccupations. This was especially true of the discourse produced by the Brazilian side, which was much closer in spirit to Rui Barbosa's social-Darwinist diagnosis and remedies than to Joaquim Nabuco's emphasis on spiritual salvation.

If official Brazil was generally more cautious or thought differently from its tactless representative in Washington, and avoided open discussion of a future ABC league,[61] it did make many deliberate and noticeable references to another triple alliance from South America's past. The Paraguayan War became a living memory during Roca's visit. The participation of this campaign's veterans in the maritime welcome was merely a prelude. The Committee of the Paraguayan War Veterans was also among the delegations that arrived to congratulate Roca during the official reception held the following day. Then, on the fourth day of the visit, came a much more visible commemoration of the 1865-1870 campaign. A military parade,

60. Jean Franco, *An Introduction to Spanish American Literature,* 3rd ed. (Cambridge: Cambridge University Press, 1994), p. 160.

61. As a matter of fact, the Brazilian foreign minister instructed Assis Brasil to refute the rumors about the formation of an Argentine-Brazilian alliance, with possible participation of other South American countries, in order to defend against North American aggression. The minister further reported that President Roca probably did not consider such an alliance, and that Campos Sales would in any case reject any suggestion of this kind. Olyntho de Magalhães, Rio de Janeiro, to Assis Brasil, Washington, 2/3 reservado, Aug. 24, 1899, AHI.

which attracted a mass of spectators, was held in Campo de São Cristovão. In the middle stood a pavilion especially built to accommodate the two presidents, their entourages and many other high ranking officials, military commanders, and upper-class men. High up, on the external part of all sides of the structure, in between garlands of flowers and leaves, were inscribed the names of the principal battles of that war, in which Brazilians fought alongside Argentines against a small neighboring country.[62]

Another, even better illustration of this intentional linking of past and present, was the inauguration of the statue of General Luiz Alves de Lima e Silva, Duke of Caxias, the Brazilian commander in chief of the allied forces during part of the Paraguayan War, in one of Rio de Janeiro's public squares, an event that also took place in the presence of the presidential entourages and amidst a big crowd. The ceremony itself typically mixed military and civil elements, combining messages of might and peace. The president of the municipal council gave a speech in which he drew a comparison between Caxias and Roca, highlighting their twofold careers as warriors and statesmen and, in the same breath, their essentially peaceful inclinations. Both believed that "intolerance is a sign of mediocrity." Afterward, the Argentine President himself spoke in praise of the Brazilian general's role in the defeat of two oppressive regimes in the Plata region, in reference to Brazil's participation in the 1852 campaign against Juan Manuel de Rosas's government and to the later campaign against Paraguay's Solano López, calling the inaugurated monument a symbol of "virtue, good citizenship and American solidarity." Next, several Brazilian and Argentine military men took a bronze wreath, especially smelted in Argentina, from Roca's hands and laid it at the feet of the statue.[63]

The symbolic centrality of the War of the Triple Alliance during the 1899 Argentine-Brazilian encounter may seem obvious. After all, it was a major event in the individual history of each country, as well as a watershed in the traditionally hostile relationship among them. Apparently, there was no better way, if at all, to produce a historical justification of the current rapprochement. But even if that is the case, we should pay attention to the specificities of its commemorations

62. Varela, *El Brasil y la Argentina*, p. 93.
63. Ibid., pp. 177-179.

and examine the messages embedded in them–intentionally and unintentionally–in connection with other parts of the show.

A comparison to the place of the Paraguayan War in the public discussion following the abolition of slavery is revealing. The emphasis on the campaign's "liberating mission," so dominant in 1888, greatly weakened now, with the distinction between Solano López and the Paraguayan people finding little expression as well. Vanquished Paraguay in general was forgotten, and so was the third ally, Uruguay. It was all about the victory of the two big and powerful partners, not the small and weak. Words were heard about "American solidarity," about America as the continent of international law and peace, but the name "Latin America" was rarely mentioned in the official Brazilian discourse. The Paraguayan War, it is important to remember, had been a brutal intra–Latin American struggle carried out in the name of civilization against barbarism. It was under this emblem, conveying a unity of values and interests–and *not* a romantic Pan-Latin Americanism based on shared ethnicity or race–that Brazil joined forces with Argentina back then. And the same was true now.

Although targeted at different enemies, there was a meaningful relationship between the publicly commemorated Triple Alliance and the future one, hovering in the background of the presidential visits. Both alliances, and their representations, were founded on and bespoke a convergence of world views and interests, much more than ethnically based conceptions of Latin American unity. Not that the two were mutually exclusive. Accompanying an assertive and well-designed policy, the Argentine diplomatic discourse on hemispheric issues had already fused "two sets of dimensions, the one civic and territorial, the other ethnic and genealogical," to use Anthony D. Smith's typology.[64] But the Campos Sales administration did not follow suit in embarking on such an ideological enterprise.

64. Smith, *National Identity*, p. 15. See, for example, the "Introduction" to Luis Vicente Varela's *El Brasil y la Argentina: Confraternidad Sud-Americana,* which stated that the aim of Argentine foreign policy under Roca was "to establish ties of international solidarity [between the Latin republics] on the basis of their already existing ties of *common origin,*" p. VI. The Argentine diplomatic discourse resembled, in this respect, a wider intellectual trend discussed in Jean H. Delaney, "Imagining El Ser Argentino: Cultural Nationalism and Romantic Concepts of Nationhood in early Twentieth-Century Argentina," *Journal of Latin American Studies* 34:3(Aug. 2002), esp. pp. 638-641.

True, signs of such fusion were evident in un- or semi-official Brazilian texts, such as Rui Barbosa's aforementioned articles, published on the eve of the presidential visit. Applauding Roca's grand regional scheme, they described Brazilians and Argentines as "peoples of the same race, the same religion, and nearly the same language."[65] It was for a reason that these words won the gratitude of the Argentine minister to Brazil, Manuel Gorostiaga who, in a pathos-filled letter to Rui, accorded the bilateral encounter continental significance, defining its ultimate goal as the "aggrandizement of Latin America."[66] Yet even Rui's incipient Latin Americanism gave precedence to shared values and historical experiences over common racial, religious, or linguistic features, and thus ultimately resembled the official language of Brazilian-Argentine rapprochement. Rui, let us recall, assigned "the three big nations of South America," Brazil, Argentina, and Chile, "a peaceful and *civilizing* solidarity." These countries were "sisters in terms of their highest interest." In the narrower context of Brazilian-Argentine relationships, he described an evolution that had begun with the "liberating alliances" of 1852 and 1865-1870, then continued with the simultaneous celebrations of the abolition of slavery across the River Plate in 1888, and culminated with the 1899 mutual embrace. A unity forged in blood led to a unity of ideals. The fundamental meaning of this moral-historical narrative, interweaving two national trajectories, was fully revealed in a subsequent reference to a key event in Roca's personal career and in the consolidation of Argentina's modernizing state, the so-called "Conquest of the Desert." Expressly designed to purge the fertile pampas of its indigenous inhabitants by either extermination or expulsion, the 1879 military campaign, led by Roca as minister of war, was, in Rui's interpretation, a great feat that had "liberated" that valuable piece of the national territory from barbarism on behalf of civilization.[67] The destruction of savage tra-

65. Barbosa, "Não desafinemos," p. 194.

66. Argentine Minister Manuel Gorostiaga, Petrópolis, to Ruy Barbosa, Aug. 2, 1899, CR 1589.1/1, ACRB.

67. Barbosa, "Um dia histórico," pp. 197-199. About the "Conquest of Desert," see Andermann, *The Optic of the State*, chap. 5; and David Viñas, *Indios, ejército y frontera*, 3rd ed. (Buenos Aires: Santiago Arcos Editor, 2003), chap. 2, passim. Viñas's interpretation is especially relevant here in that it places the event in the context of a

ditional rulers, backward populations, and outdated institutions, both inside and outside each country's borders, paved the way for bilateral solidarity and regional peace. It was all part of the advent of modernity.

Interestingly, the conquest of the Argentine "desert" was mentioned in almost identical terms the day afterward by another Brazilian senator who, unlike Rui, generally sided with the Campos Sales administration. This was former Foreign Minister Quintino Bocaiuva. The pro-Argentine statesman and publicist, who played a highly visible role in both visits, officially congratulated Roca in the name of the Brazilian Congress. In his speech, he called Roca's arrival in Rio de Janeiro the most solemn expression of the friendly sentiments and the idea of peace that currently dominated international relations in America, and which should enable all countries to develop their economies and achieve prosperity. The only enemy that the young countries of America should overcome was the desert: "a place of barbarism and the major obstacle to our progress, aggrandizement and strength." The same desert, he declared, that the visiting Argentine president had already conquered.[68]

It is in relationship, then, with the convergence of Brazilian and Argentine viewpoints and interests that the remembering of the Paraguayan War must be read. On the threshold of the new century, the political leaderships of the two traditional rivals were again ready, as they had been 30 years before, to join forces against barbarism in the name of civilization.

A Ordem por Base, o Progresso por Fim

Order and progress were on the lips of everybody, Portuguese- and Spanish-speaking alike, during the 1899/1900 visits. Order always came before progress, as in the above positivistic emblem inspired by French philosopher Auguste Comte. Nothing had been more harmful to the Latin American countries' prestige and financial

wider Latin American-wide onslaught of the modernizing elites against indigenous populations.

68. Varela, *El Brasil y la Argentina*, pp. 66-67.

credit in Europe and the United States than internal instability, usually associated with civil wars and caudillism.[69] This specific threat, which had greatly damaged Argentina's, Chile's, and especially Brazil's external image during the early 1890s, seemed now more remote. The visual and textual representations of the two visits stressed the subordination of the military to civilian rule, expressing not merely an aspiration but also a changing reality.[70] But there were other threats looming on the horizon. The traditional rivalry between Chile and Argentina acquired, during the second half of the decade, the form of an arms race that threatened regional stability and caused preoccupation in Brazil, as we have already seen. Repeated calls for continental peace should, therefore, be understood differently than similar declarations that had accompanied the birth of the republic. Bocaiuva's speeches at Rio de Janeiro and Buenos Aires in 1899/1900, for example, reproduced the same Americanist notions that he had expressed about ten years earlier in the these two capitals.[71] Yet, in the end-of-the-century context of military buildup, nationalistic competition and imperialism, they acquired a less idealistic, more pragmatic significance, regardless of the speaker's intentions.

Now, it was no longer the need to overcome the isolationist, even aggressive legacy of the Empire and win American and Latin American recognition and friendship which dominated Brazil's international relations. Nor did the republic resemble anymore the dream of a radically new Brazil, *fundamentally* more democratic and more modern, as some of its founders had dreamt. On the other hand, monarchical restoration ceased to be a realistic option. The civilian governing elite, which emerged victorious from the turbulent decade, wanted to secure its grip and continue the stabilization

69. Brazil, President (1902-1906: Rodrigues Alves), *Relações exteriores do Brazil durante a administração do Presidente Rodrigues Alves, 1902-1906* (Rio de Janeiro: Typ. do Jornal do Commercio de Rodrigues & c., 1906), p. 87; Joaquim Nabuco to Rodrigues Alves, London, Oct. 7, *Cartas a amigos*, vol. 2, p. 179; Sevcenko, *Literatura como missão*, pp. 45-49.

70. The Brazilian discourse stressed, for example, the transformation of President Roca and former President Mitre from military leaders to statesmen in the service of peace. See Varela, *El Brasil y la Argentina*, pp. 13, 133, 138, 178; Cipriano de la Peña, *Cronica illustrada y documentada de las fiestas de confraternidad brasilero-argentinas* (Buenos Aires: Compania Sud-Americana de Billetes de Banco, 1901), pp. 68, 70.

71. Varela, *El Brasil y la Argentina*, pp. 54-56, 66-67, 382-383.

process. It did not yet have the energy to get into conflict or to compete head-on with its strong neighbors over regional leadership, as could be heard in President Campos Sales's 1898 inaugural message–reproduced by an Argentine journal on the occasion of the 1900 visit–where he announced his plan of "order and peace": "As to our international relations, I am confident that it would be in accordance with the will of the nation if I were to employ a policy with the principal aims of expanding and strengthening the amicable ties of friendship that Brazil enjoys with other powers [...] no mission is more noble, and no task more gratifying to those who rule than to secure peace."[72]

The Argentines reached out at the right moment, then. The mutual vision of order and progress was best exemplified in the encounters between each of the presidents and representatives of Brazil's industrialists and businessmen. On August 13, the sixth day of Roca's visit, in between sumptuous banquets and shows of military might, thousands of workers marched before the two heads of state, who observed the procession from the balcony of the Catete palace. The first group to pass by belonged to the Companhia de Luz Esteárica, who exhibited a medal it had received in the 1882 Continental Exposition in Buenos Aires, thus reminding contemporary spectators (and us) that Luso–Hispano-American encounters of this sort were already something of a tradition. The company's president, who also served as president of the Industrial Association, greeted Roca with the following words: "Mister General, the motto of our flag, order and progress, is a literal translation of the motto of industry, *pax et labor*. Peace and labor! Labor is impossible without peace, without order; progress is the natural outcome of peace and order."[73] The next year in Buenos Aires, at a banquet offered by the Argentine *Comisión del Comercio*, Campos Sales emphasized the same notion, of order as prerequisite for economic development, thanking his

72. Brazil, *Manifesto inaugural de Manuel Ferraz de Campos Salles, presidente eleito para o quatriennio de 1898 a 1902* (Rio de Janeiro, 1898), Nov. 15, 1898, reproduced in *La Revista Patriótica, con motivo de la visita hecha á la Capital de la República Argentina por el Doctor Manuel Ferraz de Campos Salles, presidente de la república de los Estados Unidos del Brasil* (Buenos Aires: La Revista Patriótica, 1900).

73. Varela, *El Brasil y la Argentina*, p. 126.

hosts for their participation in "these festivities of peace, progress, and labor."[74]

However, common objectives did not reflect a common reality. Brazilian elite members looked at Argentina with admiring eyes. In that sense, little had changed since the *Diário de Notícias* announced, upon Joaquim Nabuco's return from his 1889 visit to Buenos Aires, that "there is no need to go to Paris anymore," and since Nabuco himself labeled Argentina "os Estados Unidos da América do Sul."[75] Telling here is the much larger number of Brazilian journalists who accompanied Campos Sales in his visit to the Plata as compared with the tiny group of Argentine reporters that arrived in Rio de Janeiro the year before. Something about the spirit that dominated the Brazilian correspondents who went south and others who stayed at home can be gleaned from a newspaper article by distinguished literary critic Tristão de Alencar Araripe Júnior, published just a short time after the presidential journey had ended. In his review of *El Brasil intelectual*–a book published by the Argentine writer and diplomat Martín García Merou as part of the celebrations in Campos Sales's honor–Araripe Júnior evoked real and imaginary recollections from Brazilian voyages to the Plata, his own and of those of others:

> I can still hear ringing in my ears, as though by some kind of telegraphic illusion, the outbursts of joy and the noisy accolades with which the people of Buenos Aires paraded the illustrious Brazilians of the presidential entourage and the representatives of our press, showing them the beauty of the city's avenues and monuments, and the lush interiors of its palaces. Having once paid a short visit to this magnificent city, the vistas of which produced in me the illusion of browsing through a photograph album, I can imagine what these festivities must have been like. Our men of letters who went there naturally have already conveyed, in the anecdotes they told their close friends, the sheer pleasure they experienced during the eight days they spent there, as though they had lived through chapters of *A Thousand and One Nights.*[76]

74. Ibid., p. 342.

75. "Uma palestra," *Diário de Notícias*, Oct. 10, 1889; Nabuco, "A nação Argentina," *O Paiz*, July 9, 1888.

76. Tristão de Alencar Araripe Júnior, "O Brazil intelectual," *Gazeta de Notícias*, Nov. 13, 1900, in *Obra crítica* vol. 3, pp. 497-498. See also the admiring descriptions of

Yet Brazil's southern neighbor's superiority was not associated only with cultural and material achievements, but also with a less mentioned factor–race. The following case is revealing. In October 1900, when the last preparations were being made for Campos Sales's trip to Argentina, a rumor spread in Rio de Janeiro that the crew of the presidential ship would consist of white sailors only. The former abolitionist leader and notable journalist José de Patrocínio protested the programmed act in a newspaper article: "Once again the navy is selecting its men on the basis of the color of their skin," he wrote. "Whites and mulattos will be preferred to man the crew of the ships that will carry Mr. Campos Sales to the Plata. This foolish selection was apparently ordered by His Excellency himself, who does not want the Argentines to suspect that there are blacks or *mestiços* in Brazil. But despite all his efforts, he is not going to achieve his objective. In order to stop Brazil from becoming a vast racial mixture, the first precaution should have been to cancel Mr. Campos Sales's visit."[77] In the same vein, a few years later, when officers of a Brazilian cruiser were refused lodging in hotels in Norfolk, Virginia, Foreign Minister Rio Branco ordered the diplomatic legations in Argentina, Uruguay, Paraguay, and Chile to deny that the incident had occurred through comments published in the local press.[78]

These two cases remind us of the ever-present racial factor in the dynamics of Brazilian-Argentine mutual perception. Even if Brazilian intellectuals did develop certain optimism at that time, putting their trust in the "whitening principle,"[79] the fact still remains that the darker skin of their people continued to be a major source of shame and unease before their Spanish American neighbors, especial-

Buenos Aires in a travel book by one of the Brazilian journalists who accompanied Campos Sales's visit: Arthur Dias, *Do Rio a Buenos Aires: Episodios e impressões d'uma viagem* (Rio de Janeiro: Imprensa Nacional, 1901), pp. 97-124.

77. José de Patrocínio, "Renegado," *Cidade do Rio*, Oct. 12, 1900, cited in Célio Debes, *Campos Salles, Perfil de um edtadista*, 2 vols., (Rio de Janeiro: Livraria F. Alves Editora, 1978), vol. 2, p. 516.

78. As acknowledged in Second Secretary of the Brazilian legation Felix Bocayuva, Buenos Aires, to Rio Branco, Rio de Janeiro, 3/8, July 1, 1905, AHI. In Argentina, the denial was published on June 29, 1905, in the following newspapers: *La Nación, La Prensa, El País, La Patria degli italiani*. See articles enclosed in Ibid., anexo no. 1. Consult also Smith, *Unequal Giants*, p. 63.

79. Skidmore, *Black into White*, pp. 64-77.

ly the more Caucasian ones. Argentina's regained stability and ostentatious prosperity, as revealed to the eyes of Campos Sales's large retinue and recounted back home, only reinforced the association between race and progress. While the official Brazilian discourse did not expose such concerns in words, it eventually revealed them by silencing.

* * *

The two presidential visits exhibited a Brazil in a moment of transition between the political and psychological insecurity of the 1890s and the relative stability and self-confidence of the new oligarchic order, a transition from passivity in the field of hemispheric politics to a much more active role. This was a Brazil conscious of its vulnerability in a more hostile international environment, and at the same time reawakened to its own imperialist legacy. Brazilian intellectuals and political leaders knew they belonged in the group of misruled, weak, and backward nations, which "the civilized world" viewed with contempt. But they believed they could make their way into the camp of the orderly, the advanced, and the powerful–if not on a world scale, then at least in the context of their peripheral South American environment. They remembered their "days of glory" in the battlefields of the River Plate, and how they, together with what was now a powerful Spanish American nation, defeated a smaller Spanish American nation. Joining forces with Argentina, past and present, held promises. Brazil envied its southern neighbor and was ready to get closer to it. Argentina stood for a vigorous European or Yankee Latin America, an escape route from the threatening degeneration associated with racially mixed populations.

The Brazilian diplomatic discourse that had been generated throughout the presidential visits, conveyed, then, a composite vision, at once pessimistic and optimistic, infused with fears and hopes, of Latin America and Brazil's place within it–a vision that formed the basis for more elaborate designs in the following years, as men of letters like Rui Barbosa, Joaquim Nabuco, and Oliveira Lima would assume leading diplomatic missions in the service of their state under Rio Branco's leadership. The movement of these intellectuals into the orbit of international relations would give rise to competing hemispheric projects, ideological extensions of a common Latin American consciousness. This was the time of the "isms." From the real and symbolic meeting point of the Third Pan-American Conference at Rio de Janeiro, three main roads diverged: Americanism, Latin Americanism and Luso-Americanism.

PART 3
THE PAN-AMERICAN CONFERENCE: AMERICANISM, LATIN AMERICANISM, LUSO-AMERICANISM

INTERWEAVING LETTERS AND DIPLOMACY IN THE RIO BRANCO YEARS

Like Roca's visit to Rio de Janeiro, the Third Pan-American Conference, which took place in the renovated Brazilian capital between July 23 and August 27, 1906, was to a large degree a well-orchestrated spectacle destined for foreign eyes. The arrival of visitors from around the continent, including U.S. Secretary of State Elihu Root, along with extensive news coverage, provided Foreign Minister Baron of Rio Branco an excellent opportunity to enhance the image of Brazil as a highly civilized nation. The conference was possibly the high point in his continuous public relations campaign, in which Joaquim Nabuco, Oliveira Lima, Rui Barbosa, and other men of letters also played central roles. The 1906 show was also a milestone in another Rio Branco project, that of a well-planned and high-profile, yet cautious, Brazil–United States rapprochement destined to aid Brazil in achieving leadership in South America without alienating the Spanish-speaking countries. It is on this latter dimension of the conference, or its identity implications, to be more precise, that this last part of the chapter focuses.[80]

Rio Branco's policy of getting closer to the United States was not revolutionary, but rather the peak of a gradual process that had started with the republic. Notwithstanding, acts like the reciprocal elevation of the two countries' diplomatic delegations to the rank of embassy (1905), Joaquim Nabuco's nomination as the first ambassador in Washington, the Pan-American Conference, and Elihu Roots's unprecedented visit, put this diplomacy at the center of attention. To this should be added the fact that the formation of what historian E. Bradford Burns dubbed the "unwritten alliance" between Brazil and the United States took place against the previously described back-

80. Wilgus, "The Third International American Conference"; Burns, *The Unwritten Alliance*, pp. 52, 108-114; Smith, *Unequal Giants*, pp. 53-57; Skidmore, *Black into White*, pp. 136-137; Needell, "The Domestic Civilizing Mission," p. 7.

ground of rising imperialism and intensifying anti-Yankee sentiments, nationalistic rhetoric, and internationalism. These factors, together with Rio Branco's exceptional public standing, extensive manipulation of the press, as well as formal and informal enlistment of leading Brazilian intellectuals to serve his goals, created an animated and meaningful discussion concerning Brazil's continental insertion. Expressing opinions on hemispheric politics, in favor or against Rio Branco's policy, could affect one's material conditions through the allotment or not of posts in the civil service, elevate one's political and intellectual status, or enhance one's public image. Personal friendships and rivalries typical of this small, intimate milieu also came into play. In short, a strong overlap developed between membership in the Brazilian Academy of Letters, journalistic, and diplomatic activity. The inner workings of the uppermost intellectual elite became closely entwined with the practice and discourse of international relations.[81]

These circumstances have since then been a rich ground for written polemics between followers of one or another of the historical figures involved. Brazilian historiography is replete with hagiographies that offer lengthy deliberations about the relationships between Rio Branco and Joaquim Nabuco, Joaquim Nabuco and Rui Barbosa, Rui Barbosa and Rio Branco, Rio Branco and Oliveira Lima, etc. Each book sings the praises of its hero, asserting the truly patriotic motives behind his actions and the immense contribution he made to Brazil's standing among the nations, while often times casting doubt about the other figures' conduct. All the same, the interested reader will find in these works a wealth of information and, in some cases, also valuable analyses of the statesmen's hemispheric

81. Burns, *The Unwritten Alliance*, p. 53-55; On the relationship between the Academy and the Foreign Office, see Teresa Malatian, "Diplomacia e letras na correspondência acadêmica: Machado de Assis e Oliveira Lima," *Estudos Históricos* 13:24 (1999), pp. 377-392. About the same issue and Rio Branco's clientelistic practices, see Lins, *Rio Branco*, pp. 426-431; Viana Filho, *A vida do Barão do Rio Branco*, pp. 420-421; Antônio Luiz Machado Neto, *Estrutura social da república das letras: sociologia da vida intelectual brasileira, 1870-1930* (São Paulo: Editora da Universidade de São Paulo, 1973), pp. 152-153; and Brito Broca, *A vida literária no Brasil-1900*, 2nd revised and enlarged ed. (Rio de Janeiro: J Olympio, 1960), pp. 155-157. The last two works also provide a good portrait and analysis of intellectual life during this period.

views.[82] What I therefore intend to do in the following pages is not so much to describe different personal stands in detail, nor to dissect the various motivations behind them, but rather to uncover their Latin American dimension and finally connect the diplomatic discourse entwined with the Pan-American Conference to the question of national and transnational identification. This line of investigation is pursued by focusing on the intimate and public exchange of views by and among the three main exponents of Brazilian diplomacy at that time, Rio Branco, Nabuco, and Oliveira Lima.

Joaquim Nabuco's American Way

In his letter written in late October 1905 (cited above), several months after his arrival in Caracas, Oliveira Lima expressed his surprise at Nabuco's extreme North Americanism. The Brazilian minister in Caracas did not agree with the enthusiastic "*Monroismo*, or more precisely, *Rooseveltismo*," of the recently nominated ambassador in Washington. This was the opening shot of a great personal/ideological duel between these two friends over Brazil's continental policy, which would bring their relationship to an end six months later. After assuming their respective posts in Venezuela and the United States, significantly described by Lima as different observatories, the two started to promote conflicting versions of Pan-Americanism, with Rio Branco standing somewhere in the middle.

"I cannot believe you are reading *A ilusão americana*, a paradox of our dear Eduardo, who, were he alive today, would have been asked to write an apologia against *A ilusão americana*, to which he would have surely agreed," wrote Nabuco to his superior in December 1905, when the preparations for the conference and Root's visit

82. See, for example, the three biographies by Luís Viana Filho, *A vida de Rui Barbosa*, *A vida de Joaquim Nabuco*, and *A vida do Barão do Rio Branco*; Alvaro Lins, *Rio Branco*; Magalhães Júnior, *Rui, o homem e o mito*; Gouvêa, *Oliveira Lima, uma biografia*; For historiographical treatments, see Phil Brian Johnson, "Uptight about Ruy: An Essay on Brazilian Cultural Nationalism and Mythology," *Journal of Inter-American Studies and World Affairs*, 15:2 (May 1973), 191-204; and Cristina Patriota Moura, "Herança e metamorfose: a construção social de dois Rio Branco," *Estudos Históricos* 25:1 (2000), pp. 81-102.

were already under way. With these words, he hinted at Rio Branco's suspicious–to say the least–attitude toward the United States and at the foreign minister's practice of assigning propaganda missions to erudite cronies. Then, after evoking the memory of their common anti-American friend, Nabuco added, "Never, in my opinion, has any Brazilian had so much responsibility for the future of our country as you now have before the two roads open to you: the American one and the other, which I don't know what to call, whether the Latin American way, the independent way, or the solitary way."[83] "Two ways" he writes, but actually specifies three continental courses of action: American, Latin American, and Luso-American.

The first was, as already indicated, most notably his. In his new post Nabuco had become, according to everybody involved including himself, the most enthusiastic supporter within Itamaraty of Brazil's strengthening of ties with the United Sates: "more Yankee than the Yankees themselves."[84] While this development took Oliveira Lima by surprise, Carolina Nabuco later claimed much continuity with regard to the foreign policy Joaquim Nabuco had desired for Brazil. In her exhaustive biography of her father, she mentions his plan of abolition, federation, and peace, from the last years of the monarchy and his support of the First Pan-American Conference in 1889, as well as of any other initiative that could secure peace in the New World. Nabuco's daughter also quotes from the 1898 interview in the *Estado de São Paulo*, already mentioned in this chapter, where Nabuco raised the question of Latin America's fate in face of Europe, Africa, and Asia's crystallization into a single political unit. "The obvious solution lay in the Monroe Doctrine," writes his biographer, "in the indestructible union of American states." Missing is the continuation of her father's reply to the interviewer, in which he did not support any clear foreign policy, but rather wondered

83. Joaquim Nabuco to Rio Branco, Washington, Dec. 19, 1905, Nabuco, *Cartas a amigos*, vol. 2, p. 238.

84. José Veríssimo to Oliveira Lima, Rio de Janeiro, Aug. 12, 1906, Oliveira Lima Library, Oliveira Lima Family Papers [Henceforth OLFP]. See also letter by Domício da Gama, who replaced Nabuco as Brazil's ambassador to the U.S., to José Veríssimo, Washington, Feb. 24, 1913, in "Epistolário acadêmico," *Revista da Academia Brasileira de Letras* 24:139 (July 1933), p. 367; Salvador de Mendonça, *A situação Internacional do Brazil* (Rio de Janeiro: Garnier, 1913), pp. 247-248.

whether Latin America should form a whole with the United States or perhaps enter the European sphere of influence.[85] In the field of diplomacy at least, things were not so clear at that time, when Nabuco was detached from politics and the meaning of the Spanish-American War probably not yet fully internalized. But the main point to be made here concerns the field of self-perceptions and perceptions of others. That is, the fundamental importance of the Spanish American Other–or more precisely the Latin American We–for the formation of Nabuco's continental views and policies, both in the 1880s, afterward in 1898, and now in 1905. True, the vision of America as the realm of peace, distinct from the European sphere of war, was in itself not new. Nabuco voiced it in Rio de Janeiro during the Pan-American Conference,[86] of which he was president, in almost identical terms to those he had used a decade and a half before, in the middle of the Argentine-Brazilian celebrations of the abolition of slavery. In that sense, he was indeed an Americanist throughout. Yet, underlying his Americanism were changing views of Spanish America and Brazil.

Nabuco's Americanist messages and peace plans from the late Empire were destined, as already discussed in this work, to counter republican propaganda, to prove that monarchical Brazil was not an aggressive and hated exception, as it had been claimed, and thus help the regime survive. They were much more about Brazil's position within South America than about its relationship with the United States, which did not look menacing yet. It all relied on Argentina's new civilized image, on its perception as a potential friendly agent of order and progress in the region. There was much optimism in the air at that moment. Later, as the reader may recall, during the turbulent years following the fall of the Empire, hopes of Latin American regeneration had given way to a fundamentally pessimistic view of

85. Carolina Nabuco, *The Life of Joaquim Nabuco*, p. 307. Note that even much later, when he was already informed of his impending nomination as ambassador to Washington, Nabuco was still far from sure as to the desired course of Brazilian foreign policy toward the U.S.: Nabuco to Graça Aranha, London, Jan., 1905, in *Cartas a amigos*, vol. 2, pp. 202-203.

86. Nabuco spoke at a banquet in his honor, held on July 19, 1906, at Rio de Janeiro's Casino Fluminense, reported in *São Paulo*, July 21, 1906, n.pag., clipping 001.16 - 74/404, AJN.

Spanish America and Brazil–independently of external factors–that was there to stay.[87]

The growth of European and American imperialism only deepened Nabuco's concerns about "the fate of *Latin America,*" as he put it in 1898. This view of Brazil as part of larger problem lay at the basis of his Monroeism as ambassador. In early 1905, after being informed about the nomination, he referred to the creation of the Washington embassy as an "act of audacity and inspiration that opened new and extended horizons for our country and *for all of Latin America.*"[88] Close relations with the United States and an unconditional acceptance of the Monroe Doctrine were the only possible guarantees against foreign aggression, he now had come to believe. He combined this policy with a complementary spiritual project of creating a unified "American opinion, an American public spirit," as he defined it in his opening speech as president of the Third Pan-American Conference. The true objective of these intercontinental conferences should have been "to unify the continent's civilization, [...] to patch up differences, to remove everything which may set us apart, to promote everything that unites."[89] Spiritual unification of the continent under the tutelage of the United States was Nabuco's formula as a man of letters back in the service of the state. This was the ideological manifestation of his Latin American consciousness, his cure for the maladies of the Portuguese- and Spanish-speaking countries of the New World. Yet the very same endeavor to construct an all-American civilization, to bridge the gaps, ultimately emphasized the notion of two essentially distinct Americas, "Anglo-Saxon" and "Latin," which were profoundly indifferent, if not hostile, to each other.[90]

87. João Frank da Costa, *Joaquim Nabuco e a política exterior do Brasil* (Rio de Janeiro: Gráfica Récord Editôra, 1968), pp. 159-162.

88. Joaquim Nabuco to Graça Aranha, Rome, Feb. 2, 1905, in *Cartas a amigos*, vol. 2, pp. 208; my italics.

89. Lecture dated July 23, 1906, transcript in Arquivo Particular de Joaquim Nabuco, Itamaraty [Henceforth AJN-I], Lata 791, maço 4; Costa, *Joaquim Nabuco*, esp. chap. 3.

90. These motifs found their fullest expression in Joaquim Nabuco, *The Approach of the Two Americas. Convocation Address before the University of Chicago, August 28, 1908*. Bulletin of the American Branch of the Association for International Conciliation, 1908, no. 10 (New York: American branch of the Association for Interna-

FIGURE 4.3
Two different Americas: Latin and Anglo-Saxon.
The Third Pan-American Conference was held in the new Senate building named "The Monroe Palace" by Rio Branco as a tribute to the United States–an act that was in perfect agreement with Nabuco's policy. Yet, as can be seen in this reproduction from *Renascença* magazine, the official symbolism also expressed the widely accepted notion of two different Americas. According to the accompanying text, the two female figures that appear on the right-hand corner of this commemorative stamp symbolize the two races that inhabit the American continent, the Latin and the Anglo-Saxon. *Renascença*, no. 29, July 1906. Courtesy of Arquivo da Casa de Rui Barbosa.

This hostility, as already mentioned, was clearly on the rise. Nabuco's project, as is clearly stated in his above letter to Rio Branco, was not the only one at play. In the aftermath of the Spanish-American War and following the announcement of the Roosevelt Corollary to the Monroe Doctrine, his stand was bound to encounter opposition. In the current continental circumstances, his idealistic discourse of American peace acquired a different meaning than it had in 1888. In a far more conscious Latin America, increasingly aware of the United States' hostile intentions and willing to reaffirm its politi-

tional Conciliation, 1908). Importantly, a Portuguese translation appeared two years later in the *Revista Americana*, 1:3 (Dec., 1909) pp. 173-181.

cal and spiritual independence, Nabuco's vision was necessarily viewed as a justification of North American hegemony in the continent. It was in this context that Rubén Darío's poem "Salutación al águila" ("Salute to the Eagle"), written during his stay in Rio de Janeiro as secretary of the Nicaraguan delegation to the Pan-American Conference, summoning the North American eagle "to spread his great continental shade over the South," won strong criticism from Spanish American intellectuals. And it was in this context that the poet, who had befriended Joaquim Nabuco aboard the ship that carried the two to the conference from New York, would apologetically confess a year later, in another famous poem, how he "Pan-Americanized [himself] with a vague fear and with very little faith in the land of diamonds and tropical bliss."[91]

Oliveira Lima's Latin American Way

Significantly, the most notable and vociferous opponent of Nabuco's project in Brazil rose from within the Foreign Office. Oliveira Lima's view of the United States' role in hemispheric politics evolved in a way opposite from that of his rival. While Ambassador Nabuco moved, upon arriving in Washington, from suspicion to trust–at least publicly–in the host country's intentions toward Latin America, Lima's stand on international relations became more and more critical of the northern power after he had left his diplomatic post in the same capital. In 1899, during his fourth year of service as first secretary in the Brazilian legation to the United States, he published a book titled *Nos Estados Unidos,* recounting his impressions of the English-speaking country. It was a compilation of articles previously published in Brazilian journals, some of them written after the end of the Spanish-American War, assessing its significance. Lima acknowledged that the occupation of Cuba and the Philippines marked the beginning of a new phase in U.S. foreign policy, but ruled out the

91. Fred P. Ellison, "Rubén Darío and Brazil," *Hispania*, 47:1 (1964), pp. 24-35; Alberto Acereda; and Rigoberto Guevara, *Modernism, Rubén Darío, and the Poetics of Despair* (Lanham, MD: University Press of America, 2004), p. 279.

option that this fresh kind of imperialism would be directed violently against other countries in the continent. Moreover, in a chapter providing an overview of Brazil's relations with the United States, he argued directly with Eduardo Prado's *A ilusão americana* and claimed that these relations had been traditionally friendly and beneficial for both sides throughout the century, and would continue to be so in the future. In the same vein, Lima assigned a positive role to the Monroe Doctrine, albeit with one important condition: that responsibility for its implementation would be shared among all the countries of the continent, respecting their sovereignty.[92]

As far as inter-American affairs were concerned, then, *Nos Estados Unidos* stood in stark contradiction to the general awakening to the North American peril, so notable in the writings of Joaquim Nabuco and Rui Barbosa. Yet underlying the conflicting predictions were similar geocultural concepts, evidenced in and constructed by identical terminology and textual references. Lima, too, framed his discussion of Brazil–U.S. relationships in the wider terms of "Latin" versus "Anglo-Saxon," the weak versus the strong, putting forth both the problem and its solution through allusions to the same Spanish American writers also cited by Rui.[93] One was "our intelligent enemy Alberdi, who accurately observed that a country's borders are like the clothes that people wear over their body: they stretch or they shrink according to the strength or weakness of the organism, and therefore the safest way to fortify them is to fortify the country from within."[94] That was the proper answer to César Zumeta's diagnosis, mentioned next, of Latin America as a sick continent in graver condition than the Ottoman Empire and China.

Zumeta's warnings against North American expansionism, so avidly reproduced by Rui Barbosa, nevertheless did not find their way into Lima's *Nos Estados Unidos*. While sharing with his fellow Brazilian a social-Darwinist reading of international relations and a basically pessimistic conception of the Latin American reality–typically describing Chile and Argentina as positive exceptions to the

92. Manuel de Oliveira Lima, *Nos Estados Unidos: Impressões politicas e sociaes* (Leipzig, F. A. Brockhaus, 1899), p. 452.

93. Lima, *Nos Estados Unidos*, pp. 382-385.

94. Ibid., pp. 453-454.

rule–Lima was not as resolute with regard to the imminence of danger, evoking long-term means of salvation instead of immediate military buildup and regional alliances. He overwhelmingly rejected the idea that the United States might try to annex other American nations, but then went on to claim, paradoxically, that it was ultimately up to the Latin American countries themselves whether they were going to become "victims" of the colossus of the North. Their efforts should concentrate, he suggested in the spirit of Alberdi, on strengthening themselves from within by achieving higher levels of industriousness, political stability, and tolerance. "It is better to promote national prosperity than to imagine dreadful chimeras," was the rationale.[95]

There was also another important precondition for survival, namely, whitening. Engaging in a dialogue with Benjamin Kidd's 1898 *The Control of the Tropics*, which foresaw an inevitable takeover of Latin America's warm areas by the Anglo-Saxon race, the Brazilian diplomat set forth his racist understanding of the region's weaknesses. Having made a faint protest against the European author's excessively harsh indictment of Brazil as a racially mixed nation incapable of successfully absorbing immigrants, Lima proceeded to explain the crucial importance of improving the local stock. Following up on the Englishman's prevision that Central and South America would soon be exclusively populated by blacks and Indians, he declared that "almost all of our Latin American countries, unless saved by the healthy influx of European immigration, with all its moral implications and the exercise of virtues that explain the might of the Saxon race, will thus fall into the general category of tropical territories inhabited by inferior races; and for which it is becoming imperative to prepare the humanitarian prescription of domination by those better qualified for colonization and progress."[96]

Nos Estados Unidos presented, then, the widely accepted notion of two different Americas, inhabited by two distinct races, one supe-

95. Ibid., p. 452.

96. Ibid., p. 457. Lima's racial interpretation and suggested solutions were exceptionally overt in comparison with Nabuco, who expressed some similar notions, but in private: Joaquim Nabuco to Oliveira Lima, Rio de Janeiro, Nov. 28, 1896, OLFP; Joaquim Nabuco to Tobias Monteiro, Jackson, NH, Aug. 20, 1905, in *Cartas a amigos*, vol. 2, p. 223.

rior to the other in terms of material progress and military power, if not in terms of cultural production and moral values. This vision would inform Lima's subsequent writings on continental affairs, evolving by 1903, into a politico-cultural project. In that year, Lima published an article in the *Diário de Pernambuco* dedicated to the Drago Doctrine, the famous Argentine response to the forcible coercion of Venezuela by England, Germany, and Italy in 1902, named after Roca's Foreign Minister Luis María Drago. In a note sent to the U.S. government, Drago stated that no public debt should be collected from a sovereign American state by a foreign power through armed force or the occupation of territory. Lima applauded every aspect of Argentina's conduct surrounding the Venezuelan case, from the typographic quality of a recently published volume comprising Drago's treatise alongside other related documents, to the assertiveness and foresight embedded in the anti-interventionist plan, stressing Brazil's inferiority to its southern neighbor in both respects. Drago's great achievement lay in "latinizing the Monroe Doctrine." He divested it of its North American exclusiveness and distasteful protectionist overtones, thus granting it the support of Latin America and, most importantly, "of the nation that aspires to lead the other countries of Spanish origin, showing, at the same time, that the great Republic [of the United States] is not the sole arbiter on this side of the Atlantic."[97]

Underlying this strong affirmation of Latin American unity under Argentine leadership were deep preoccupations with racial inferiority and chronic anarchy, as revealed in other writings of a less political and more scholarly nature from that period. In Lima's eyes, Argentina–where the whites made the blacks and the Indians disappear–stood out among the ex-Portuguese and ex-Spanish colonies, representing, together with Chile–where the landed aristocracy refrained from interbreeding–a Latin America rich in promises.[98] This familiar division of the region was largely informed by northern views: most

97. "O Sr. Drago, o caso da Venezuela e a doutrina de Monroe," in Lima, *Panamericanismo*, p. 21.

98. See, for example, Oliveira Lima, *Impressões da América Espanhola, 1904-1906*, prefaced and annotated by Manoel da Silveira Cardozo, introduction by Gilberto Freyre (Rio de Janeiro: Livraria J. Olympio, 1953), pp. 53-62, 105-106, 120-121.

U.S. papers which had dealt with Drago's message, noted Lima, "classified the Argentine republic as the most civilized, the most progressive and the most important country in South America."[99] Yet it was the very view from the North, ultimately condescending toward the South as a whole, against which the Brazilian diplomat had been revolting.

Fusing the notion of a distinct Latin American identity with anti-Yankee sentiments and indicating concrete measures to confront U.S. continental hegemony, Lima's 1903 article marked the beginning of his Latin Americanism. It was followed, after his arrival in Venezuela, by a growing stream of journalistic writings that reproduced this basic formula in greater detail and in a more assertive tone, highly critical of Theodore Roosevelt's hemispheric policies. The first first-hand encounter with the Spanish American reality in Caracas was stamped by the same ambivalence already apparent in his essays. The city was a "pestilent hell" from which he wanted to flee, as he confided at one point to a relative,[100] but it was also the place, as already mentioned in beginning of the chapter, where the Brazilian learned that Europeans and Americans were "by no means morally superior" to the local people. There, he also pursued a rich social and intellectual life, attending the meetings of the National Academy of History and making many contacts with local statesmen and writers. Intense and full of conflicting emotions, the relatively short Venezuelan experience (mid-1905 to mid-1906) enhanced Lima's interest in the neighboring countries and his active identification with "Latin America." From that point onward he had grown to be the most prolific writer about Spanish American themes in Brazil, the best connected to Spanish American intellectual circles, and the most notable Portuguese-speaking exponent of *latinoamericanismo*.[101]

99. Lima, *Pan-americanismo*, p. 26.

100. Cited by Manoel da Silveira Cardozo, "Preface," in Lima, *Impressões da América Espanhola*, , p. 41.

101. See Lima's *The Evolution of Brazil Compared with That of Spanish and Anglo-Saxon America*, (Stanford: Stanford University Press, 1914), translated into Portuguese as *America Latina e America Ingleza: A Evolução Brazileira comparada com a Hispano-Americana e com a Anglo-Americana* (Rio de Janeiro/Paris: Garnier, 1914?), and *Impressões da América Espanhola*. Discussion of his continental views and interest in Spanish America is provided in Barbosa Lima Sobrinho, "Oliveira

So unrelenting were the articles dispatched regularly from Caracas to the *Estado de São Paulo* that Joaquim Nabuco was seriously concerned they might ruin the forthcoming Pan-American Conference. This specific concern and other worries over hostile reactions to Root's visit did not materialize. Even Rui Barbosa's refusal to his request to deliver a speech in Root's honor at the Brazilian Senate did not manage to spoil the good spirit of the ambassador to Washington, who ultimately went back North generally satisfied with the conference's intangible results, albeit not completely free of preoccupations about the future harm that the "diplomatic torpedo," as he came to refer to Oliveira Lima, might cause.[102]

The combined battle over Brazil's political and cultural orientation and for personal prestige was to be continued on the many fronts it had been waged so far, the private and the public, the diplomatic and the literary, the national and the international. Writing right before his departure to intellectual and politician Artur Orlando, who had recently added his own voice to the discussion about inter-American relationships with a volume titled *Pan-americanismo* (1906), Nabuco lamented the fact that he could not invite this potential ally for a joint dinner with the U.S. ambassador and then proceeded to express his hope that Orlando would become "the apostle" of Brazil–United States rapprochement, counteracting Oliveira Lima's continuous effort to spread distrust against the North American power.[103]

Several months after the conference had ended, now back in Brazil, Oliveira Lima also found reasons to be satisfied. Continuing his journalistic reflections on hemispheric politics, Lima acknowledged that Root's visit to Rio de Janeiro had managed to mislead

Lima: Sua vida e sua obra," in Oliveira Lima, *Obra seleta*, ed. by Barbosa Lima Sobrinho (Rio de Janeiro: Instituto Nacional do Livro, 1971), pp. 110-115; and in the abovementioned "Preface" and "Introduction" by Manoel da Silveira Cardozo and Gilberto Freyre, respectively, in Lima's *Impressões da América Espanhola*.

102. Joaquim Nabuco to Graça Aranha, Washington, March 2, 1906, in *Cartas a amigos*, vol. 2, pp. 248-250.

103. Joaquim Nabuco to Artur Orlando, Rio de Janeiro, Oct. 15, 1906, AJN 754. This letter also reveals Nabuco's own mistrust of the United States even at that time: "Even if they are justified," he wrote with regard to the suspicions spread by Lima, "the right policy for us is still to be friends with the U.S. rather than its enemies."

many Brazilians to believe that the United States would stand behind their country in case of European aggression or armed conflict with Spanish American countries. However, the Brazilian government itself, remained immune to illusions of this sort, the correct official line artfully put forth by Rio Branco in the inaugural speech to the Pan-American Conference. The foreign minister did not go out of his way to praise the United States, nor did he spare good and warm words for Europe, thus striking the right balance between "what our attitude should be toward a nation that requires our moral support as much as we require hers, and a continent to which we are strongly bound by bonds of blood, economy and civilization."[104] Brazil, in other words, was profoundly Latin, a fact of history and race from which foreign policy could not be detached.

Significantly, following his deliberations on Brazil's position vis-à-vis the great centers of power, Lima went on to comment on the recent deterioration of relations with Argentina, which had no real reason in his view. Turning to the South-South context, he recalled Campos Sales's contribution to the rapprochement between the two countries in a positive light and asserted that their interests were basically the same: "moral resistance to foreign influences, a resistance for which we are not as prepared as we tend to think, and material progress that naturally involves competition but should not provoke enmity." After all, they were neighbors "of the same race with generally similar objectives of culture and grandeur." In a manner reminiscent of Rui Barbosa, Lima weaved the Arielist thread of cultural confrontation between Latin and Anglo-Saxon values and traditions with earthly principles of power relations. Thus, there was no denial of Argentina's aggressive potential. In view of its strength, it was only natural that Brazil's southern neighbor should aspire to take over Uruguay, but this aspiration might not necessarily materialize. Instead, Argentine strength could be harnessed to confront U.S. predominance in the continent. While it was too early to speak about a change of hegemony in the southern part of the continent, Latin American solidarity should and could turn U.S. hegemony into a thing of the past.[105]

104. Lima, *Pan-americanismo*, p. 110.
105. Ibid., pp. 110-111.

The articles discussed, from before and after the conference, together with many others on the same issues, were published in book form in 1907 under the title *Pan-americanismo (Monroe-Bolívar-Roosevelt)*. The epigraph on the work's title page was borrowed from an old book, published in Brazil back in 1840, about the 1817 revolution in Pernambuco. Brazilian revolutionaries of the time had been wrong, according to the excerpt, when they counted on the United States to help them in their struggle, because "this nation has a mercantile spirit, and merchants are avaricious," and would not lend any help to the insurgents until sure of their victory. Reproducing these lines, Oliveira Lima inserted himself in a long tradition of constructing the neighbor to the north as a materialist utilitarian Other–a tradition not only Spanish American but also Brazilian. As Barbosa Lima Sobrinho has argued, this might not have been a statement of *antiamericanismo*,[106] but it suggested that, grouped together, the essays should be read not only as a diplomatic treatise but also as an act of national and transnational identification.

Rio Branco's Luso-American Way

Oliveira Lima's *Pan-Americanismo* bore a dedication "to the Baron of Rio Branco, who in the opening speech to the Pan-American Conference in Rio de Janeiro indicated to this continental assembly the right course, calmly preventing the feudalization of Brazil, a country with aspirations and traditions of its own, to the North American system."[107] One may suspect the motives behind these words, but there was certainly more to them than simple flattery of a civil servant to his superior, as is evident in both public and private reactions to the book upon its publication. José Veríssimo, who reviewed Lima's book for *Jornal do Comércio* alongside Artur Orlando's work bearing the same title, thought for example that of all the speeches made during the conference, Rio Branco's address was "possibly the only one of real value and importance." In Veríssimo's view, the foreign minister actually expressed the same ideas that his

106. Barbosa Lima Sobrinho, "Oliveira Lima: Sua vida e sua obra," p. 113.
107. Lima, *Pan-americanismo*, p. 17.

former ambassador to Caracas had been advocating since 1903.[108] In the same vein, Lima's friend from the years of service in the Spanish American capital, the Venezuelan intellectual Ángel César Rivas, who had been sent a copy of *Pan-americanismo* by mail, found the dedication to Rio Branco "very serious, noble, and well deserved."[109] Last, Euclides da Cunha reported to Lima that he had discussed the book with Rio Branco in private, and had gotten the impression that the foreign minister agreed with its general thrust and was delighted with the dedication.[110]

Indeed, Rio Branco's diplomatic discourse contained several points of convergence with Lima's writings, the rejection of U.S. hegemony being only one of them. In his inaugural speech, the foreign minister also emphasized the important role of the continental meeting in reconciling opposing interests in order to achieve the ideal of "progress amidst peace." Like Nabuco, Rio Branco spoke repeatedly of peace, only in his case the notion was not identified so closely with America, painting instead a bright picture of *universal* transition from the law of the strongest to a peaceful and law-abiding conduct among nations. The peace congresses of the day were convened in quiet times and not in the aftermath of wars. They did not serve the victorious side as a means of dictating its conditions to the defeated, but rather regulated normal international activity, with "equal respect for the rights of the weakest as to the rights of the most powerful."[111] Here was an image of world politics almost completely opposite from the Hobbesian view advanced by Oliveira Lima and Rui Barbosa, albeit not incompatible. For as already indicated, the pursuit of international peace went hand in hand with speeding armament races, jingoism, and imperialism. Many states-

108. José Veríssimo, "O Perigo Americano," *Jornal do Commercio*, Feb. 2, 1908, n.pag., clipping in Joaquim Nabuco's papers with his inscription: "Oliveira Lima persecutes me with his resentment without affecting me or even arousing my curiosity. Resentment is what his life is all about. Poor thing! He must be filled with resentment to the bone. I, however, always felt friendship for him." 001.16-74/619, AJN.

109. Ángel César Rivas to Oliveira Lima, Caracas, May 9, 1908, OLFP.

110. Euclides da Cunha to Oliveira Lima, Rio de Janeiro, May 25, 1908, in "New Light on Euclides da Cunha," p. 41.

111. José Maria de Silva Paranhos Júnior, Barão do Rio Branco, *Obras do Barão do Rio Branco*, 9 vols. (Rio de Janeiro: Ministério das Relações Exteriores, 1945-1948), vol. 9, *Discursos*, pp. 86-87.

men of the period combined all of these. Theodore Roosevelt, let us remember, carried a "big stick," receiving at the same time the Nobel Peace Prize for his successful mediation to end the war between Russia and Japan.

This same duality also characterized Rio Branco. In an interview he gave during the first days of the Pan-American Conference to the Argentine daily *La Nación*, one of Spanish America's most influential newspapers, and which was reproduced by the Rio de Janeiro press, the Brazilian statesman spoke differently about international relations in general, and specifically about the Latin American sphere. The contents of the interview, its location and timing, the nationality of the two sides involved, as well as its almost simultaneous publication in both Spanish and Portuguese, all make it an exemplary case of Luso-Hispano-American dynamics in the Age of Empire and worthwhile to quote at some length:

> –Many people think, Minister, that you fear Europe too much, whereas the United States may represent a more immediate threat.
>
> –They are mistaken. The threat of North American expansionism is a fiction. The United States only wishes to encourage the prosperity of the other American republics and help them increase their population, so that the *European immigrants* might come and contribute with their work toward the advancement of these nations, in such a way that the natural increase of the foreign population might make it unnecessary for it [the U.S.] to invade the less-populated republics. The United States is far away from us and can only exercise its direct influence in the Caribbean, not here.
>
> –And what about the republics of Central America?
>
> –In this regard I have often stated my opinion–to which I still hold–that *countries that are incapable of governing themselves* and lack the means to prevent the incessant outbreak of revolutions and civil wars that plague them do *not have the right to exist and must give way to a stronger, better organized, more progressive, and more virile nation.*
>
> –Would this not be dangerous?
> –Not at all. It only shows that it is time to act, that everybody should be concerned with the progress of their nation and allow the state and com-

> merce to prevail; this is the policy that each and every country should adopt for its own benefit. This could be achieved by reaching *an agreement between Argentina, Chile, and Brazil. I mention these three nations because they are the strongest and the most progressive*, and because it is impossible to forge agreements with 21 republics. These three countries would exercise their influence over the rest, thus preventing the wars that are so common among certain nations.[112]

Whitening, internal political order, virility, regional cooperation, and progress were all intimately connected in the mind and actions of the foreign minister. In this vision of Latin America in the making there was no room for the "sick" ones. Evidently, unequal power relations within the Latin American periphery could override (but not eliminate) ethnic and cultural closeness.

Where the Three Ways Converged

After the interview had ended, the Brazilian foreign minister showed the Argentine correspondent around the Itamaraty Palace. Among the objects he pointed out to the guest was Benjamin Parlagreco's painting depicting Roca's arrival in Rio de Janeiro in 1899. Although many things had changed since then, others apparently had not. By 1906 continental diplomatic initiatives, as is evident above, were no longer an Argentine prerogative. With Rio Branco in office, Brazil had also become a leading player in hemispheric politics, which were now dominated by the North American threat. This constellation gave rise to three main diplomatic-identitarian projects that signified the ideologization of a shared Latin American consciousness.

Underlying the splits at the ideological level was a common vision. Like other key Brazilian men of state and/or letters, Nabuco, Lima, and Rio Branco envisaged two distinct Latin Americas: one that was racially mixed and anarchical, and therefore also inferior, weak, and vulnera-

112. *Jornal do Commercio*, Aug. 4, 1906, a clipping in AJN-I, Lata 791, maço 5; my italics throughout. Originally published in *La Nación* (Buenos Aires), July 26, 1906. Rio Branco was considering a treaty among Brazil, Argentina, and Chile on similar moral and pragmatic grounds, as early as 1904. See Burns, *The Unwritten Alliance*, p. 153.

ble to external aggression, as was the case of Venezuela; and another that was white, stable, prosperous, *relatively* strong and secure,–civilized, that is–like Chile or Argentina, a synthesis of so-perceived "Latin" and "Anglo-Saxon" traits. In 1906, the old negative stereotype of Spanish America, the origins of which stretched back to the early nineteenth century, was still in place. The great difference from the past was that it had been gradually joined by a contradictory image. Brazil itself was commonly associated with both images. The country was by now relatively stable and prosperous (as far as the ruling upper class was concerned), yet the caudillistic experience of the previous decade was still fresh in mind, and the continuous stream of European immigration could not do away with racial preoccupations. Argentina, therefore, still stood as a radiant example, the embodiment of an ideal Latin America, European in its culture and Yankee in its conduct.

Nabuco, possibly the most idealistic and pessimistic of all, could not envision Latin America making a great material leap forward in the foreseeable future, nor did he believe in its power to defend itself. Fearful of foreign aggression, he thought the South should throw in its lot with the North, emphasizing shared continental values. Oliveira Lima went in an opposite direction. He stressed Latin America's separate identity and political autonomy, singling out Argentina as a leader to be followed. With relation to these two paths, Rio Branco's was clearly a middle route.[113] It might be called Luso-American. While less inclined to openly identify himself or his country as American or Latin American than his two apostles sent on missions to the North and to the South, the Baron actually did so through their voices, allowing them enough leeway to express their conflicting visions from within Itamaraty. The way of the Foreign Office, which in the final analysis was Rio Branco's way, was thus at once northbound and southbound, successfully synthesizing cultural and diplomatic elements from both paths into a project of wide and lasting influence upon Brazil's self-perception, as will be further explained in the concluding chapter.

113. Viana Filho, *A vida do Barão do Rio Branco*, p. 408.

Chapter 5
Recreating the Island, Maintaining the Bridges: Rio Branco, Spanish America, and the Myth of *Paz e Concórdia*

"*Not* a Monster Country"

In May 2000, shortly before being appointed foreign minister of Brazil for the second time, Celso Lafer delivered a lecture at Tel Aviv University, in celebration of the Brazilian quincentenary. The title of the lecture was "The Continental Scale of Brazil's International Identity." Afterward, Lafer repeated some of the main elements of this talk in an academic article he published, also on the occasion of the *quinto centenário*, entitled "Brazilian International Identity and Foreign Policy: Past, Present and Future." The protagonist of both texts was the Baron of Rio Branco, who, in Lafer's words, "peacefully drew the Brazilian map." He first did so as the Brazilian representative in cases of international arbitration, beginning in 1895, and later as foreign minister from 1902 to 1912. "Not only did Rio Branco bequeath to Brazil a peacefully obtained map of continental proportions," declared Lafer, "he was also the great institution-builder of Itamaraty [...] The Baron inspired a diplomatic style which characterizes Brazil's international identity in the light of its circumstances, its history and its experience, a style of constructive moderation and de-dramatization of foreign policy, by relying on diplomacy and law." Stressing the point further, the future head of Itamaraty (2001-2002) said that Brazil "is *not* a scary 'monster country,'" and its nationalism is "*not* expansionist."[1]

1. Celso Lafer, "The Continental Scale of the Brazilian International Identity: the Role of History," unpublished lecture delivered at Tel Aviv University, May 25, 2000;

A few days before Celso Lafer's talk in Tel Aviv, President Fernando Henrique Cardoso expressed some identical notions, in a very similar language, in Brasília, at the graduation ceremony of the Rio Branco Institute, which trains Brazil's diplomats: "It is worth remembering that Rio Branco's great effort of consolidating our frontiers, which everybody always mentions, is what made possible this type of relationship between Brazil and its neighbors: a quiet, calm, peaceful relationship, with no territorial disputes. That allows us, and here is the challenge for our diplomacy, to consolidate the task, under Rio Branco's inspiration, of looking at South America as a peaceful home. Of looking at South America *not* as a hunter eyeing his prey. *No*, *not* in our case. We *don't* want that, we have *never* been like that."[2]

I would argue that these sentences belong to a long discursive tradition that reproduces an old myth, not only about the history of Brazil's conduct in the international sphere, but also about its national character.[3] Brazilian foreign policy discourse is not solely responsible for disseminating the story of a friendly and law-abiding nation. This myth is hardly distinguishable from other myths or widely accepted interpretations, such as that of racial democracy, lenient slavery, cordial people, and nonviolent historical evolution, which have constructed the Brazilian self- and outer image. Some of these myths, interpretations, and images–which are not only creations of political and intellectual leaders, but which also resonate in the popular imagination–have received much scholarly attention, while others have not. In general, though, we still know very little about their historical origins, mutual relationships, and evolution through time. Yet,

and Celso Lafer, "Brazilian International Identity and Foreign Policy: Past, Present, and Future," *Daedalus*, 129:2 (Spring 2000), pp. 215, 221-222; my italics.

2. Fernando Henrique Cardoso, "Discurso do Senhor Presidente da República, Fernando Henrique Cardoso, na Solenidade de Formatura dos Alunos do Instituto Rio Branco," Palácio Itamaraty, May 18, 2000, http://www.mre.gov.br/portugues/politica_externa/discursos/discurso_detalhe3.asp?ID_DISCURSO =1206; my italics.

3. I use the term myth to mean not necessarily a falsification of reality, but principally "a process of continual work on a basic narrative pattern that changes according to the circumstances." For a more elaborate definition, see Chiara Bottici and Benoît Challand, "Rethinking Political Myth: The Clash of Civilizations as a Self-Fulfilling Prophecy," *European Journal of Social Theory* 9:3 (2006), pp. 315-321.

it seems quite safe to assert that the different components of this imaginary compendium, which are mutually reinforcing, join together to characterize Brazil as a peaceful nation.[4]

This chapter attempts to show how one type of public discussion, which has been examined throughout the work, namely the political and diplomatic discourse about Brazil's relations with its Spanish-speaking neighbors, contributed to the construction of the image of Brazil as a cordial and peace-loving nation, and helped to consolidate this as a central component of the country's national and international identity. As will be demonstrated, it is the intra–Latin American axis of the Brazilian elites' self-definition process that accounts for Cardoso and Lafer's many significant "no's." These are "no's" that express, and this is the main point to be stressed, Brazil's ultimate rebirth as an "island" in the 1900s while maintaining the bridges that had been built during the previous three decades. These are "no's" that manifest a regained insular and secure identity that, unlike in the imperial past, expresses the struggle for recognition and acceptance by the Spanish American Other.[5]

4. On the myth of racial democracy, see Viotti da Costa, *The Brazilian Empire*, chap. 9; Jorge Reid Andrews, *Blacks and Whites in São Paulo, Brazil, 1888-1998* (Madison: University of Wisconsin Press, 1991) pp. 7-10, 129-134. About representations of Brazilian slavery as lenient, consult, Skidmore, *Black into White, pp.* 70-77; Suely Robles Reis de Queiroz, "Brandura da escravidão brasileira: Mito ou realidade?" *Revista de História*, 52:103 (1975), pp. 443-447; Brookshaw, *Race and Color*, p. 54. H. H. Keith wrote about "The Nonviolent Tradition in Brazilian History: A Myth in Need of Explosion?" in Keith and S. F. Edwards, eds., *Conflict and Continuity in Brazilian Society* (Columbia: University of South Carolina Press, 1969), p. 231. About the notion of cordiality, see Octavio Ianni, "Tipos e mitos do pensamento brasileiro," *Revista Brasileira de Sciências Sociais* 17:49 (June 2002), p. 6; Kelly Cristiane da Silva, "A nação cordial: Uma análise dos rituais e das ideologias oficiais de 'comemoração dos 500 anos do Brasil,'" *Revista Brasileira de Sciências Sociais* 18:51 (Feb. 2003), pp. 141-159; José Murilo de Carvalho, "Dreams Come Untrue," *Dadealus* 129:2 (Spring 2000), pp. 72, 75-76; Sommer, *Foundational Fictions*, p. 153.

5. On the relationship between "the struggle for recognition" and formation of personal and collective identities, see Larraín, *Identity and Modernity in Latin America*, pp. 28-29.

"The God Terminus of Our National Integrity": Rio Branco as a National Symbol

The final stage in the evolution of Brazilian elite views of Spanish America and of their own reality between 1888 and 1912 was strongly related, as suggested by the opening quotations, to the diplomatic undertakings and public image of the Baron of Rio Branco; "The God Terminus of our national integrity," in Rui Barbosa praising words.[6] While Rio Branco's diplomatic-identitarian path converged at many points with those of Oliveira Lima and Joaquim Nabuco, it was ultimately distinct. Whereas Lima singled out Argentina as a model of strength and prosperity, and Nabuco exalted the role of the United States, Rio Branco did not go that far in either direction. If the first two clearly associated themselves and their country with Latin America or America, Rio Branco emphasized and represented Brazil's singularity in the continent. And while the hemispheric projects of his opinionated subordinates entailed the construction of supranational identities, Rio Branco's grand project, of which these were a part, ultimately fashioned a uniquely Brazilian one. Lima's and Nabuco's contrasting Pan-Americanisms represented a high point in the continentalization of Brazil's national identity following the collapse of its double slaveholding and imperial wall. It fell to Rio Branco to redraw the nation's real and imagined boundaries and thus become a living symbol of a new-old insular Brazil.

That Rio Branco became a national hero and icon during the last phase of his long diplomatic career, and continues to be regarded as such, is commonplace in Brazilian lore (the two speeches cited above are again a good illustration). While José Murilo de Carvalho asserts that Brazil has always had a modest pantheon and that the only Brazilian figure approaching the status of national hero is Tiradentes,[7] other scholars readily confer this distinction on the Baron. According to E. Bradford Burns, who has meticulously investigated the life and times of the foreign minister, "[Rio Branco's] diplomatic victories had raised him to the rank of a national hero [...], throughout his long term in office the chancellor was extremely popular with the

6. Rui Barbosa, "Rio Branco," *Revista Americana* 4:4 (April 1913), p. 3.
7. Carvalho, "Dreams Come Untrue," pp. 68-70.

Brazilian people." Burns goes on to cite several contemporary observers who described Rio Branco as being generally and enormously admired, and claims that these personal opinions "were representative of the attitude of *the entire nation.*"[8] While contradicting the notion of an almost empty national pantheon, this statement may indeed seem too sweeping. But even if public opinion had not been as unanimous as Burns would have us believe, the fact still remains that in turn-of-the-century Rio de Janeiro and beyond, Rio Branco and his foreign policy were widely and repeatedly represented as embodying the aspirations of the Brazilian nation and its ideal character.

As João Felipe Gonçalves has observed in his study of the funeral of Rui Barbosa and of other public figures during the Old Republic, that period witnessed a general trend of hero-making through various kinds of public rituals.[9] The men and events we have discussed so far played leading roles in this drama. President Roca's visit to Rio de Janeiro and the Third Pan-American Conference can be added to the list of what Gonçalves describes as spectacles by the elite for the people. For, although the 1899 presidential visit and the 1906 international conference were primarily intended for the eyes and minds of foreigners, they also constituted an effort to buttress the image of the republican regime and elevate the status of certain Brazilian figures within the local context.[10] The same is true with respect to the public displays and discourse involving Rio Branco, as we are about to see. The head of Itamaraty was probably the most celebrated figure among the different candidates for the Brazilian pantheon during the 1900s. And no one, with the possible exception of Rui Barbosa, had become so identified with the nation itself, through a process of construction that was at once planned and spontaneous.[11]

8. Burns, *The Unwritten Alliance*, pp. 55-56; my italics.

9. João Felipe Gonçalves, "Enterrando Rui Barbosa: Um estudo de caso da construção fúnebre de heróis nacionais na Primeira República," *Estudos Históricos* 14:25 (2000), pp. 148-157.

10. According to one historian, for example, Rio Branco's approach toward the 1906 conference was rather cold because it put him in the shadow of Joaquim Nabuco. Afonso Arinos de Melo Franco, *Rodrigues Alves: Apogeu e declineo de presidencialismo*, 2 vols. (Rio de Janeiro: José Olympio, 1973), vol. 1, p. 293.

11. Gonçalves, "Enterrando Rui Barbosa," pp. 148-153; Herman Lima, *História da caricatura no Brazil*, 3 vols. (Rio de Janeiro: José Olympio, 1963), vol. 1, pp. 293-

And yet, Rio Branco's name rarely appears in historical accounts of Brazil's national identity. If at all, he is mentioned because of his efforts to conceal the real Brazil by "selling" it as a white, ordered, and progressive nation–"selling" it to "the civilized world," that is, to Europe and the United States. The historiographical focus remains largely there.[12] It is usually forgotten that much of the propaganda and of the general discourse of international relations that emanated from Itamaraty itself and affiliated sources during Rio Branco's tenure was a product of interaction along the Luso–Hispano-American axis, and destined for consumption in the neighboring countries. The same applies to the public discussion that Rio Branco and his actions elicited both within and outside Brazil. This animated and extensive discussion sprang from within the context of Brazil's relations with Spanish America, functioning as a reproduction site of national and international images and myths. The construction of Rio Branco as a national symbol was an integral part of this process, the origins of which stretch back to the imperial period.

It should be remembered that for Rio Branco and his generation, the Paraguayan War was a formative experience. Rio Branco in particular had been totally and passionately immersed in it, as well as in other violent encounters between Portuguese- and Spanish-speaking neighbors in the region. His emotional and intellectual involvement in these events had much to do with his father's career as a leading imperial statesman, closely connected to Platine affairs. The son's interest in Brazil's military history, and his preoccupation with the country's standing vis-à-vis the other side–first and foremost Argentina–was almost an obsession, and manifested itself in his journalistic and historical writings since the age of sixteen. Thus, when the Baron stepped into office, he brought with him many personal and collective memories. He was identified and identified himself as the Viscount of Rio Branco's son, and through the father's image,

307, esp. 302. "Not only the triumphs he personified but also his contribution to the consolidation of the republican regime turned Rio Branco into the great statesman and hero of the Old Republic. A figure of extraordinary popularity." Danese, *Diplomacia presidencial,* p. 256.

12. Freyre, *Order and Progress*, pp. 202-203, 255, 339; Skidmore, *Black into White*, pp. 133-136; Carvalho, "The Force of Tradition," p. 158;

also with Brazil's mixed regional legacy of aggression and conciliatory diplomacy, glory and humiliation.[13]

That being said, the personal motivations of the second Rio Branco will remain outside the scope of this study. Instead, the focus will be on the construction of his public image. A critical survey of his spoken, written, and illustrated road to becoming a symbol of a powerful yet peace-loving Brazil will serve to elucidate the points just mentioned, as well as to bring together some of the issues raised in the previous chapters. This short journey, which will bring this work to a close, begins in 1895.

Rio Branco and "the First Great Conquest of *Paz e Concórdia*"

After the fiasco of 1890, Brazil and Argentina submitted the Missões controversy to U.S. arbitration, in accord with an older agreement signed in the last days of the Empire. In 1893, the Baron of Rio Branco was recalled from his relatively minor diplomatic post in Paris to replace Brazil's original representative for the case, who had died. Two years later Brazil was declared the winner. The award gave it the entire disputed territory. Back home, the news had a strong impact. Public buildings throughout the country were adorned with flags and illuminated at night. In towns such as Ouro Preto and Natal, work in government offices was suspended and bands marched through the streets; São Paulo's *fina flor* celebrated with a ball where money was raised to purchase an award for the new hero, while in Rio de Janeiro the public was invited to attend a demonstration in the Largo de São Francisco.[14]

"People of all classes"–to use the term of the contemporary press–came, and according to one journal, spirits were so high that even José Bonifácio's statue joined the party.[15] Speeches were also

13. Lidia Besouchet, *Rio-Branco e as relações entre o Brasil e a República Argentina* (Rio de Janeiro: Ministério das Relações Extereriores, 1949), p. 8, passim; Raul do Rio Branco, *Reminiscencias do Barão do Rio Branco* (Rio de Janeiro: José Olympio, 1942), pp. 33-43; Burns, *The Unwritten Alliance*, pp. 21-28, 181-190.

14. *Gazeta de Noticias*, various news items, Feb. 10 and 11, 1895.

15. Caption of the front cover illustration, *Don Quixote*, 1:4 (Feb. 16, 1895).

given. Then a telegram addressed to Rio Branco was read, in which the organizers thanked him in the name of the entire nation, whose unanimous sentiments they aspired to express, adding that he also deserved the gratitude of *republican America*, since–according to them–what had just happened was a "victory of peace and justice" that both Brazil and Argentina celebrated. At this point, the crowd marched toward the Presidential Palace. The general tone of the day was quite uniform, from the respected *Jornal do Comércio*, whose editorial stated that "the Brazilian nation could be proud of this victory, which, being nonviolent, was even more glorious,"[16] to the more popular *Gazeta de Notícias*, which dubbed the outcome of the arbitration "the first great conquest of American politics, the positive politics of *paz e concórdia*, the only one which is appropriate for these new nations, which are the great nations of the future."[17]

A comparison of the reactions to the two different solutions of the Missões controversy–the hostile reception that greeted the 1890 agreement and the 1895 celebrations–is enlightening. Although the pacifying Americanist discourse, strongly present in both instances, had annoyed some monarchists, it had not been the major cause of the resistance to Bocaiuva's move in 1890. This can be partially concluded from an official explanation, designed to quell criticism, published by the regime about a month after the signing of the Montevideo agreement. The document emphasized that nothing was final, since the approval of the Congress was still pending, but it also stated that whatever the outcome, the case would serve as a starting point for an "ample American policy of *paz e concórdia*."[18] The principal reason for Bocaiuva's failure, then, lay somewhere else: in the sense of loss, both of territory and of honor. It was precisely in preventing this loss, in securing victory over Brazil's traditional rival through peaceful means, which the secret of the construction of Rio Branco as a national symbol resided. The appeal of this formula, combining a

16. *Gazeta de Noticias*, "A questão das Missões," p. 1, Feb. 8, 1895;

17. *Jornal do Commercio*, "A questão das Missões," p. 1, Feb. 8, 1895.

18. Published in *Diário Oficial*, Feb. 12, 1890, cited in Nicélio César Tonelli, "De rivais a aliados: A Argentina e o Brasil na Década de 1890," in Eliane Garcindo Dayrell and Zilda Márcia Gricoli Iokoi, eds., *América Latina contemporânea: Desafios e perspectivas* (Rio de Janeiro/São Paulo: Expressão e Cultura/Edusp, 1996), p. 140.

nationalist sense of strength and pride with a message of peace, will be further explained through the story of one painting.

Rio Branco Steps into *Paz e Concórdia* and Both Enter the Itamaraty

In April 1904, Pedro Américo's imposing canvas *Paz e Concórdia* (300 x 431 cm) was hung in the main reception hall of the Itamaraty Palace in Rio de Janeiro, then the residence of the Ministry of Foreign Affairs [Figure 5.1].[19] In this way the allegorical work, which celebrated the place of the young Brazilian republic in America and in the civilized world, and conveyed a message of international peace, became part of the official foreign policy discourse.[20] The first arrangements for purchasing the painting were made by Rio Branco in October 1903. During this same month, Rio de Janeiro's *Jornal do Comércio* published an article that described and interpreted Pedro Américo's work in detail:

> At the entrance to the temple of Pax e Concórdia, there is a reproduction of the painting of Ipiranga [describing the declaration of Brazilian independence in 1822]. In front of the temple, two processions, one representing ancient society and the other modern society, approach each other. Also in front stand two statues, one of Columbus holding an anchor in his right hand and a globe in his left hand, and, on the other side, a statue of Cabral raising the cross of the sword, the symbol of conquest and domination. Below, at the bottom of the steps leading to the temple, a chorus of vestal virgins sings a hymn to peace, while the Brazilian nation, inspired by the two traditions–the Christian and the pagan–and crowned by Glory, follows the path illuminated by civilization on the way to receiving homage from the principal nations of the world led by the United States, it being the most enlightened or strongest

19. Liana Rosemberg, "Da imagem retórica: A questão da visualidade na pintura de Pedro Américo no Brasil oitocentista" (Ph.D. diss., University of São Paulo, 1999), p. 138.

20. And it has actually remained so. See the direct reference to this painting and the insertion of Rio Branco's figure into it in Celso Lafer, "Mudanças na Continuidade," *Gazeta Mercantil*, Aug. 31, 2001, http://ftp.unb.br/pub/UNB/ipr/rel/discmin/2001/ 3444.pdf

FIGURE 5.1
Pedro Américo, *Paz e Concórdia,* 1902.
Museu Histórico e Diplomático do Itamaraty, Rio de Janeiro.

> nation in the American continent. Two youths offer these nations sparkling wine and fruit, while History records a memorable date, and the Angel of Evil, lying on the ground, breaks the sword rendered useless by the triumph of Justice.[21]

In the right-hand corner of the painting [Figure 5.2] Rio Branco himself appears, dressed in a toga and bearing the Cross of the Order of Christ–a symbol of the Portuguese colonization project–around his neck;[22] in his hand he carries a volume with the word *Lex* inscribed on it. The middleman who brokered the deal between the foreign minister and the painter instructed the latter to portray the

21. Cited in J. M. Cardoso de Oliveira, *Pedro Américo: Sua vida e suas obras*, special revised and enlarged ed. (Rio de Janeiro: Imprensa Nacional, 1943), p. 186.

22. The identification of this object is drawn from Rubens Ricupero, *José Maria da Silva Paranhos, Barão do Rio Branco: Uma biografia fotográfica, 1845-1995*, iconography and captions by João Hermes Pereira de Araujo (Brasília: Fundação Alexandre de Gusmão, 1995), n.pag.

FIGURE 5.2
A detail from *Paz e Concórdia.* Rio Branco appears in the right corner.

Baron in consonance with his actual physical appearance: imposing and serene.[23] In a sense, these details turn Rio Branco's image in the foreground into a condensed version of the larger composition, embodying the overall message of nationalism and universalism, force and lawfulness.

What led Rio Branco to purchase this particular work and put it on display in the Itamaraty Palace? Why was he portrayed in this way, and to whom were the imbedded messages addressed? One clue might be found in the fact that at the time, continuous negotiations with Bolivia over the disputed Amazonian territory of Acre were nearing their conclusion. Violence had erupted in that area in 1899, when the predominantly Brazilian population rebelled against the Bolivian government, and declared independence. Rio Branco entered office when the crisis reached its peak. The political leadership and the press in both countries spoke the language of nationalism, and patriotic passions ran high. There were popular demonstrations calling for violent action, and a full-scale confrontation seemed imminent. Relying on Brazil's stronger presence in the region and military might, the Baron played a major role in avoiding a full-scale war, bringing the Bolivians to the negotiation table and securing a huge territorial gain of approximately 73,000 square miles for his country.[24] According to the Treaty of Petrópolis, signed on November 17, 1903, Bolivia received two million pounds sterling in return, as well as a small strip of land that gave it access to one of the tributaries of the Amazon and thus to the Atlantic, a Brazilian promise to build a railway that would bypass the rapids that hindered navigation in that waterway, and perpetual rights to free transit through Brazilian territory.

The two houses of the Brazilian Congress approved the treaty by a wide margin, but only after an extensive and heated debate in the

23. Rosemberg, "Da imagem retórica," p. 137.

24. Burns, *The Unwritten Alliance*, p. 46. According to a later detailed study of this case, it was President Rodrigues Alves who played the key role on the Brazilian side. See Charles E. Stokes, "The Acre Revolutions, 1899-1903: A Study in Brazilian Expansionism," (Ph.D diss., Tulane University, 1974), chap. 13, esp., pp. 414-418. Notwithstanding, Moniz Bandeira, in what is probably the most recent treatment of the issue, reasserts Rio Branco's centrality in *Brasil, Argentina e Estados Unidos*, chap. 2, esp., p. 77. For an account of the conflict and its resolution, see these three works and Lins, *Rio Branco*, pp. 270-301.

chambers and in the press. Central political leaders, among them Rui Barbosa, who had initially participated in the negotiations with Bolivia, objected to the settlement for being too generous. Rio Branco himself became a target of harshly critical newspaper articles and cartoons [Figure 5.3], accusing him of violating the territorial integrity of the nation. But there were other influential voices that criticized the treaty for opposite reasons. Barbosa Lima, the main opponent of the treaty in the lower house, accused Rio Branco of having "bellicose instincts" and of belonging to the same school as the French statesman Jules Ferry, who had been responsible for imperialist adventures in Asia and Africa. Senator Lauro Sodré, for his part, called Rio Branco's policy "imperialistic" and asserted that Brazil had begun a period of conquests following in the footsteps of France, England and the United States: "This last-minute imperialism makes Brazil look ridiculous," he stated.[25]

Indeed, Brazil's incorporation of the then rubber-rich Amazonian territory had imperialistic overtones that resuscitated traditional Spanish American allegations of Luso-American expansionism dating back to the colonial period. These were not limited to Bolivia, but could be heard from other neighbors as well. Newspapers in Buenos Aires and Rio de Janeiro cited each other and exchanged barbs over the matter [Figure 5.4]. For example, in early 1903, *Jornal do Brasil* reproduced *El Diario's* depiction of what was taking place in Brazil as an "epileptic bellicose outburst." The Argentine paper reportedly described this combative spirit as especially lamentable and unjustified, since it was directed at weak and strangled Bolivia.[26]

Rio Branco was well aware of this criticism. He did not need to rely only on reports in Brazilian newspapers. The Brazilian legation

25. Quoted in Leandro Tocantins, *Formação histórica do Acre*, 3 vols. (Rio de Janeiro: Conquista, 1961), vol. 3, pp. 662, 664. About the debates surrounding the treaty, see also ibid., vol. 3, chap. 60; Lins, *Rio Branco*, pp. 293-301; Viana Filho, *A vida do Barão*, pp. 386-392; Stokes, "The Acre Revolutions," p. 444; Rodrigo M. F. de Andrade, *Rio-Branco e Gastão da Cunha* (Rio de Janeiro: Ministério das Relações Exteriores, Instituto Rio-Branco, 1953), pp. 121-190.

26. See reviews of the Argentine press in reports from Buenos Aires, *Jornal do Brasil*, Jan. 30 and 31, 1903; Burns, *The Unwritten Alliance*, pp. 55, 183; Stokes, "The Acre Revolutions," p. 443; Cervo and Bueno, *História da política exterior*, pp. 176-177. About the deep history of these accusations, see Burns, *The Unwritten Alliance*, pp. 204-205; and McCann, "The Brazilian General Staff," pp. 300-301.

FIGURE 5.3

"In the Butcher Shop." This cartoon, published shortly before the signing of the Treaty of Petrópolis, portrays Rio Branco as a butcher cutting pieces of Brazil's body (i.e., territory) in order to hand them over to Bolivia. It illustrates the harsh public criticism that foreign policymakers such as Quintino Bocaiuva and Rio Branco had to contend with and take into account in their dealings with Spanish America. Relationships with the neighboring countries were a touchy issue, easily translated into feelings of hurt pride and accusations of treason. Cover of *A Avenida*, Oct. 31, 1903.

FIGURE 5.4
"Bad Neighborliness." Argentine newspapers attack Brazil's conduct during the Acre affair. *O Malho*, Feb. 7, 1903. Courtesy of Arquivo da Casa de Rui Barbosa.

in Buenos Aires furnished him with newspaper clips and summaries of the coverage of the Acre conflict in the Argentine press.[27] Especially interesting in this regard is a handwritten copy, found in his personal archive, of an article published in the Argentine *Revista de*

27. Brazilian Minister, Buenos Aires, to Minister of Foreign Relations, Rio de Janeiro, 16 reservado, Aug. 17, 1903, AHI; Minister of Foreign Relations, Rio de Janeiro, to Brazilian Minister, Buenos Aires, 2/3 reservado, Oct. 31, 1903, AHI.

Derecho, Historia y Letras.[28] The article alluded to the United States' takeover of Cuba and awoken lust for expansion: "This illness now seems to be spreading to the south, to judge by the Acre affair; that is, in light of the blatant and overtly frank policy, without scruples or considerations, adopted by the Brazilian Chancellor, the Baron of Rio Branco [...] This distinguished personage, usually perceived as an able statesman and an honest diplomat, seems to have broken away from the old chivalrous tradition [...] that characterized almost all the foreign ministers of his country, who, it is true, always sought to satisfy the territorial greed they inherited from their Portuguese ancestors through advantageous pacts and treaties, but they at least were determined to fulfill or honor them once these were achieved, in accordance with Dom Pedro's policy."[29]

Evidently, the acquisition of the Acre gave birth to what Alvaro Lins, author of the semi-official and probably most widely cited biography of the Baron, has dubbed "the *legend* of Rio Branco's Imperialism."[30] Other students of Brazilian foreign policy would be more hesitant to employ the term "legend" in this regard. North American historian E. Bradford Burns, for example, whose *The Unwritten Alliance* is generally favorable to Brazil and tends to celebrate Rio Branco's peaceful conduct in South America, compared the Acre story to events in Texas some 75 years earlier, when United States–backed settlers won independence from Mexico through armed struggle.[31] A more recent study by a Brazilian scholar acknowledges, along the same lines, that Brazil's behavior in South America took a turn that in some way signified a reappearance of the foreign policy of the monarchy, "dressed in new clothes."[32]

28. The editor of this respected journal was former foreign minister Estanislao Zeballos (1889-90, 1891-92), who had signed the 1890 agreement with Quintino Bocaiuva and lost, five years later, to Rio Branco in the arbitration over Missões.

29. "Brasil-Bolivia," 858/3/8, Arquivo Particular do Barão do Rio Branco, Itamaraty [Henceforth ARB-I].

30. Lins, *Rio Branco*, p. 290; my italics. This could be the reason why Charles Stokes, who wished to investigate the matter further, was denied access to the Itamaraty archives by Ambassador Miguel Rio Branco, the Baron's grandson ("The Acre Revolutions," p. 427n). Brazil had been and remains, as we have seen at the beginning of this chapter, sensitive to accusations of aggressiveness toward its neighbors.

31. Burns, *The Unwritten Alliance*, p. 43.

32. Cervo and Bueno, *História da política exterior*, p. 176.

As a matter of fact, the foreign minister himself acknowledged that Brazilian foreign policy had entered a new phase, in an official report that provided the rationale for the Petrópolis agreement. In this document, submitted to the president of the republic before the treaty's ratification, Rio Branco evoked his two previous diplomatic achievements, the 1895 award in the Missões arbitration case with Argentina and the 1900 triumph in a second international arbitration over a disputed area in the northern border with French Guiana. In these two instances, stated the Baron, Brazil had merely secured possession of territories that had always belonged to it, "real territorial expansion is only taking place now."[33]

Yet, such overtly imperialist language quickly gave place, once the Treaty of Petrópolis was ratified, to a discourse of what can be termed "patriotic pacifism." In late February 1904, a popular demonstration in Rio Branco's honor took place at the Itamaraty Palace. Those among the crowd who had managed to make their way inside the building heard a flowery speech by Brazil's leading poet, Olavo Bilac. Bilac eulogized the foreign minister for placing the national good above personal interest, saving once again the territorial integrity of the nation and bringing the Brazilian inhabitants of the Acre into the homeland. And all that through peaceful measures. Nonviolence loomed large in the poet's rhetoric. With his "love of peace," Rio Branco exercised tolerance instead of force, thus avoiding massacres and bloodshed.[34]

A blend of patriotic notions and peaceful messages also marked Rio Branco's own public address at the occasion. He opened his speech with a reference to the strong criticism he had suffered and expressed his gratitude for the words of support he had received from "across the country." These had helped him, he said, to continue serving the *Pátria*, indifferent to internal political cleavages, and to keep calm in the face of danger. Only then, after identifying himself with the national interest and constructing a serene but powerful self-

33. Rio Branco, *Obras Completas do Barão do Rio Branco*, 9 vols. (Rio de Janeiro: Ministério das Relações Exteriores, 1945-1948), vol. 5, *Questões de limites. Exposições de motives*, pp. 26-30.

34. Published in *Jornal do Commercio*, Feb. 21, 1904, cited in Tocantins, *Formação histórica do Acre*, vol. 3, p. 667.

image, did he move on to discuss the international matter and its allegedly nonviolent nature. Disagreeing only on this point with Bilac, who sealed his speech with an impassioned reference to Rio Branco's "victorious intelligence," the foreign minister lowered the tone negating any suggestion of victory. "The occasion that you passionately and patriotically celebrate today," Rio Branco told his audience–and notice here the negation reminiscent of those we encountered at the beginning of the chapter–"was *not* and can*not* be called a victory of Brazilian diplomacy. In the pact we signed with Bolivia, there were *neither* winners *nor* losers." He spoke about conciliating the interests of two friendly nations, "two sister republics," proclaiming continuity between his conduct and earlier policies from the time of the Empire. Bolivia obtained a maritime outlet to the Atlantic Ocean, so essential to its economy, in agreement with the liberal policy promoted by some of the Empire's most notable statesmen. Brazil, for its part, "redeemed through amicable transaction the immensely vast territories it had generously ceded" decades before, when circumstances were different, thus expanding its borders and bringing back home thousands of its sons. "I am very pleased," concluded Rio Branco, "to have been able to collaborate in this endeavor of peace and fraternity."[35]

In Rio Branco's speech, national politics met international relations. Sentiments and perceptions from both spheres intersected, responding to foreign and domestic needs alike. It was a masterful synthesis of the opposing kinds of criticism that he and his policy had endured and which, in turn, reflected the contradictory trends of the age of empire, already described in detail in the previous chapter. The combination of nationalism and internationalism, expansionism and lawfulness, strength and cordiality, triumphalism and generosity, both in action and text, proved to be a winning proposition. And indeed, Rio Branco's image as the embodiment of this formula, which had begun to appear in the Rio de Janeiro press throughout the different stages of the Acre affair [Figures 5.5, 5.6.], would dominate the Brazilian public discussion in the following years.

35. Rio Branco, *Obras Completas*, vol. 9, *Discursos*, pp. 67-68. It is important to note that the text of the speech was also published in *Jornal do Commercio*, Nov. 11, 1906.

Photographias, vistas instantaneas, desenhos e caricaturas

REVISTA DA SEMANA

Edição semanal illustrada do JORNAL DO BRASIL

Redactor-gerente, Dr. CANDIDO MENDES — Redactor-chefe, Dr. FERNANDO MENDES DE ALMEIDA — Director-technico, GASPAR DE SOUZA

Anno IV — N. 142 | DOMINGO, 1 DE FEVEREIRO | Numero : 300 réis

FIGURE 5.5

Rio Branco balances between law and force.

"While in the scales of my conscience law weighs more than force, fearless of destiny's fists, I'll prove to the entire world that if you search for Brazil you're bound to find it." The caption and the image together place law above violence while simultaneously conveying military strength–symbolized by the canon–and patriotic readiness to use it. Patriotism and pacifism are intimately connected in the figure of Rio Branco who provides the balance between them. *Revista da Semana*, Feb. 1, 1903. Courtesy of Arquivo da Casa de Rui Barbosa.

FIGURE 5.6

"The Baron of Rio Branco and the Acre." Battleships are already en route to the Acre; the minister of war prepares and tests his artillery; the minister of navy inspects and prepares his ships; the reporters work unceasingly. They see everything, know everything, and report everything; soldiers are marching from every corner; ... Ouvidor street fills with demonstrators who are waving flags and calling for battle; [...] But all of a sudden a telegram arrives from Bolivia, accepting Rio Branco's proposals. A victory for the Baron and for all of us." Notice that Rio Branco, to whom the illustration is dedicated, appears at the center of the bellicose atmosphere, but at the same time–serene in civilian attire–seems somehow above or outside it. *Don Quixote*, Feb. 14, 1903. Courtesy of Arquivo da Casa de Rui Barbosa.

To be sure, Rio Branco himself had a hand in his construction as national symbol. This is widely documented, even in the most favorable studies about him. Financial resources and a strong network of patronage, as seen in the previous chapter, enabled him to influence public discussion within Brazil and without. One of the critics of the deal that the Baron had brokered with Bolivia confided to Joaquim Nabuco, several days after the aforementioned demonstration at the Itamaraty, that the foreign minister "had bought the entire press," with the exception of two opposition newspapers.[36] The first issue of the stylish *Renascença* magazine, which appeared just then, might be a case in point. It carried Rio Branco's photo on the front cover and devoted the opening article to him. The text repeated almost verbatim the main points and terminology of the two speeches by Bilac and Rio Branco: "[Thanks to the] immediate and peaceful solution that he has managed to find to the grave question of the Acre–a constant threat of South American conflagration–Rio Branco's name is in the mouths and hearts of everybody [...] At this moment, after the energetic and patriotic action of this great citizen has endowed the nation with a vast and rich territory, no other figure merits so much esteem and gratitude as this illustrious Brazilian."[37] And so the author continued with his flattery.

These words return us to *Paz e Concórdia* and its very similar messages. The motives behind the purchase of Pedro Américo's work for exhibition in the Itamaraty Palace, and the specific way in which Rio Branco was portrayed in it, should have become clear by now. The close match between the visual and the textual components of the discourse that came out of Itamaraty was not incidental. It was all part of a well-orchestrated propaganda campaign and a conscious exercise in personal and international image-building. The emphasis on Rio Branco's and Brazil's peaceful and law-abiding conduct was strongly linked to the aforementioned turn in foreign policy, represented by the acquisition of the Acre. Brazil, which in 1899 was still basically responding to Argentine initiatives in the diplomatic field, now began to promote its own regional plan. Yet, notwithstanding

36. Barão de Jaceguay to Joaquim Nabuco, Feb. 29, 1904, cited in Viana Filho, *A vida do Barão*, p. 387.

37. João de Barro, "Chronica," *Renascença*, 1:1 (March 1904), p. 3.

the renewed expansionist thrust and the practical steps taken to achieve a leading role in the southern part of the continent, the ruling class of the oligarchic republic was interested in maintaining stability in the region. At that time of authoritarian modernization, let us recall, order was widely perceived as a prerequisite for progress. This is where the discourse of patriotic pacifism came in. It was directed mainly toward Argentina. War with that powerful and rapidly developing rival, which the Brazilian elite, and Rio Branco in particular, generally viewed with a mixture of admiration and awe, was to be avoided. Despite, or maybe because of, his clear superiority-inferiority complex vis-à-vis the *porteños* and his basic suspicions of their intentions, the Baron wanted to appear strong before these Spanish-speaking neighbors, but did not want to alienate them. In this sense, *Paz y Concórdia* served him well, but not well enough.

The United States had a very strong presence in this painting, while Spanish America had none. This was very likely the reason why Benjamin Parlagreco's large canvas commemorating President Roca's historic visit to Rio de Janeiro in 1899 was also put on display at the Itamaraty Palace, in a hall not far from *Paz e Concórdia* [Figures 5.7 and 5.8]. While the latter emphasized Brazil-U.S. rapprochement, the former painting highlighted, as already noted, Brazil's friendly relations with Argentina. In this way, the two works of art balanced and complemented each other, constituting a perfect representation of Rio Branco's maneuver between North and South. When viewed together, these works conveyed in color the same composite message, combining elements from Olivera Lima's Latin Americanism and Joaquim Nabuco's North Americanism, which the foreign minister expressed in words in his previously cited interview to *La Nación* during the Third Pan-American Conference. And let us remember how, following the conversation, he himself personally presented the two paintings to the Argentine correspondent.[38]

38. For further proof of Rio Branco's conscious coupling of the two paintings, see a note in his handwriting, found among his personal papers, listing them among other paintings that were on display at the Itamaraty Palace during his years in office. ARB-I 880/2/7

FIGURES 5.7 AND 5.8
Paz e Concórdia and *Visita do General Roca* on display at the Itamaraty Palace during Rio Branco's years in office. From Marie Robinson Wright, *The New Brazil, its Resources and Attractions* (Philadelphia: G. Barrie & Sons, 1907). Courtesy of Ibero-Amerikanisches Institut, Berlin.

The Discursive Origins of Rio Branco's Patriotic Pacifism

Yet, with all of this in mind, calculated interests alone cannot account for the message of patriotic pacifism that accompanied Rio Branco's policy. Nor can the massive amount of propaganda that emanated from Itamaraty during his years in office fully explain the wide reception of his image–acknowledged posthumously even by his great Argentine rival, Estanislao Zeballos–as supreme arbiter of the national interest and a messenger of continental peace, both within and outside Brazil [Figure 5.9].[39] The successful construction of Rio Branco as a symbol of a vigorous but essentially cordial Brazil also derived from continuities–conscious and unconscious–in both the diplomatic and the discursive realms.

The Baron's use of Parlagreco's work, which had been painted before he assumed office, shows that neither his policy nor the accompanying discourse were *completely* new. This is also proved by the existence of an earlier and slightly different version of *Paz e Concórdia* published in 1900 in the Argentine magazine *Caras Caretas* [Figure 5.10], when President Campos Sales returned Roca's visit to Rio de Janeiro and traveled to Buenos Aires. In that earlier version, Rio Branco does not appear in the picture, and the colors of the U.S. flag are also missing. Otherwise, the details and overall impression remain almost exactly the same. It is significant that both paintings were first woven into the Brazilian foreign policy discourse within the context of Brazilian-Argentine rapprochement and the convergence of elite ideals and values in 1899/1900. This fact indicates to what extent Rio Branco's more assertive diplomacy and its visual representation had assimilated already existing notions of national strength and international order and progress.

39. See, for example, U.S. Minister Nicolay A. Grevstad, Montevideo, to Secretary of State, Washington, no. 108, Feb. 13, 1912, in U.S., Department of State, *Records of the Department of State Relating to Political Relations Between Brazil and Other States, 1910-1929*, (Washington, DC: National Archives and Records Administration, 1969), Microfilm Copy M526; E. S. Zeballos, "Rio Branco," *Revista de Derecho, Historia y Letras* 14:41 (March 1912), p. 424; and various obituaries by both Brazilian and Spanish-American intellectuals in *Revista Americana* 4:4 (April 1913).

FIGURE 5.9
Rio Branco's image in Argentine eyes.
An imposing, resolute Rio Branco with the Brazilian flag in the background, in a cartoon published in the popular Argentine magazine *Caras y Caretas* on Aug. 25, 1906, in the context of the Pan-American Conference in Rio de Janeiro. It provides a good illustration–possibly cynical in this case–of the foreign minister's projected image in Spanish America. "His oratory destroys his rival and tears him apart," says the caption below, thus suggesting violence but transferring it from the physical to the symbolic realm.

FIGURE 5.10
Paz e Concórdia in the Argentine magazine *Caras y Caretas* (Oct. 27, 1900) during President Campos Sales's visit to Buenos Aires.

In fact, the genealogy of *Paz e Concórdia* leads us to an even earlier time, to the period when the first bridges between Brazil and Spanish America were erected. The origins of Pedro Américo's work stretch back to another painting of his–*Libertação dos escravos* (1889)–commissioned by the late imperial regime and designed to commemorate the abolition of slavery [Figure 5.11]. Some of the main elements of *Paz e Concórdia*, such as the angel of evil and the main feminine figure representing the nation, were already sketched here. Also connecting the two works is the overall triumphant spirit blending patriotism and internationalism. And, most importantly, from our perspective, both paintings convey a message of peace.

Libertação dos escravos highlighted the peaceful nature of Brazilian abolition, concealing the social unrest and slave resistance that had contributed to it.[40] This was in tandem with a general tendency to portray

40. Conrad, *The Destruction of Brazilian Slavery*, pp. 239-257.

FIGURE 5.11
Pedro Américo, *Libertação dos escravos*, 1889.
Acervo Artístico Cultural do Governo do Estado de São Paulo.

the event in such colors, also evident in the inflamed rhetoric that could be heard in Brazil and in neighboring Spanish American countries in the aftermath of May 13, 1888. For example, Argentina's former president, Bartolomé Mitre, in his already mentioned public address to the joyous crowds in Buenos Aires, said that "[while] all slave emancipations took place amid great crises or bloody struggles, Brazil, like England, did it peacefully." In order to press the point, Mitre turned to the past and quoted a U.S. diplomat who, some three decades earlier, had contrasted the quietly legislated Brazilian Law of the Free Womb with the bloody Civil War in the United States. The Brazilian minister in the Argentine capital replied in a similar vein, reminding the audience in his speech that the complicated feat of finally extinguishing slavery in his country had been achieved "without bloodshed or use of force."[41]

41. *La fiesta de la libertad*, pp. 24, 26. The Brazilian minister's emphasis on the peaceful nature of the event was highlighted in a report from Buenos Aires, *Jornal do Commercio*, May 18, 1888, p. 1.

Similar views were exchanged between Brazilians and Chileans during the visit of the Chilean battleship *Admiral Cochrane* to Rio de Janeiro in late 1889. Among the many festivities surrounding the visit was a special session of the Brazilian Historical and Geographical Institution in honor of the Spanish-speaking officers. Present were the imperial couple, as well as leading statesmen, intellectuals, military officers, foreign diplomats, and journalists. In his welcome address, the vice president of the institute recited a poem that had been written in Chile on the occasion of the abolition of slavery in Brazil and translated into Portuguese by Emperor Dom Pedro II himself. One stanza read:

Assim, á sombra de uma paz ditosa
Sem violencia que a ordem perturbasse
Sem que se ouvisse discordante nota
Ou fosse derramado sangue irmão,
Naquelle vasto e dilatado império
Do Brasil a augusta soberana
Com generosa e bemfazeja mão
Lavou do mundo de Colombo a mancha.

Thus, in the shadow of a blissful peace
Without violence to disturb order
Without a sound of discord
Or shedding of fraternal blood
In that vast extensive Empire
Of Brazil the august sovereign
With a generous and benevolent hand
Erased the stain from the world of Columbus.[42]

The Chilean visitors had barely left when the military coup brought down the monarchy. Somewhat paradoxically, this event also

42. Pantaleon Velis Silva, "A lamentação de um escravo," in Instituto Historico e Geographico Brasileiro, *Chile e Brazil; sessão solemne do Instituto Historico e Geographico Brazileiro em homenagem á nação chilena e consagrada á officialidade do encouraçado Almirante Cochrane* (Rio de Janeiro: Dias da Silva Junior, 1889), p. 37. For details about the meeting, see ibid., pp. 5-7. The poem was originally published in Brazil within a series of articles by the Chilean Justo Abel Rozales entitled "Brazileiros e Chilenos: Páginas de história antiga, media e contemporânea," published in Rio de Janeiro's *Jornal do Commercio* between June and July 1889.

served to buttress the narrative of Brazil's uniquely peaceful historical trajectory. As we have already seen in previous chapters, while opponents of the newly established regime emphasized its caudillistic qualities, its defenders–aided by the general apathy with which it was initially received–stressed time and again the nonviolent character of the transition, constructing what one modern historian has called "the myth of peace and consensus" regarding the birth of the republic.[43] A good example of this counterinterpretation is Oliveira Lima's article "Sept ans de République au Brésil," published in the Parisian *Nouvelle Revue* in 1896. Much like Pedro Américo's *Paz e Concórdia*, Lima's overview silenced the turmoil and civil war of the early 1890s, but through a different procedure. Instead of completely obliterating scenes of fratricide violence and dictatorial rule, it presented them as an abnormal hiatus between "forty years of internal peace" under the reign of Emperor Dom Pedro II and the recent signs of political and financial stabilization under the first civilian president of the republic, Prudente de Morais (1894-98). Here came the familiar comparison to Spanish America. Since independence, Brazil had enjoyed an exceptionally peaceful existence due to two distinguishing factors: the one historical, namely the institution of the monarchy; and the other psychological and unchanging, "the more tranquil nature of its [Brazil's] sons." According to Lima's explanation, "the bloodshed and the pointless barbaric killings" of the first years of the republic "nearly altered the pacific Brazilian character," but only nearly.[44]

Interestingly, this pro-republican narrative had actually coincided with monarchist interpretations of the coming of the republic as a rupture in Brazil's special historical path in Latin America, as well as a breakdown of the nation's identity. The tones were highly contradictory, of course, but underlying them were common perceptions. In other words, competing ideologically informed interpretations of

43. Maria de Lourdes Monaco Janotti, "O diálogo convergente: Políticos e historiadores no início da República," *Luso-Brazilian Review* 36:2 (1999), pp. 93-94.

44. Oliveira Lima, "Sete anos de república no Brazil (1889-1896)," trans. by Sheila Schvarzman, in Manoel Ernesto de Campos Porto, *Apontamentos para a história da República: Um registro centenário*, ed. by José Sebastião Witter (São Paulo: Editora Brasiliense, 1990), pp. 12, 39.

the transition from monarchy to republic at once drew on and fed an old, widely held image of Brazil as a distinctively peaceful nation. The story of *Paz e Concórdia* formed part of this broader process of self-identification. If *Libertação dos escravos* concealed slave insurgency and social unrest under the screen of state benevolence, its subsequent reworking, *Paz e Concórdia,* buried the violent chaos of the early republic beneath the façade of international harmony, its only remnant possibly being the vanquished Angel of Evil and its broken sword. The historical subject matter changed, as did some of the details, but the main pictorial narrative and the fundamental notion of peace (i.e., order) that brought together republicans and monarchists, Brazilians and Spanish Americans, remained the same.

The trajectory of *Paz e Concórdia* shows that the image of Brazil as a uniquely peaceful nation and its reproduction in Brazilian foreign policy discourse predated Rio Branco's years in office. This discourse, which turned at times into a Luso-Hispano-American dialogue, accompanied the growing interest of Latin America's modernizing oligarchies in *ordem e progresso*, *paz y administración*, both within and outside their national borders.[45] It was entwined with the upper classes' common fears of social unrest and external war that might hinder development and endanger their position, and of their beliefs concerning their own ability to check these dangers and ensure progress. In Brazil, high hopes followed the abolition of slavery, as portrayed in *Libertação dos escravos*. Not only slavery and its memory were to be erased, but also the old tradition of violent conflicts in the Plata region. Thus, Quintino Bocaiuva, in his capacity as first foreign minister of the republic, rushed to the Plata to sign the generous 1890 agreement with Argentina, too generous to be accepted. The ostensibly unpatriotic treaty was rejected, but already then, the words *paz e concórdia* could be heard against the background of the turmoil of the republic's first years. The new climate of political unrest and violence diminished the hopes for a better future of order and progress, but it did not

45. As José Luis Romero has noted, "Peace, to Roca" who coined the latter phrase in 1880, "meant not only the repression of all revolutionary attempts [...] but also the determined elimination of any fair and open struggle for power." *A History of Argentine Political Thought*, trans. by Thomas F. McGann (Stanford: Stanford University Press, 1968), p. 185.

silence the political and diplomatic discourse of peace, because the chaotic circumstances called for order, and *order* and *peace* were quite synonymous terms. In the midst of these difficult times came the victory over Argentina in the 1895 arbitration of Missões. Rio Branco, representing Brazil, secured for the nation the same territory that Bocaiuva had so easily given away, in what was described as the "first great conquest of *paz e concórdia*," the motto that harbored the core of his construction as a national symbol. Then, around the turn of the century, the country's internal economic and political situation stabilized and a bright American future again seemed possible. The painting *Paz e Concórdia* represented it well, and so did Rio Branco, who in 1902 stepped into the picture both as an icon and a leading player.

Recreating the Island, Maintaining the Bridges

After gaining the Acre from Bolivia in 1903, other bilateral agreements followed with the rest of Brazil's neighbors, bringing additional territorial gains and increasing the foreign minister's prestige. Rio Branco was becoming a national symbol in a process based mainly on a combination of expanding the nation's borders and, at the same time, defining them by legal means. Each component of this formula had its own unique value in the context of Brazilian attitudes toward its Spanish-speaking neighbors, as described throughout this study. Territorial gains and the ensuing sense of victory sat well with patriotic sentiments, ingrained animosities, and feelings of superiority or inferiority, whereas settling border disputes without war held the promise of Latin American order and progress. Rio Branco's diplomacy combined all these elements, reconciling conflicting interests of competition and cooperation, contradictory sentiments of rejection and identification, memories of a tumultuous past and dreams of a stable future.

By the time he died in 1912, Rio Branco was an integral part of Brazil's foreign policy discourse that had evolved out of the country's relationships with its South American neighbors and that assumed, under his leadership, a transnational character. Among those who mourned his loss was the main advocate of Latin American cultural unity José Enrique Rodó. The laudatory eulogy by the famous Uruguayan appeared the year after the Baron's death in a commemorative issue of the *Revista Americana*. Importantly, this journal had been launched by Itamaraty in 1909 with the declared mission of promoting intellectual exchange between the countries of the continent as a means to political rapprochement, featuring articles by Brazilian and Spanish American –but not U.S.–statesmen and writers in both Portuguese and Spanish.[46] Rodó's praise of the foreign minister echoed nearly verbatim all the main tropes of Brazilian diplomatic discourse. The greatness of the deceased lay "in his victorious patriotic conduct, expanding the boundaries of his people; in his unparalleled fortune, winning immense fertile lands," as well as in "the bloodless, purely intellectual manner in which he had achieved his triumphs." This is what made him "a great honor to American civilization."[47]

Indeed, the formula that Rio Branco created in his dealings with Spanish Americans–expansion and diplomatic settlement through negotiation–infused the Brazilian discourse of peace with patriotic vitality, at the same time that it reinforced a national and transnational myth. Consolidating Brazil's borders in this particular way led to the formation of a new–old national identity, that of a powerful, proud, and peaceful island, an island with bridges. This was a singular Luso-American identity that embodied the will to be recognized by neighboring Others instead of rejecting them out of hand; an identity that remains amply evident in the statements made by Fernando Henrique Cardoso and Celso Lafer almost a century later. These men-of-state-and-letters surely had some new reasons, arising from their contemporary concerns, for reproducing the identification between Rio Branco, the nation, and a peaceful stance in the world, and for stating what Brazil was not. By now, the older reasons have become clearer.

46. Cândido, "Os brasileiros e a nossa América," pp. 134-135; Alvaro Fernández Bravo, "Utopías americanistas: la posición de la *Revista Americana* en Brasil (1909-1919)," in Paula Alonso, ed., *Construcciones impresas: Panfletos, diarios y revistas en la formación de los estados nacionales en América Latina, 1820-1920* (Buenos Aires: Fondo de Cultura Económica, 2004), pp. 321-338.

47. José Enrique Rodó, "Rio Branco," *Revista Americana* 4:4 (April 1913), pp. 181-183; also published in his *El mirador de Próspero* (Montevideo: José María Serrano, Editor, 1913), pp. 344-347.

Conclusion
An Island with Bridges

"Together with this letter I am sending a copy of *Os Sertões* for the Library in Lima; more books, by other authors, will be shipped later on." Thus wrote Euclides da Cunha to the Brazilian minister to Peru in August 1907, exactly two years before his tragic death, asking the latter to send him in return modern historical and geographical studies concerning that country. "I am contemplating writing a book, *essencialmente sul-americano*," he explained, "and I need to learn a lot, and in fact I am learning a lot, but we don't have any relevant books around here."[1]

By that time *Os Sertões* had already been acclaimed as a foundational interpretation of Brazil. And so it remains today, an almost obligatory reference source. No history of the country's national identity seems complete without it. The other book Euclides mentioned in his letter, dedicated in its entirety to South American themes, he never completed.[2] In that sense and others, the words quoted above can be read both as a condensed example and a

1. Euclides da Cunha to Domício da Gama, Aug. 15, 1907, in Euclides da Cunha, *Correspondência de Euclides da Cunha* (ativa), edited by Walnice Nogueira Galvão and Oswaldo Galotti (São Paulo: Edusp, 1997), p. 336.

2. However, he did leave behind him a few separate essays on Latin American themes included in his collected volumes *Contrastes e Confrontos* (1907) and *À Margem da História* (1909), as well as *Peru versus Bolívia* (1907)–a study of the border question between these two countries, first published in installments in the *Jornal do Commercio* before the above letter was written.

metaphor for the larger story of Brazilian attitudes toward Spanish America around the turn of the nineteenth century, a story I have tried to tell in the preceding pages. To a large extent, it is indeed a tale of scarce knowledge and of books never written, a "non-story," as various colleagues have told me. Yet as da Cunha's unfulfilled intention suggests, and as the discourse by other Brazilian literati of his generation we have examined thus far shows, it is also a story of growing interest, increased contact, and nascent awareness of shared pasts, presents, and futures, a story of an island with bridges.[3]

Running across national borders within the Latin American periphery, those newly erected bridges linking Luso and Spanish America formed part of the same transportation system, so to speak, as the older (or, in any case, heavier) bridges that had connected Brazil to the North Atlantic centers–as well as the shaky, if not broken, bridges between Brazilian men-of-state-and-letters and their national circumstances. Interaction along any one of these three axes of differentiation and identification should be understood in connection with the other two. Brazilian attitudes toward Spanish America, approving and disapproving, evolved in conjunction with the pendulum-swing between dreams and realities, that "schizophrenia" often attributed to the lettered elites of nineteenth-century Latin America. Preoccupations with political instability, material backwardness, and a large non-white population–reinforced by constant exposure to Western chauvinism and aggression–on the one hand, and the corresponding desire to remake Brazil according to overseas models, on the other, constituted a catalyst for interest in the neighboring countries, a source of standards by which to judge them as well as motivations for rapprochement or distancing. That partially explains why eyes were fixed first and foremost on Argentina, the one Spanish-American country which best represented the region's transition from the times of the caudillos to those of "order and progress." It was the so-perceived miraculous *transformation* from the first into

3. In fact, significant similarities with Domingo Faustino Sarmiento's *Facundo: Civilización y barbarie* (1845) suggest that *Os Sertões* itself may constitute a case–albeit implicit–of Brazilian familiarity with and borrowing from Spanish-American letters. See Leopoldo Bernucci, *A imitação dos sentidos: Prólogos, contemporâneos e epígonos de Euclides da Cunha* (São Paulo: EDUSP, 1995), chap. 3.

the second which fascinated Brazilians, elicited glorifying value judgments, and opened the way for closer ties. But then, eventually, here was a lesson that only close neighbors, facing similar problems, could provide. The southern neighbor's relevance and elevated status derived, in other words, from its successful dealing with local conditions and growing proximity–proximity, not identity–to higher, more distant ideals of civilization. In that it was original, "pride of the Latin race *in America*," embodying the promise of a distinct modernity.

However, these *gradual*, interconnected processes in the national, regional, and global spheres form only part of the story. It was the War of the Triple Alliance, fought in the name civilization against barbarism, that opened first cracks in the island mentality, and it was the cumulative impact of the abolition of slavery and the fall of the monarchy that finally broke it down. Transnational gazes and dialogues across the River Plate and the Amazon basins turned these two events into a critical moment of discovery and construction transcending the Brazilian self. Here was a discovery and construction–simultaneously hopeful and threatening, conscious and unconscious–of sameness with the neighbors grounded in shared historical experiences and common fates; the discovery and construction of a Janus-faced "Latin America," at once ordered and disordered, backward and advanced, civilized and barbaric. Later on, Latin American consciousness in Brazil would be bolstered, as elsewhere in the continent, by the growing menace of U.S. and other imperialisms, and translated into various hemispheric policies and official or semi-official discourses. Nevertheless, it did not spring from outside threats, nor did it solely rely on them for its continued existence. It was born from relationships within and across the South, relationships which kept it alive even when Brazilians regained their sense of distinctiveness during the 1900s, as is evident in the discourse of *Paz e Concórdia*, activated in the context of the Acre conflict with Bolivia and still reproduced today.

Bibliography

Archival Sources

Arquivo da Casa de Rui Barbosa, Rio de Janeiro.
Arquivo Histórico do Itamaraty, Rio de Janeiro.
Arquivo de Joaquim Nabuco, Arquivo Nacional, Rio de Janeiro.
Arquivo Particular do Barão do Rio Branco, Itamaraty, Rio de Janeiro.
Arquivo Particular de Joaquim Nabuco, Itamaraty, Rio de Janeiro.
Arquivo Quintino Bocaiúva, Centro de Pesquisa e Documentação de História Contemporânea do Brasil, Fundação Getúlio Vargas, Rio de Janeiro.
Oliveira Lima Family Papers, Oliveira Lima Library, Catholic University of America, Washington, D.C.
Vicente G. Quesada Papers, Ibero-Amerikanisches Institut, Berlin.

Contemporary periodical sources

Anales de la Sociedad Científica Argentina (Buenos Aires)
A Avenida (Rio de Janeiro)
Caras y Caretas (Buenos Aires)
Cidade do Rio (Rio de Janeiro)
Correio do Brasil (Lisbon)
El Diario (Buenos Aires)
Diário de Notícias (Rio de Janeiro)
Don Quixote (Rio de Janeiro)
Estado de São Paulo (São Paulo)
El Ferrocarril (Santiago de Chile)

Gazeta da Comarca (São Fídelis, RJ)
Gazeta de Noticias (Rio de Janeiro)
A Illustração: Revista quinzenal para Portugal e Brazil (Paris)
A Imprensa (Rio de Janeiro)
Jornal do Brasil (Rio de Janeiro)
Journal do Commercio (Rio de Janeiro)
La Libertad Electoral (Santiago de Chile)
O Malho (Rio de Janeiro)
La Nación (Buenos Aires)
La Nación (Asunción)
La Opinión Nacional (Caracas)
O Novo Mundo (New York)
El País (Buenos Aires)
O Paiz (Rio de Janeiro)
La Patria degli italiani (Buenos Aires)
La Prensa (Buenos Aires)
Provincia de São Paulo (São Paulo)
Renasença (Rio de Janeiro)
Revista Americana (Rio de Janeiro)
Revista da Semana (Rio de Janeiro)
Revista de Derecho Historia y Letras (Buenos Aires)
Revista de Portugal (Porto)
Revista do Instituto Historico e Geographico Brasileiro (Rio de Janeiro)
Revista Illustrada (Rio de Janeiro)
La Revista Patriotica (Buenos Aires)
El Siglo (Caracas)
El Siglo (Montevideo)

Official publications

Argentina. Legación de la República (Brazil). *La fiesta de la libertad en el imperio do Brazil; Testimonios de amistad fraternal á la República Argentina. Colección hecha por Enrique B. Moreno*. Rio de Janeiro: Imprensa Nacional, 1888.

— *Tratado de Misiones. Litigio solucionado. Las Republicas Brasilera y Argentina. Homenajes al Ministro Brasilero Bocayuva en el El Plata. Firma del tratado en Montevideo. Resumen general de las fiestas 1889-90*. Buenos Aires: Sommaruga, 1890.

Brazil. *Annaes do Parlamento Brazileiro, Camara dos Srs. Deputados – Terceira sessão da vigesima legislatura de 4 de julho a 2 de agosto de 1888*. vols. 2,3. Rio de Janeiro: Imprensa Nacional, 1888.

— *Manifesto inaugural de Manuel Ferraz de Campos Salles, presidente eleito para o quatriennio de 1898 a 1902. 15 de novembro de 1898.* Rio de Janeiro, 1898.

— *Mensagem dirigida ao Congresso Nacional pelo Generalíssimo Manuel Deodoro da Fonseca, Chefe do Governo Provisório da República dos Estados Unidos do Brasil, em 15 de novembro de 1890.* Rio de Janeiro: Imprensa Nacional, 1890.

— *Mensagem apresentada ao Congresso Nacional na abertuta da terceira sessão da terceira legislatura pelo presidente da republica M. Ferraz de Campos Salles, 1899.* Rio de Janeiro, 1899.

— *Mensagem apresentada ao Congresso Nacional na abertura da primeira sessão da quarta legislatura pelo presidente da republica M. Ferraz de Campos Salles,* 1900. Rio de Janeiro, 1899.

— President. *Relações exteriores do Brazil durante a administração do Presidente Rodrigues Alves, 1902-1906.* Rio de Janeiro: Typ. do Jornal do Commercio de Rodrigues & c., 1906.

— "Discurso do Senhor Presidente da República, Fernando Henrique Cardoso, na Solenidade de Formatura dos Alunos do Instituto Rio Branco." Palácio Itamaraty, May 18, 2000. <http://www.mre.gov.br/portugues/politica_externa/discursos/discurso_detalhe3. asp?ID_DISCURSO=1206>.

— *Relatorio do Ministerio das Relações Exteriores.* Rio de Janeiro, 1891.

— *Relatorio do Ministerio do Imperio.* Rio de Janeiro: Imprensa Nacional, 1885, 1886, 1888.

U.S. Department of State. *Papers Relating to the Foreign Relations of the United States Transmitted to Congress with the Annual Message of the President, Dec. 3, 1888.* Washington, DC: 1889.

— *Records of the Department of State Relating to Political Relations Between Brazil and Other States, 1910-1929.* Washington, DC: National Archives and Records Administration, 1969.

Books and articles

"Epistolário acadêmico" [letters by Domício da Gama]. *Revista da Academia Brasileira de Letras* 24:139 (July 1933), pp. 367-370.

Abranches, Dunshee de. *Actas e actos do governo provisorio.* 3rd. ed. Rio de Janeiro: Jornal do Brazil, 1953.

Acereda, Alberto and Guevara, Rigoberto. *Modernism, Rubén Darío, and the Poetics of Despair.* Lanham, MD: University Press of America, 2004.

Alambert, Francisco. "Civilização e barbárie, história e cultura: Representações literárias e projeções da guerra do Paraguay nas crises do segundo reinado e da primeira república." In *A guerra do Paraguay: 130 anos depois*. Edited by Eduarda Castro Maglhães Marques. Rio de Janeiro: Relume-Dumará, 1995, pp. 83-96.

ALBERDI, Juan Bautista. *Historia de la guerra del Paraguay*. Buenos Aires: Ediciones de la Patria Grande, 1962.

ALONSO, Angela. *Idéias em movimento: A geração 1870 na crise do Brasil-Império*. São Paulo: Paz e Terra, 2002.

ANDERMANN, Jens. *The Optic of the State: Visuality and Power in Argentina and Brazil*. Pittsburgh: Pittsburgh University Press, 2007.

ANDERSON, Benedict. *Imagined Communities: Reflections on the Origin and Spread of Nationalism*. 2nd revised and extended ed. London: Verso, 1991.

ANDRADE, Rodrigo M. F. de. *Rio-Branco e Gastão da Cunha*. Rio de Janeiro: Ministério das Relações Exteriores, Instituto Rio-Branco, 1953.

ANDREWS, George Reid. *Blacks and Whites in São Paulo, Brazil, 1888-1998*. Madison: University of Wisconsin Press, 1991.

— *Afro-Latin America, 1800-2000*. New York: Oxford University Press, 2004.

ARARIPE JÚNIOR, Tristão de Alencar. *Obra crítica de Araripe Júnior*. 5 vols. Rio de Janeiro: Ministério da Educação e Cultura, Casa de Rui Barbosa, 1958-1970.

ARDAO, Arturo. *Génesis de la idea e el nombre de América Latina*. Caracas: Centro de Estudios Latinoamericanos Rómulo Gallegos, 1980.

AZEVEDO, José Affonso Mendonça de. *Vida e obra de Salvador de Mendonça*. Brasília: Divisão de Documentação, Seção de Publicações, 1971.

BAGGIO, Kátia Gerab. "A América Latina e os Estados Unidos na visão de Euclides da Cunha." *Estudos de História* 7:2 (2000), pp. 55-68.

BANDEIRA, Moniz. *Brasil, Argentina e Estados Unidos: Conflito e integração na América do Sul (Da Triplice Aliança ao Mercosul, 1870-2003)*. 2nd revised and extended edition. Rio de Janeiro: Revan, 2003.

— *Presença dos Estados Unidos no Brasil*. 2nd ed. Rio de Janeiro: Civilização Brasileira, 1978.

BARBOSA, Rui. *Meu caro Rui, meu caro Nabuco*. Edited by José Almino de Alencar and Ana Maria Pessoa dos Santos. Rio de Janeiro: Casa de Rui Barbosa, 1999.

— *O estado do sitio*. Rio de Janeiro: Companhia Impressora, 1892.

— *Mocidade e exílio*. São Paulo: Companhia Editora Nacional, 1934.

— *Obras Completas de Rui Barbosa*. Rio de Janeiro: Ministério da Educação e Cultura, 1942-.

BARMAN, Roderick J. *Citizen Emperor: Pedro II and the Making of Brazil, 1825-1891*. Stanford: Stanford University Press, 1999.

BARRETO, Lima. *Toda crônica: Lima Barreto*. Edited by Beatriz Resende and Rachel Valença, 2 vols. Rio de Janeiro: Agir, 2004.

BASTOS, Aureliano Cândido de Tavares. *Os males do presente e as esperanças do futuro.* 2nd ed. São Paulo: Companhia Editora Nacional, 1939 [1862].

— *A província: estudo sobre a decenralização do Brasil.* Facsimile ed. Brasília: Senado Federal, 1996 [1870].

BEATTIE, Peter. *The Tribute of Blood: Army, Honor, Race, and Nation in Brazil, 1864-1945.* Durham: Duke University Press, 2001.

BERNUCCI, Leopoldo. *A imitação dos sentidos: prólogos, contemporâneos e epígonos de Euclides da Cunha.* São Paulo: EDUSP, 1995.

BESOUCHET, Lidia. *José Maria de Silva Paranhos: Visconde do Rio Branco.* Rio de Janeiro/Brasília: Nova Fronteira/INL, 1985.

— *Rio-Branco e as relações entre o Brasil e a República Argentina.* Rio de Janeiro: Ministério das Relações Extereriores, 1949.

BETHELL, Leslie. "O Brasil e a ideia de 'América Latina' em perspectiva histórica." *Estudos Históricos* 22:44 (2009), pp. 289-321.

BEST, Geoffrey. "Peace Conferences and the Age of Total War: The 1899 Hague Peace Conference and What Came After." *International Affairs* 75:3 (1999), pp. 619-634.

BLANCAS, Alberto. *Anécdotas y recuerdos.* Buenos Aires: Editorial Tor, 1936.

BLOOM, William. *Personal Identity, National Identity and International Relations.* Cambridge: Cambridge University Press, 1990.

BOCAIÚVA, Quintino. *Idéias políticas de Quintino Bocaiúva.* Edited by Eduardo Silva. Brasilia/Rio de Janeiro: Senado Federal/Casa Rui Barbosa, 1986.

BOEHRER, George C. A. "José Carlos Rodrigues and *O Novo Mundo*, 1870-1879," *Journal of Inter-American Studies* 9:1 (Jan., 1967), pp. 127-144.

BORGES, Dain. "Intellectuals and the Forgetting of Slavery in Brazil." *Annals of Scholarship* 11 (1996), pp. 44-46.

BOULDING, K. E. "National Images and International Systems." *Journal of Conflict and Resolution* 3 (1959), pp. 120-131.

BOTTICI, Chiara and Benoît CHALLAND. "Rethinking Political Myth: The Clash of Civilizations as a Self-Fulfilling Prophecy," *European Journal of Social Theory* 9:3 (2006), pp. 315-336.

BRAVO, Alvaro Fernández. "Ambivalent Argentina, Nationalism, Exoticism, and Latin Americanism, at the 1889 Paris Universal Exposition." *Nepantla: Views from South* 2:1 (2001), pp. 115-139.

— "Utopías americanistas: la posición de la *Revista Americana* en Brasil (1909-1919)." In *Construcciones impresas: Panfletos, diarios y revistas en la formación de los estados nacionales en América Latina, 1820-1920.* Edited by Paula Alonso. Buenos Aires: Fondo de Cultura Económica, 2004, pp. 321-338.

BROCA, Brito. *A vida literária no Brasil - 1900*. 2nd revised and enlarged ed. Rio de Janeiro: J. Olympio, 1960.

BROOKSHAW, David. *Race and Color in Brazilian Literature*. Metuchen: Scarecrow Press, 1986.

BRUBAKER, Rogers, Mara LOVEMAN and Peter STAMATOV. "Ethnicity as Cognition." *Theory and Society* 33:1 (2004), pp. 31-46.

BUENO, Clodoaldo. *A república e sua política exterior (1889 a 1902)*. São Paulo/Brasília: Editora UNESP/IPRI, 1995.

BURNS, E. Bradford. *The Poverty of Progress: Latin American in the Nineteenth Century*. Berkeley: University of California Press, 1980.

— *The Unwritten Alliance: Rio-Branco and Brazilian-American Relations*. New York: Columbia University Press, 1966.

CÂNDIDO, Antônio. *On Literature and Society*. Translated, edited, and introduced by Howard S. Becker. Princeton: Princeton University Press, 1995.

— *Recortes*. São Paulo: Companhia das Letras, 1993.

CARVALHO NETO, Paulo de. "Folclore da guerra do Paraguai." *Journal of Inter-American Studies* 3:2 (April 1961), pp. 273-280.

CARVALHO, José Murilo de. "Brasil naciones marginadas." In *De los imperios a las naciones*. Edited by Antonio Anino, Luis Castro Leiva and François-Xavier Guerra. Saragosa: Ibercaja, 1994, pp. 401-423.

— "Brazil 1870-1914: The Force of Tradition." *Journal of Latin American Studies* 24, Quincentenary Supplement (1992), pp. 145-162.

— *A construção da ordem: A elite política imperial/Teatro de sombras: A polítlica imperial*. 2nd revised ed. Rio de Janeiro: Editora UFRJ, Relume-Dumará, 1996.

— "Dreams Come Untrue." *Dadealus* 129:2 (Spring 2000), pp. 57-82.

— *A formação das almas: O imaginário da república no Brasil*. São Paulo: Companhia das Letras, 1993.

— *Os bestializados: O Rio de Janeiro e a República que não foi*. São Paulo: Companhia das Letras, 1987.

CARVALHO, Maria Alice Rezende de. "André Rebouças: Un americanista del imperio." In *Estados Unidos desde América Latina: Sociedad, política y cultura*. Edited by Víctor A. Arriaga Weiss and Ana Rosa Suárez Argüello. Mexico City: Colegio de Mexico, 1995, pp. 197-216.

CASSELS, Alan. *Ideology and International Relations in the Modern World*. London: Routledge, 1996.

CELSO, Afonso. *Guerrilhas*. Rio de Janeiro: Typ. Moraes, 1895.

CENTENO, Miguel Angel. *Blood and Debt: War and the Nation-State in Latin America*. University Park: Pennsylvania State University Press, 2002.

CERQUEIRA, Dionísio. *Reminiscências da campanha do Paraguay, 1865-1879*. Rio de Janeiro: Biblioteca do Exército Editora, 1980.

CERVO, Amado Luiz and Clodoaldo BUENO. *História da política exterior do Brasil.* São Paulo: Editora Atica, 1992.

CERVO, Amado Luiz. *O parlamento brasileiro e as relações exteriores: 1826-1889.* Brasília: Editora Universidade de Brasília, 1981.

CHASTEEN, John Charles. *Heroes on Horseback: A Life and Times of the Last Gaucho Caudillos.* Albuquerque: University of New Mexico Press, 1995.

CHIARAMONTE, José Carlos. "Formas de identidad en el Río de la Plata luego de 1810." *Boletín del Instituto de Historia Argentina y Americana Dr. Emilio Ravignani* 3:1 (1989), pp. 71-92.

COLLIER, Simon. "Nationality, Nationalism, and Supranationalism in the Writings of Simón Bolívar." *Hispanic American Historical Review* 63:1 (1983), pp. 37-64

CONRAD, Robert. *The Destruction of Brazilian Slavery, 1850-1888.* Berkeley: University of California Press, 1972.

COOPER, Sandi E. *Patriotic Pacifism: Waging War on War in Europe, 1815-1914.* New York: Oxford, 1991.

COSTA, Emília Viotti da. *The Brazilian Empire: Myths and Histories.* Chicago: Chicago University Press, 1985.

COSTA, João Frank da. *Joaquim Nabuco e a política exterior do Brasil.* Rio de Janeiro: Gráfica Récord Editôra, 1968.

CUNHA, Euclides da. *Correspondência de Euclides da Cunha (ativa).* Edited by Walnice Nogueira Galvão and Oswaldo Galotti. São Paulo: Edusp, 1997.

— *Contrastes e confrontos.* São Paulo: Cultirx, 1975 [1907].

CUNHA, Francisco Xavier da. *Propaganda contra o imperio; Reminiscencias na imprensa e na diplomacia, 1870 a 1910.* Rio de Janeiro: Imprensa Nacional, 1914.

DABOVE, Juan Pablo. *Nightmares of the Lettered City: Banditry and Literature in Latin America, 1816-1929.* Pittsburgh: University of Pittsburgh Press, 2007.

DANESE, Sérgio. *Diplomacia presidencial: História e crítica.* Rio de Janeiro: Topbooks, 1999.

DEBES, Célio. *Campos Salles: Perfil de um edtadista.* 2 vols. Rio de Janeiro: Livraria F. Alves Editora, 1978.

DELANEY, Jean H. "Imagining El Ser Argentino: Cultural Nationalism and Romantic Concepts of Nationhood in early Twentieth-Century Argentina." *Journal of Latin American Studies* 34:3 (Aug., 2002), pp. 625-658.

DEUTSCH, Sandra McGee. *Las derechas: The Extreme Right in Argentina, Brazil, and Chile, 1890-1939.* Stanford: Stanford University Press, 1999.

DIAS, Arthur. *Do Rio a Buenos Aires: Episodios e impressões d'uma viagem.* Rio de Janeiro: Imprensa Nacional, 1901.

DONGHI, Tulio Halperín. *The Contemporary History of Latin America*. Translated and edited by John Charles Chasteen. Durham: Duke University Press, 1993.

DORATIOTO, Francisco. *Maldita guerra: Nova história da duerra do Paraguai*. São Paulo: Companhia das Letras, 2002.

EARLE, Rebecca. *The Return of the Native: Indians and Myth-making in Spanish America, 1810-1930*. Durham: Duke University Press, 2007.

ELLISON, Fred P. "Rubén Darío and Brazil." *Hispania*, 47:1 (1964), pp. 24-35.

ERIKSEN, Thomas Hylland. *Ethnicity and Nationalism: Anthropological Perspectives*. Chicago: Pluto Press, 1993.

EU, Conde d' (Prince Gastão de Orléans). *Viagem militar ao Rio Grande do Sul*. Belo Horizonte: Editora Itatiaia; São Paulo: Editora da Universidade de São Paulo, 1981.

FAORO, Raimundo. *Os donos do poder: Formação do patronato político brasileiro*. 13th ed. São Paulo: Globo, 1998.

FAUSTO, Boris. "Brazil: The Social and Political Structure of the First Republic (1889-1930)." In The *Cambridge History of Latin America*. Edited by Leslie Bethell. vol. 5. Cambridge: Cambridge University Press, 1986, pp. 779-829.

FEY, Ingrid E. "First Tango in Paris: Latin Americans in Turn-of-the-Century France, 1880-1920." Ph.D. diss., University of California Los Angeles, 1996.

FRAGA, Rosendo and Luiz Felipe de SEIXAS CORRÊA. *Argentina Brasil: Centenario de 2 visitas: Historia fotográfica*. Buenos Aires: Editorial Centro de Estudios Unión para la Nueva Mayoría, 1998.

FRANCO, Afonso Arinos de Melo. *Rodrigues Alves: Apogeu e declínio do presidencialismo*. 2 vols. Rio de Janeiro: J. Olympio, 1973.

FRANCO, Jean. *An Introduction to Spanish American Literature*. 3rd ed. Cambridge: Cambridge University Press, 1994.

— *The Modern Culture of Latin America : Society and the Artist*. Harmondsworth, Middlesex: Penguin, 1970.

FREYRE, Gilberto. *Order and Progress: Brazil from Monarchy to Republic*. Edited and translated by Rod W. Horton. Berkeley: University of California Press, 1986.

GALASSO, Norberto. "Prólogo." In *La nación latinoamericana*, by Manuel Ugarte. Caracas: Biblioteca Ayacucho, 1978, pp. ix-xxv.

GOMES, Ângela de Castro and Marieta de MORAES FERREIRA. "Primeira República: Um balanço historiográfico." *Estudos Históricos* 2:4 (1989), pp. 244-280.

GONÇALVES, João Felipe. "Enterrando Rui Barbosa: um estudo de caso da construção fúnebre de heróis nacionais na Primeira República." *Estudos Históricos* 14:25 (2000), pp. 148-157.

— *Rui Barbosa: Pondo as idéias no lugar*. Rio de Janeiro: FGV Editora, 2000.

GOUVÊA, Fernando da Cruz. *Joaquim Nabuco entre a Monarquia e a República.* Recife: Fundação Joaquim Nabuco, Editora Massangana, 1989.

— *Oliveira Lima, uma biografia.* 3 vols. Recife: Instituto Arqueológico, Histórico e Geográfico Pernambucano, 1976.

GRAHAM, Maria. *Journal of a Voyage to Brazil, and Residence There During Part of the Years 1821, 1822, 1823.* London: Longman & C. & J. Murray, 1824.

GRAHAM, Richard. *Britain and the Onset of Modernization in Brazil, 1850-1914.* Cambridge: Cambridge University Press, 1968.

— "Joaquim Nabuco, Conservative Historian." *Luso-Brazilian Review*, 17:1 (1980), pp. 1-16.

GREENFIELD, Gerald Michael. "The Great Drought and Elite Discourse in Imperial Brazil." *Hispanic American Historical Review* 72:3 (1992), pp. 375-400.

GUERRA, Francisco-Xavier. "The Implosion of the Spanish Empire: Emerging Statehood and Collective Identities." In *The Collective and the Public in Latin America.* Edited by Luis Roniger and Tamar Herzog. Brighton: Sussex Academic Press, 2000, pp. 71-94.

GUIMARAES, Argeu. *Diccionario bio-bibliographico brasileiro, de diplomacia, politica externa e direito internacional.* Rio de Janeiro: Published by the author, 1938.

HAHNER, June Edith. *Civilian-Military Relations in Brazil, 1889-1898.* Columbia: University of South Carolina Press, 1969.

— *Emancipating the Female Sex: The Struggle for Women's Rights in Brazil, 1850-1940.* Durham: Duke University Press, 1990.

— "Jacobinos versus Galegos: Urban Radicals versus Portuguese Immigrants in Rio de Janeiro in the 1890s." *Journal of Interamerican Studies and World Affairs* 18:2 (May 1976), pp. 125-154.

HALE, Charles. "Political and Social Ideas in Latin America, 1870-1930." In The *Cambridge History of Latin America.* Edited by Leslie Bethell. vol. 4. Cambridge: Cambridge University Press, 1984, pp. 367-441.

HELG, Aline. "Race in Argentina and Cuba, 1880-1930: Theory, Policies, and Popular Reaction." In *The Idea of Race in Latin America.* Edited by Richard Graham. Austin: University of Texas Press, 1990, pp. 37-69.

HARDMAN, Francisco Foot. *Trem Fantasma: A modernidade na selva.* São Paulo: Companhia das Letras, 1982.

HILTON, Stanley. "The Argentine Factor in Twentieth-Century Brazilian Foreign Policy Strategy." *Political Science Quarterly* 100:1 (1985), pp. 27-51.

HOBSBAWM, E. J. *Nations and Nationalism since 1780*. 2nd ed. Cambridge: Cambridge University Press, 1992.

HOLANDA, Sérgio Buarque de. *Do Império a República*. t. 2, vol. 5, of *História geral da civilização brasileira*. Edited by Idem. São Paulo: Difusão Europeia do Livro, 1972.

HORNE, John. "Masculinity in Politics and War in the Age of Nation-States and World Wars, 1850-1950." In *Masculinities in Politics and War: Gendering Modern History*. Edited by Stefan Dudink, Karen Hagemann and John Tosh. Manchester: Manchester University Press, 2004, pp. 22-40.

IANNI, Octavio. "Tipos e mitos do pensamento brasileiro." *Revista Brasileira de Sciências Sociais* 17:49 (June 2002), pp. 5-10.

INSTITUTO HISTORICO E GEOGRAPHICO BRASILEIRO. *Diccionario historico, geographico e ethnographico do Brasil*. Rio de Janeiro: Imprensa Nacional, 1922.

— *Chile e Brazil; sessão solemne do Instituto Historico e Geographico Brasileiro em homenagem á nação chilena e consagrada á officialidade do encouraçado Almirante Cochrane*. Rio de Janeiro: Dias da Silva Junior, 1889.

JAGUARIBE, Helio. "Brazil-Argentina. Relações de conflito e cooperação." *Revista Brasileira de Política Internacional* 25 (1982), pp. 131-143.

JANOTTI, Maria de Lourdes Monaco. "O diálogo convergente: Políticos e historiadores no início da República," *Luso-Brazilian Review* 36:2 (1999), pp. 93-102.

— "The Monarchist Response to the Beginnings of the Brazilian Republic." *The Americas* 48:2 (Oct., 1991), pp. 223-243.

— *Os subversivos da República*. São Paulo: Brasiliense, 1986.

JARDIM, Antônio da Silva. *Propaganda republicana (1888-1889): Discursos, opúsculos, manifestos, e artigos coligidos, anotados e prefaciados por Barbosa Lima Sobrinho*. Rio de Janeiro: Ministério da Educação e Cultura/Fundação Casa de Rui Barbosa, 1978.

JOHNSON, Phil Brian. "Uptight about Ruy: An Essay on Brazilian Cultural Nationalism and Mythology," *Journal of Inter-American Studies and World Affairs*, 15:2 (May 1973), pp. 191-204

JORGE, Araujo. *Ensaios de historia diplomatica do Brasil no regimen republicano (1889-1912)*. Rio de Janeiro: n.p., 1912.

JOSEPH, Gilbert M. "Close Encounters: Toward a New Cultural History of U.S.-Latin American Relations." In *Close Encounters of Empire: Writing the Cultural History of U.S.-Latin American Relations*. Edited by

Gilbert M. Joseph, Catherine LeGrand and Ricardo D. Salvatore. Durham: Duke University Press, 1998, pp. 3-46.

KEITH, Henry H. "The Nonviolent Tradition in Brazilian History: A Myth in Need of Explosion?" In *Conflict and continuity in Brazilian Society.* Edited by Idem and S. F. Edwards. Columbia: University of South Carolina Press, 1969, pp. 231-240.

KIDDER, Daniel P. *Sketches of Residence and Travels in Brazil Embracing Historical and Geographical Notices of The Empire and its Several Provinces*, 2 vols. Philadelphia: Sorin and Ball, 1845.

KIRKENDALL, Andrew. *Class Mates: Male Student Culture and the Making of a Political Class in Nineteenth-Century Brazil.* Lincoln: University of Nebraska Press, 2002.

LAFER, Celso. "Brazilian International Identity and Foreign Policy: Past, Present, and future." *Daedalus* 129:2 (Spring 2000), pp. 207-238.

— "Mudanças na Continuidade." *Gazeta Mercantil*, Aug. 31, 2001. <http://ftp.unb.br/pub/UNB/ipr/rel/discmin/2001/3444.pdf>.

LARRAÍN, Jorge. *Identity and Modernity in Latin America.* Malden, Mass.: Polity Press, 2000.

LAUERHASS JUNIOR, Ludwig. *Getulio Vargas e o triunfo do nacionalismo brasileiro.* Belo Horizonte/Sao Paulo; Itatiaia/Editora da Universidadede Sao Paulo, 1986.

LECLERC, Max. *Cartas do Brasil.* Translated by Sérgio Milliet. São Paulo: Companhia Editora Nacional, 1949.

LEERSSEN, Joep. "The Rhetoric of National Character: A Programmatic Survey." *Poetics Today* 21:2 (2000), pp. 267-292.

LESSER, Jeffrey. *Negotiating National Identity: Immigrants, Minorities, and the Struggle for Ethnicity in Brazil.* Durham: Duke University Press, 1999.

LEVI, Darrel. *The Prados of São Paulo, Brazil: An Elite Family and Social Change, 1840-1930.* Athens: University of Georgia Press, 1987.

LEVINE, Robert M. "Elite Perceptions of the Povo." In *Modern Brazil: Elites and Masses in Historical Perspective.* Edited by Michael L. Conniff and Frank D. McCann. Lincoln: University of Nebraska Press, 1989, pp. 209-224.

LEVINE, Robert M. and Steven C. TOPIK. "Introduction." *The Americas* 48:2 (1991), pp. 131-138.

LIMA SOBRINHO, Barbosa. "Oliveira Lima: Sua vida e sua obra." In *Obra seleta*, by Oliveira Lima. Edited by Barbosa Lima Sobrinho. Rio de Janeiro: Instituto Nacional do Livro, 1971, pp. 17-131.

LIMA, Herman. *História da caricatura no Brazil*, 3 vols. Rio de Janeiro: José Olympio, 1963.

LIMA, Oliveira. *The Evolution of Brazil Compared with that of Spanish and Anglo-Saxon America*. Stanford: Stanford University Press, 1914.

— *Impressões da América Espanhola, 1904-1906*. Prefaced and annotated by Manoel da Silveira Cardozo. Introduction by Gilberto Freyre. Rio de Janeiro: Livraria J. Olympio, 1953.

— *Nos Estados Unidos: Impressões politicas e sociaes*. Leipzig: F. A. Brockhaus, 1899.

— *Pan-americanismo: Monroe, Bolivar, Roosevelt*. Brasília/Rio de Janeiro: Senado Federal/Fundação Casa de Rui Barbosa, 1980 [1907].

— "Sete anos de república no Brazil (1889-1896)." Translated by Sheila Schvarzman. In *Apontamentos para a história da República: Um registro centenário*, by Manoel Ernesto de Campos Porto. Edited by José Sebastião Witter. São Paulo: Editora Brasiliense, 1990, pp. 11-49.

LINS, Alvao. *Rio-Branco (o barão do Rio-Branco) biografia pessoal e história política*. 2nd revised ed. São Paulo: Companhia Editora Nacional, 1965.

LOBO, Helio. *O Pan-americanismo e o Brasil*. São Paulo: Companhia Editora Nacional, 1939.

LOVE, Joseph. *Rio Grande do Sul and Brazilian Regionalism, 1882-1930*. Stanford: Stanford University Press, 1971.

— *São Paulo in the Brazilian Federation, 1889-1937*. Stanford: Stanford University Press, 1980.

LUQUE, Fermín Vicente Arenas. *Enrique B. Moreno, un gran diplomático argentino*. 2 vols. Buenos Aires: Editorial "La Facultad," 1945-1946.

MACHADO NETO, Antônio Luiz. *Estrutura social da república das letras: sociologia da vida intelectual brasileira, 1870-1930*. São Paulo: Editora da Universidade de São Paulo, 1973.

MACIEL DE BARROS, Roque Spencer. *A ilustração brasileira e a idéia de universidade*. São Paulo: Universidade de São Paulo, 1959.

MAGALHÃES JÚNIOR, R. *Rui, o homem e o mito*. 2nd revised and enlarged ed. Rio de Janeiro: Editôra Civilização Brasileira, 1965.

MALATIAN, Teresa. "Diplomacia e letras na correspondência acadêmica: Machado de Assis e Oliveira Lima." *Estudos Históricos* 13:24 (1999), pp. 377-392.

MALLON, Florencia E. *Peasant and Nation: The Making of Postcolonial Mexico and Peru*. Berkeley: University of California Press, 1995.

MARTIN, Gerald. "Literature, Music and the Visual Arts." In *A Cultural History of Latin America: Literature, Music, and the Visual Arts in the 19th and 20th Centuries*. Edited by Leslie Bethell. New York: Cambridge University Press, 1998, pp. 47-131.

MCCANN, Frank D. "The Brazilian General Staff and Brazil's Military Situation: 1900-1945." *Journal of Interamerican Studies and World Affairs* 25:3 (1983), pp. 299-324.

MCGANN, Thomas F. *Argentina, the United States, and the Inter-American System, 1880-1914*. Cambridge: Harvard University Press, 1957.

MENDES, Raimundo Teixeira. *Benjamin Constant: Esboço de uma apreciação sintética da vida e da obra do fundador da República brazileira*. 2nd ed. Rio de Janeiro: Séde central da Igreja pozitivista do Brazil, 1913.

MENDONÇA, Salvador de. *A situação Internacional do Brazil*. Rio de Janeiro: Garnier, 1913.

MIGNOLO, Walter. *The Idea of Latin America*. Malden: Blackwell, 2005.

MILLER, Nicola. *In the Shadow of the State: Intellectuals and the Quest for National Identity in Twentieth-Century Spanish America*. London: Verso, 1999.

— "The Historiography of Nationalism and National Identity in Latin America." *Nations and Nationalism* 12:2 (2006), pp. 201-221.

MOSSÉ, B. [pseudonym for Barão do Rio Branco] *Dom Pedro II, imperador do Brasil*. Translated by Herminia Lessa. São Paulo: Edições Cultura Brasileira, n.d. [1889].

MOURA, Cristina Patriota. "Herança e metamorfose: a construção social de dois Rio Branco." *Estudos Históricos* 25:1 (2000), pp. 81-102.

NABUCO, Carolina. *The Life of Joaquim Nabuco*. Translated by Ronald Hilton. Stanford: Stanford University Press, 1968.

NABUCO, Joaquim. *Abolitionism: The Brazilian Antislavery Struggle*. Translated by Robert Conrad. Urbana: University of Illinois Press, 1977 [1883].

— *The Approach of the Two Americas. Convocation Address before the University of Chicago, August 28, 1908*. Bulletin of the American Branch of the Association for International Conciliation, 1908, no. 10. New York: American Branch of the Association for International Conciliation, 1908.

— *Balmaceda. A intervenção estrangeira durante a revolta de 1893*. São Paulo: Instituto Progresso Editorial, 1949 [1895].

— *Cartas a amigos*. Edited and annotated by Carolina Nabuco. 2 vols. São Paulo: Instituto Progresso Editorial, 1949.

— *Diários*. 2 vols. Prefaces and annotations by Evaldo Cabral de Mello. Rio de Janeiro/Recife: Bem-Te-Vi/Fundação Joaquim Nabuco, Editora Massangana, 2005.

— *Discursos parlamentares*. Rio de Janeiro: Imprensa Nacional, 1949.

— *Escritos e discursos literários. L'option*. São Paulo: Instituto Progresso Editorial, 1949.

— *Porque continuo a ser monarchista*. London: Abraham Kingdon & Newnham, 1890.

— *Minha formação*. 9th ed. Rio de Janeiro: Livraria J. Olympio Editora, 1976 [1900].

— *Nabuco e a república*. Edited and introduced by Leonardo Dantas Silva. Recife: Fundação Joaquim Nabuco, Editora Massangana, 1990.

— *Resposta às mensagens do Recife e Nazareth*. 2nd ed. Rio de Janeiro: Leuzinger, 1890.

— *Um estadista do Império*. 2 vols. 5th ed. Rio de Janeiro: Topbooks, 1998 [1898-1900].

NEEDELL, Jeffrey. "The Domestic Civilizing Mission: The Cultural Role of the State in Brazil, 1808-1930," *Luso-Brazilian Review* 36:1 (Summer 1999), pp. 1-18.

— "A Liberal Embraces Monarchy: Joaquim Nabuco and Conservative Historiography." *The Americas* 48:2 (1991), pp. 159-179.

— "Rio de Janeiro and Buenos Aires: Public Space and Public Consciousness in *Fin-de-Siècle* Latin America." *Comparative Studies in Society and History* 37:3 (July 1995), pp. 519-540.

— *A Tropical Belle Époque: Elite Culture and Society in Turn-of-the-Century Rio de Janeiro*. Cambridge: Cambridge University Press, 1987.

NOGUEIRA, Aurélio. *As desventuras do liberalismo: Joaquim Nabuco, a monarquia* e a república. Rio de Janeiro: Paz e Terra, 1984.

NOVAIS, Fernando A. "O significado da 'guerra do Paraguay' na história do Brasil." In *A guerra do Paraguay: 130 anos depois*. Edited by Eduarda Castro Maglhães Marques. Rio de Janeiro: Relume-Dumará, 1995, pp. 77-82.

OCTAVIO, Rodrigo. *Constituições Federaes*. São Paulo/Rio de Janeiro: Livraria Clasica de Alves & C., 1897.

OLIVEIRA, J. M. Cardoso de. *Pedro Américo: Sua vida e suas obras*. Special revised and enlarged ed. Rio de Janeiro: Imprensa Nacional, 1943.

OLIVEIRA, Lúcia Lippi. *A questão nacional na Primeira República*. São Paulo: Brasiliense, 1990.

ORTIZ, Renato. *Cultura brasileira e identidade nacional*. São Paulo: Brasiliense, 1985.

PARANHOS, José Maria da Silva (Visconde do Rio Branco). *A convenção de 20 de fevereiro demonstrada à luz dos debates do Senado e dos successos da Uruguayana*. Rio de Janeiro: B.L. Garnier, 1865.

PEIXOTO, Artur Vieira, et al., eds. *Floriano: Memórias e documentos*. 5 vols. Rio de Janeiro: Serviço Gráfico do Ministério da Educação, 1939-.

PEÑA, Cipriano de la. *Cronica illustrada y documentada de las fiestas de confraternidad brasilero-argentinas*. Buenos Aires: Compania Sud-Americana de Billetes de Banco, 1901.

POMER, Léon. "A guerra do Paraguay e a formação do estado na Argentina." In *A guerra do Paraguay: 130 anos depois*. Edited by Eduarda Castro Maglhães Marques. Rio de Janeiro: Relume-Dumará, 1995, pp. 113-120.

PONTES, Carlos. *Tavares Bastos*. 2nd ed. São Paulo/Brasília: Ed. Nacional/ INL, 1975.

PRADO, Eduardo. *A ilusão Americana*. São Paulo: Brasiliense, 1958 [1893].

— "Destinos políticos do Brasil." *Revista de Portugal* I (1889), pp. 467-491.

— *Fastos da dictadura militar no brasil*. São Paulo: Escola Typografica Salesiana, 1902.

— *Viagens: América, Oceania e Asia*. São Paulo: Salesiana, 1902.

PRATT, Mary Louise. *Imperial Eyes: Travel Writing and Transculturation*. 2nd ed. London: Routledge, 2008.

QUEIRÓS, Eça de. "Eduardo Prado." *Revista do Livro*, 18 (June 1960), pp. 101-124.

QUEIROZ, Suely Robles Reis de. *Os radicais da república. Jacobinismo: Ideologia e ação, 1893-1897*. São Paulo: Brasiliense, 1986.

— "Brandura da escravidão brasileira: Mito ou realidade?" *Revista de História* 52:103 (1975), pp. 443-482.

QUESADA, Vicente G. *Mis memorias diplomáticas, misión ante el gobierno del Brasil*. 2 vols. Buenos Aires: Imprensa de Coni hermanos, 1907-1908.

RAMA, Angel. *The Lettered City*. Translated by John Charles Chasteen. Durham: Duke University Press, 1996.

RANGEL, Vicente Marrota. "Direito internacional e relações internacionais: a teoria tridimensionalista no contexto brasileiro." In *Teorías de relaciones internacionales y de derecho internacional en América Latina*. Bogotá: Fundación Simón Bolívar: Departamento de Asuntos Culturales de la OEA, 1989, pp. 462-483.

REBOUÇAS, André. *Diário e notas autobiográficas*. Edited by Ana Flora and Ignacio José Verissimo. Rio de Janeiro: José Olympio, 1938.

RETAMAR, Roberto Fernández. *Caliban and other Essays*. Translated by Edward Baker. Minneapolis: University of Minnesota Press, 1989.

La Revista Patriótica, con motivo de la visita hecha á la Capital de la República Argentina por el Doctor Manuel Ferraz de Campos Salles, presidente de la república de los Estados Unidos del Brasil. Buenos Aires: La Revista Patriótica, 1900.

RIBAS, A. J. *Perfil biographico do Dr. Manoel Ferraz de Campos Salles*. Rio de Janeiro: Typ. Leuzinger, 1896.

RIBEIRO JÚNIOR, José. "O Brasil monárquico em face das repúblicas americanas." In *Brasil em perspectiva*. Edited by Carlos Guilherme Mota. 2nd ed. São Paulo: Difusão Européia do Livro, 1969, pp. 146-161.

RICUPERO, Rubens. *José Maria da Silva Paranhos, Barão do Rio Branco: Uma biografia fotográfica, 1845-1995*. Iconography and captions by João Hermes Pereira de Araujo. Brasília: Fundação Alexandre de Gusmão, 1995.

RIO BRANCO, José Maria da Silva Paranhos, Jr., Barão do. *Obras do Barão do Rio Branco*. 9 vols. Rio de Janeiro: Ministério das Relações Exteriores, 1945-1948.

RIO BRANCO, Raul do. *Reminiscencias do Barão do Rio Branco*. Rio de Janeiro: José Olympio, 1942.

ROCK, David. "The Collapse of the Federalists: Rural Revolt in Argentina 1863-1876." *Estudios Interdisciplinarios de América Latina y el Caribe* 9:2 (July-Dec., 1998). pp. 5-20.

RODÓ, José Enrique. *Ariel.* Translated by Margaret Sayers Peden. Austin: University of Texas Press, 1988 [1900].

— "Rio Branco." *Revista Americana* 4:4 (April 1913), pp. 181-183.

RODRIGUES, João Paulo Coelho de Souza. *A dança das cadeiras: Literatura e política na Academia Brasileira de Letras*. Campinas: Editora da Unicamp, 2001.

RODRIGUES, José Honorio. *Conhecimento dos países hispano-americanos no Brasil.* Washington: Unión Panamericana, 1956.

— *História da História do Brasil.* 2 vols. in 3. São Paulo: Companhia Editora Nacional, 1979. Vol. 2, tomo 1, *A historiografia conservadora.*

ROMERO, José Luis. *A History of Argentine Political Thought*. Translated by Thomas F. McGann. Stanford: Stanford University Press, 1968.

ROMERO, Sílvio. *Novos estudos de litteratura contemporanea.* Rio de Janeiro: H. Garnier, 1899.

ROSEMBERG, Liana. *"Da imagem retórica: A questão da visualidade na pintura de Pedro Américo no Brasil oitocentista."* Ph.D. diss., University of São Paulo, 1999.

SALLES, Ricardo. *Guerra do Paraguay: Escravidão e cidadania na fomação do exército.* Rio de Janeiro: Paz e Terra, 1990.

SALVATORE, Ricardo. "The Enterprise of Knowledge: Representational Machines of Informal Empire." In *Close Encounters of Empire: Writing the Cultural History of U.S.-Latin American Relations*. Edited by Gilbert M. Joseph, Catherine LeGrand and Ricardo D. Salvatore. Durham: Duke University Press, 1998, pp. 69-104.

SANTOS, Lúis Cláudio Villafañe G. "A América do sul no discurso diplomático brasileiro." *Revista Brasileira de Política internacional*, 48:2 (2005), pp. 185-204.

SARMIENTO, Domingo Faustino. *Viajes por Europa, África y América, 1845-1847.* Madrid: ALLCA XX, 1996 [1849].

SCHEFF, Thomas J. "Emotions and Identity: A Theory of Ethnic Nationalism." In *Social Theory and the Politics of Identity.* Edited by Craig Calhoun. Oxford, UK: Blackwell, 1994, pp. 277-303.

SCHNEIDER, Ronald M. *Order and Progress: A Political History of Brazil.* Boulder: Westview Press, 1991.

SCHWARCZ, Lilia Moritz. *As Barbas do imperador: D. Pedro II, um monarca nos trópicos*. São Paulo: Companhia das Letras, 1998.

— "A Mestizo and Tropical Country: The Creation of the Official Image of Independent Brazil." *European Review of Latin American and Caribbean Studies*, 80 (2006), pp. 25-42.

SCHWARZ, Roberto. "Brazilian Culture: Nationalism by Elimination." *New Left Review* 167 (Jan.-Feb., 1988), pp. 77-90.

SCOBIE, James R. *Argentina: A City and a Nation*. 2nd ed. New York: Oxford University Press, 1971.

SECKINGER, Ron. *The Brazilian Monarchy and the South American Republics, 1822-1831: Diplomacy and State Building*. Baton Rouge: Louisiana State University Press, 1984.

Segunda reunión del Congreso científico latino americano celebrada en Montevideo del 20 al 31 de marzo de 1901. Montevideo, Tip. y enc. "Al libro inglés," 1901.

SEVCENKO, Nicolau. *Literatura como missão: Tensões sociais e criação cultural na Primeira República*. São Paulo: Brasiliense, 1983.

SEYFERTH, Giralda. "Construindo a nação: Hierarquias raciais e o papel do racismo na política de imigração e colonização." In *Raça, ciência e sociedade*. Edited by Marcos Chor Maio and Ricardo Ventura Sanots. Rio de Janeiro: Centro Cultural Banco do Brasil / Editora FIOCRUZ, 1996, pp. 41-58.

SHUMWAY, Nicolas. *The Invention of Argentina*. Berkeley: University of California Press, 1991.

SILVA, Eduardo. *Prince of the People*. London: Verso, 1993.

SILVA, Kelly Cristiane da. "A nação cordial: Uma análise dos rituais e das ideologias oficiais de 'comemoração dos 500 anos do Brasil,'" *Revista Brasileira de Sciências Sociais* 18:51 (February 2003), pp. 141-159.

SKIDMORE, Thomas. *Black into White: Race and Nationality in Brazilian Thought*. New York: Oxford University Press, 1974.

— "Brazil's American Illusion: From Dom Pedro II to the Coup of 1964." *Luso-Brazilian Review* 23:2 (1986), pp. 71-84.

— Eduardo Prado: A Conservative Nationalist Critic of the Early Republic, 1889-1901." *Luso-Brazilian Review* 12:2 (1975), pp. 149-161.

— "Racial Ideas and Social Policy in Brazil, 1870-1940." In *The Idea of Race in Latin America*. Edited by Richard Graham. Austin: University of Texas Press, 1990, pp. 7-36.

SKIDMORE, Thomas and Thomas HOLLOWAY. "New Light on Euclides da Cunha: Letters to Oliveira Lima, 1903-1909." *Luso-Brazilian Review* 8:1 (1971), pp. 30-55.

SMITH, Anthony D. *National Identity*. Reno: University of Nevada Press, 1991.

SMITH, Joseph. *Unequal Giants: Diplomatic Relations Between the United States and Brazil, 1889-1930*. Pittsburgh: University of Pittsburgh Press, 1991.

SOCIEDADE BRASILEIRA DE GEOGRAFIA. *Catalogo da exposição de geographia sul-americana realizada pela Sociedade de geographia do Rio de Janeiro e inaugurada em 23 de fevereiro de 1889.* Rio de Janeiro: Imprensa Nacional, 1891.

SODRÉ, Lauro. *Crenças e opiniões.* Facsimile ed. Brasília: Senado Federal, 1997 [1896].

SOMMER, Doris. *Foundational Fictions: The National Romances of Latin America.* Berkeley: University of California Press, 1991.

STEIN, Stanley. "The Historiography of Brazil 1808-1889." *Hispanic American Historical Review* 40:2 (1960), pp. 234-278.

STOKES, Charles E. "The Acre Revolutions, 1899-1903: A Study in Brazilian Expansionism." Ph.D diss., Tulane University, 1974.

SÜSSEKIND, Flora. "Shifting Frontiers–Manuel Bonfim [sic] and *A América Latina*: An Introduction." *Journal of Latin American Cultural Studies*, 11:1 (2002), pp. 65-76.

TENORIO-TRILLO, Mauricio. *Argucias de la historia: Siglo XIX, cultura y 'América Latina'*. Mexico City: Paidós, 1999.

— *Mexico at the World's Fairs: Crafting a Modern Nation.* Berkeley: University of California Press, 1996.

TOCANTINS, Leandro. *Formação histórica do Acre*, 3 vols. Rio de Janeiro: Conquista, 1961.

TODOROV, Tzvetan. *The Conquest of America: The Question of the Other.* Translated by Richard Howard. New York: Harper Perennial, 1992.

TONELLI, Nicélio César. "De rivais a aliados: A Argentina e o Brasil na década de 1890." In *América Latina contemporânea: Desafios e perspectivas.* Edited by Eliane Garcindo Dayrell and Zilda Márcia Gricoli Iokoi. Rio de Janeiro/São Paulo: Expressão e Cultura/Edusp, 1996, pp. 133-144.

TOPIK, Steven C. *Trade and Gunboats: The United States and Brazil in the Age of Empire.* Stanford: Stanford University Press, 1996.

URRUTIA, Manuel Vicuña. *El París americano: La oligarquía chilena como actor urbano en el siglo XIX.* Santiago, Chile: Universidad Finis Terrae/ Museo Histórico Nacional, 1996.

VARELA, Luis Vicente. *El Brasil y la Argentina: confraternidad sud-americana; obra descriptiva, ilustrada con fotograbados de las más importantes festividades; pub. por la Intendencia municipal de la capital de la República Argentina.* Buenos Aires: Impr. de J. Peuser, 1901.

VENTURA, Roberto. *Estilo tropical.* São Paulo: Companhia das Letras, 1991.

VERÍSSIMO, José. *A Educação nacional*. 3rd ed. Porto Alegre: Mercado Aberto, 1985 [1890].

— *Homens e cousas estrangeiras*. 3 vols. Rio de Janeiro: Garnier, 1902, 1905, 1910.

— *José Veríssimo, teoria, crítica e história literária*. Edited by João Alexandre Barbosa. São Paulo: Brasiliense, 1986.

VIANA FILHO, Luís. *A vida de Joaquim Nabuco*. São Paulo/Brasília: Martins/INL, 1973.

— *A vida de Rui Barbosa*. 8th revised ed. Rio de Janeiro: Livraria J. Olympio Editora, 1977.

— *A vida do Barão do Rio Branco*. 2nd ed. São Paulo: Martins, 1967.

VIANNA, Luiz Verneck. *A revolução passiva: Iberismo e americanismo no Brasil.* Rio de Janeiro: Revan, 1997.

VIÑAS, David. *Indios, ejército y frontera*. 3rd ed. Buenos Aires: Santiago Arcos Editor, 2003.

WEINSTEIN, Barbara. "The Decline of the Progressive Planter and the Rise of Subaltern Agency: Shifting Narratives of Slave Emancipation in Brazil." In *Reclaiming the Political in Latin American History*. Edited by Gilbert Joseph. Durham: Duke University Press, 2001, pp. 81-101.

WHIGHAM, Thomas and Barbara POTTHAST. "The Paraguayan Rosetta Stone: New Insights into the Demographics of the Paraguayan War, 1864-1870." *Latin American Research Review* 34:1 (1999), pp. 174-186.

WHIGHAM, Thomas and Hendrik KRAAY. "Introduction: War, Politics, and Society in South America, 1820s-60s." In *I Die with My Country: Perspectives on the Paraguayan War, 1864-1870*. Edited by Thomas Whigham and Hendrik Kraay. Lincoln: University of Nebraska Press, 2004, pp. 174-186.

WILGUS, A. Curtis. "The Third International American Conference at Rio de Janeiro, 1906." *Hispanic American Historical Review* 12:4 (Nov., 1932), pp. 420-456.

WOGAN, Daniel S. *A literatura hispano-americana no Brasil: 1877-1944*. Baton Rouge: Louisiana State University Press, 1948.

WOLL, Allen L. *A Functional Past: The Uses of History in Nineteenth-Century Chile*. Baton Rouge: Louisiana State University Press, 1982.

WRIGHT, Marie Robinson. *The New Brazil, its Resources and Attractions*. Philadelphia: G. Barrie & Sons, 1907.

ZEA, Leopoldo. *The Latin American Mind*. Translated by James H. Abbott and Lowell Dunham. Norman: University of Oklahoma Press, 1963.

ZEBALLOS, E. S. "Rio Branco." *Revista de Derecho Historia y Letras* 14:41 (March 1912), pp. 411-439.

Index of names